NORFOLK

ISLAND OF SECRETS

NORFOLK
ISLAND OF SECRETS

THE MYSTERY OF JANELLE PATTON'S DEATH

TIM LATHAM

A SUE HINES BOOK
ALLEN & UNWIN

First published in 2005

A Sue Hines Book
Allen & Unwin
83 Alexander Street
Crows Nest NSW 2065
Australia
Phone: (61 2) 8425 0100
Fax: (61 2) 9906 2218
Email: info@allenandunwin.com
Web: www.allenandunwin.com

National Library of Australia
Cataloguing-in-Publication entry:
Latham, Tim.
Norfolk : island of secrets.

ISBN 1 74114 373 X.

1. Patton, Janelle - Death and burial. 2. Murder -
Investigation - Norfolk Island. 3. Murder victims -
Norfolk Island. 4. Norfolk Island - Social conditions.
I. Title.

364.1523

Edited by Jo Jarrah
Text design by Phil Campbell
Map designed by Guy Holt Illustration and Design
Typesetting by Midland Typesetters
Printed in Australia by Griffin Press

10 9 8 7 6 5 4 3 2

CONTENTS

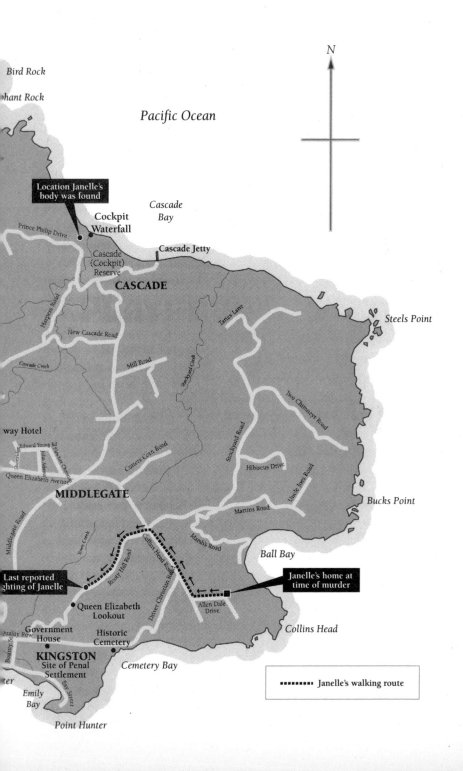

N

Bird Rock

hant Rock

Pacific Ocean

Location Janelle's
body was found

Cascade
Bay

Cockpit
Waterfall

Prince Philip Drive

Cascade Jetty

Cascade
(Cockpit)
Reserve

CASCADE

Harpers Road

Tartes Lane

Steels Point

New Cascade Road

Mill Road

Stockyard Creek

Cascade Creek

way Hotel

Edward Young Rd

Two Chimneys Road

Shortridge

John Adams Close

Queen Elizabeth Avenue

Country Corn Road

Stockyard Road

Hibiscus Drive

Uncle Tom's Road

MIDDLEGATE

Bucks Point

Middlegate Road

Town Creek

Rocky Hill Road

Collins Head Road

Martins Road

Marsh's Road

Ball Bay

Last reported
ghting of Janelle

Driver Christian Road

Janelle's home at
time of murder

Allen Dale
Drive

Queen Elizabeth
Lookout

Government
House

quality Row

Historic
Cemetery

Collins Head

Bounty Row

KINGSTON
Site of Penal
Settlement

Bay Street

Cemetery Bay

·········· Janelle's walking route

ter

Emily
Bay

Point Hunter

PROLOGUE

Unique is a tired word but in the case of Norfolk Island it is an exquisite fit. Norfolk has no comparison, nor equal. There is no other place like it in Australia, or the Pacific. It is an island rich in many things, especially anomalies.

It has its own government, flag, stamps, immigration, health and welfare systems, there is no taxation and it sends its own team to the Commonwealth Games. Norfolk is wonderfully and strangely *different*, so it comes as no surprise the island is never on the weather map. 'We are on the commercial TV weather!' said the vivacious clerk of the Island Assembly, an Australian-born Norfolk patriot who over a cup of tea was eager to challenge my conclusion that this tiny speck in the Pacific was never on the charts.

Other than her parliamentary post, the clerk was also an amateur mystic, spiritually connected to a wider world which spoke of harmony, love and compassion. She couldn't understand why Australia was so *afraid* of little Norfolk: 'What have they got to fear? We are only eighteen hundred people.'

We were sitting in a local café where feral chickens pecked at loose salad droppings on the veranda. She was adamant Norfolk was on the weather map so I watched the nightly broadcasts with new enthusiasm. Whenever I could I dashed home in time for the weather. I watched all four TV channels in case the island suddenly appeared, like a cameo performance, or a lost world surfacing for air. I have no idea what channel she was watching but I never saw Norfolk mentioned. No matter how many times I watched the weather I never saw it appear.

I couldn't even pinpoint Norfolk on the satellite chart on page two of the weekly paper, the *Norfolk Islander*. Norfolk was, as I suspected, literally off the map. Even for locals. This is despite the existence of a federal weather monitoring station next to the airport.

'I almost got the island onto the SBS weather,' said Mike King, one-time public servant, trade unionist, restaurant owner, tour operator, immigration officer, tourism and finance minister and manager of Austote, an online punting business. Like most people on Norfolk he's embarked on a number of careers, including the frustration of local politics. 'When I was Chief Minister we had discussions with SBS about being included in the w-w-w—that's the world weather wrap.' Mike has his legs stretched out on a coffee table, cradling a scotch whisky in his hand. He rattles the glass to crack the ice and takes another sip. 'They said they would.'

'And?' I ask.

'I got voted out of office. Nobody followed through. It came to nothing.'

He runs his fingers down his moustache and grins. 'So we're still off the map.'

I always thought the biggest coup for Norfolk Island would be to get *on* the map, the big blue TV weather map, to be broadcast to millions of viewers in mainland Australia who would say 'So *that's* where Norfolk Island is.'

Instead, Norfolk Island got on a different map and it had nothing to do with sunshine or rain. On the afternoon of Easter Sunday 2002, somebody killed a woman. A vicious, nasty, prolonged attack. The crime pitted a feisty, pretty brunette against a person of great strength, anger and hatred. She fought with muscle and sinew. She was stabbed, gashed and bruised, kicked, defaced and broken. She was a woman who punched above her weight but she never got one over her attacker. She fought for her life. And died.

Then it rained and in a daylight gamble which astounds police, the person who killed her took the body to a grassy reserve and, like it was a slaughtered animal, dumped it on the ground.

Her name was Janelle Patton. The 29-year-old had been living on Norfolk Island for two and a half years. She loved to sing, laugh and drink. She was loyal to those who were loyal to her. The person who murdered her put Norfolk Island on the map for all the wrong reasons.

I first went to Norfolk Island on the strength of Janelle Patton's unsolved murder. I wasn't there to break the case, but to understand why it wasn't breaking; why it had gone *quiet*. Like all first time visitors what I found was something of an unpolished gem. A rural early eighties backwater with a tough exterior, common-sense decency and old-fashioned prices—especially for cigarettes and alcohol. I was struck by the quiet, the solitude and the feeling of being surrounded by nothing but ocean. Even in the shadow of its convict ruins Norfolk is wrapped in a peaceful idleness; the wind speaks of nothing urgent, nothing pressing. It has the charm of yesterday without the burden of tomorrow.

My first visit was in February 2003. I was working at *Background Briefing*, a feature length documentary program on ABC Radio National. The crime was eleven months old and for some time the story floated the corridors with no takers. When I arrived on the island I understood why. I rushed about in a controlled panic, trying to find people to talk into a microphone. Nobody was very keen to say anything on the record. Off the record was like a stream of consciousness. It's here I realised Norfolk Island itself was as fascinating and strange as Janelle Patton's murder.

My visit coincided with the return of Janelle's parents, Ron and Carol Patton, to Norfolk Island, their first journey there since Janelle's death. It was also the first time they had publicly spoken about her murder and they did so graciously, finishing off each other's sentences as married couples tend to do: they needed little prompting. Their story was one of excitement, confusion, disbelief, then anguish. The Pattons arrived on Norfolk Island twenty-six hours before their daughter's murder on 31 March 2002. They had come for a holiday. It ended in a nightmare.

When I left Norfolk Island, I swore I would never return. It was for holidays not journalists. Questions and the people who ask them are unwanted intrusions. But I did return, four times in all, and each journey was as difficult as the first. But a few people helped and some were generous with their time. It's thanks to them the door creaked ajar, enough for me to persist, and persist some more.

Most books centred on a 'true crime' are written after trial and sentencing. At the author's disposal are a plethora of documents including statements, court proceedings, transcripts and appeals. It's this evidence which forms the backbone of a narrative. In the case of Janelle Patton it is the opposite. The crime is unsolved, the investigation active and ongoing. There has never been an arrest or a key suspect named by police. This book is written within these constraints. At all times Detective Sergeant Bob Peters and the Australian Federal Police have done their best to accommodate my needs as a journalist without compromising their investigation. For the most part, though, our differing needs are incompatible. I was denied access to every document tendered at the June 2004 coronial inquest into Janelle's death, except for two exhibits. I was permitted to view the crime scene photographs of Janelle, which reveal more horror than words can impart, and I was allowed to read the autopsy report.

When people on Norfolk Island declined to talk to me (which many did) they often said, 'Read my police statement, I've nothing else to say.' But this was not possible either. I was refused permission to read any individual statement. The basis for my information remains my own interviews and observations, Bob Peters' 227-page statement to the coronial inquest, which Islanders were later able to buy for five dollars a copy, and the transcript of the overall proceedings. Requests to see Janelle's 2001 and 2002 diaries were also denied on the grounds that my seeing them might compromise the investigation. For reasons unknown, Janelle's last diary entry for 2002 was on 9 February, fifty days before her death on 31 March.

CHAPTER I

OFF THE MAP

THE FLIGHT from Sydney to Norfolk takes two and a half hours and costs $900 return. There're cheaper places to go in the Pacific but they're not nearly as intriguing. Norfolk is called an 'external territory' of Australia and to get there involves an international flight. This is the first of the anomalies—without a passport there's no entry.

Carrying me is Air Nauru, perhaps the most optimistic case study of a Pacific carrier. The jet and crew from the bankrupt Pacific nation are leased by Brisbane company Norfolk Jet. On board is a large tour group with matching holiday blazers. During the flight one of them, in excitement and confusion, asks a Nauruan flight attendant if he's a Norfolk Islander. It's not the first or last time someone's been confused about what constitutes a Norfolk Islander—even the island isn't sure. The issue of identity is something of a sticky wicket.

I arrive in darkness on a Sunday evening. The landing comes out of nowhere and takes me by surprise. The plane doesn't touch down on the tarmac, it sort of flops out of the sky. With so few lights below, it feels like we're ditching into the ocean. Travelling to Norfolk is like camping in the bush after months in the city—you forget how dark darkness can be. It will take a while for my city-flared eyes to assimilate to the overall dimness.

Outside the window I see the haughty silhouettes of the island icon—the Norfolk pine. You haven't seen the species in its native glory until you visit its homeland. The pines which dot the east coast of Australia and the beaches of Sydney are usually tired, sick, buckled or deformed from pollution. When the pine needles lose their protective wax coating they find it difficult to prosper. But on Norfolk, adrift in the pure ocean air, they retain the majestic, soaring look which so appealed to Captain Cook when he stumbled across this curvaceous isle on his way to New Zealand in 1774.

The plane pulls up at the terminal like a car in a driveway. I've always enjoyed small island destinations where the trolley-stairs are rolled to the back door of the plane. It makes for a casual yet graceful exit, one which says 'now you're on holiday'. I step out of the cabin and inhale a bouquet of Pacific dew, pine needles and jet fuel. It's a heady mix.

Locals wave and smile from a grass lawn in front of the terminal. A sign in Norfolk says 'Welkam tu Norfolk Ailen'. In the bad light I interpret it as 'Welcome to Norfolk, Aliens'. Depending on who you talk to, Norfolk is a language in its own right, a quaint patois, or a bastardised version of pidgin English. Either way it's the first point of difference from Australia.

The island's airport terminal opened in 1999 and like all issues which burn the bellies of Islanders, it was subjected to a petition and then a referendum. The in-flight infomercials don't mention the spit and sizzle of Norfolk politics but the airport terminal is one of many decisions to be democratically road-tested by an indecisive island averse to change. Overnight the community turned into a vocal pack of architecture critics.

The story of the airport terminal is the story of Norfolk politics, the embodiment of consensus decision making and its strengths and weaknesses. The $2.6 million project was approved by the Norfolk Assembly but several politicians baulked when the community savaged the plans. The initial design by Sydney architect Desmond Freeman in 1996 was a tribute to the history of the island. One end of the terminal was Polynesian, the other end a two-storey Georgian building reflecting the convict era; the roof in between was said to be Victorian. The local paper called it 'absolutely brilliant' but the swell of disapproval was festering. One letter writer questioned the need for fake Georgian buildings when the island had real ones in the capital (Kingston). Norfolk has two centres, the convict-built ocean front of Kingston dating from the 1840s, which locals call 'town', and Burnt Pine, which is the commercial hub and home to many of the island's watering holes. The terminal design proved too ambitious for the community and sixty-five per cent of the island voted NO in the referendum, which by then was really a vote of no-confidence in the Assembly.

In 1997 the dejected architect was dispatched to his drawing board to knock up simpler, less grand alternatives. These were put to the islanders in an informal poll and what now stands is a non-offensive terminal without the bells or whistles once envisioned by an architect who dared to dream he could reflect the character of Norfolk in a building.

The island elects politicians to do the housekeeping but when it comes to the big decisions, the nine members are expected to defer to the community. Decision making on Norfolk is circular; it's hard to pinpoint where it begins and ends, not unlike the luggage carousel inside the immigration hall, where a scrum of eager folk huddle around impatiently.

I glimpse my bag spin past three times before I manage to cut through the crowd and snatch it off the conveyor belt, dumping it on a secondhand luggage cart from Auckland International Airport. At the end of the room are two passport counters with locals in smart but plain uniforms, and no hibiscus flowers in sight. A serious woman in shirt, black skirt, stockings and hair pulled back in a taut knot, like a pastry chef, opens my passport and stamps it with 'Norfolk Customs'. In a world where passport stamps are becoming a fragment of the past, Norfolk still thumps the ink to declare your arrival. As an Australian citizen I get a thirty-day permit. It's illegal to camp, and there's no caravan park or budget accommodation. Every visitor must state where they are staying. If you're staying privately, then names are required. It's a bit like going to Russia, except the Union Jack is everywhere and 'God Save the Queen' is the national anthem.

'Enjoy your holiday,' she says.

I step beyond the terminal into a twilight zone. Sunday night is the start of the tourism working week and bump-in hour for travel oper-ators. I'm grappling with the handle of a borrowed red suitcase which looks far too corporate for this breezy destination. I'm ready to pick up a hire car but the darkness bundles me up. The car voucher is hand-written in blue ballpoint pen on a green slip. There is no company name and no details. It's part of a seven-day package deal.

I approach some locals loitering in the spot where the airport lights dim and the black hole of the car park looms. They're leaning against the fence rails like a posse of cowboys, some with hands around placards, several wearing Hawaiian shirts and name badges. One flaps his placard like he's fanning a camp fire.

'I'm looking to pick up a car?'

'Righto, champ.' He gives me a friendly nod. 'Got a piece of paper somewhere?'

I hand him the voucher and he turns to the available light, squinting at the print, holding his glasses out like binoculars.

'You need Greg.' He looks around. 'I'll go find him.'

I watch the other visitors totter towards the waiting minibuses. I've never seen such a large pack of elderly tourists. I'll see them again on the streets of Burnt Pine, but for now they look like they've escaped from a nursing home. Everywhere I turn I see puffy skin and radiant expressions, crinkles and pearls, broad smiles and high hair. Some men wear khaki shorts with thick cream socks, doubled over at the top in a neat fold, pulled to the rim of their knobbly knees; spectacle cases are clipped to breast pockets of short-sleeved shirts. The women wear white blouses, navy-blue jackets and ill-coloured slacks. Collectively they all lean forward, like bamboo in the wind. Their postures may be cruelled by age but their excitement is adolescent. Cackling and wheezing with laughter the elderly hordes squeeze into the waiting vans and shuffle about in their seats. Some are escorted by a granddaughter or niece. I see them later at breakfast, helping pour their tea, explaining the itinerary of daytime tours and evening events.

Every person arriving on Norfolk is given a booklet of activities with a seven-day calendar on the back page. Cramming the gamut of historical tours, convict dinners and sunset fish fries into those seven days is proof Norfolk is no idle destination. It's nonstop. For some visitors this is their final holiday in a lifetime of little travel. A chance to step back to the shadow of their younger years, a safe and fulfilling destination with the added thrill of an international departure and no

GST. For these visitors it's full throttle forward—there's literally no time to waste. Norfolk's tourism market is known as the 'newlyweds and nearly deads'. But unless the young brides have already fled, all I can see are the senior citizens. I'm the youngest by an island mile.

On cue, the flock of silver-tops now in the bus swivel in their seats and eyeball me, the lone man standing at the gutter with a red suitcase at his feet. I feel older than them and terribly isolated.

A gentleman I presume is Greg rescues me from my social stigma and leads me away from the fleet of buses. A quick handshake, car keys and I'm standing in front of a boot having blindly followed him into the car park. Greg is tossing my suitcase in the back, telling me the engine won't start unless I put a foot on the brake. 'It's an automatic,' he says. 'Come in during the week and fill out the paperwork.'

I don't know where the car is from or what the company is called. This is certainly no Hertz affair. Before I can inquire about these minor details, a hand grabs my shoulder.

'Are you Tim?'

Seeing I might know someone, Greg introduces himself faster than a game show host. In a gabble of names and more names, the people around me figure out where they're from, where they work and who they know in a matter of seconds. I'm surprised all the locals haven't already met but in this darkness it's hard to make out much. I find out later there's as many definitions of locals as there are colours in the rainbow and the order in which they sit is just as rigid.

The two meeting me are friends of a friend. Simon and Lee are two of the four hundred or so TEPs—holders of Temporary Entry Permits which allow them to live and breathe on Norfolk Island, as well as earn tax-free dollars. On this island, friends of friends are good enough to open the lines of hospitality. I just didn't realise it would be so soon.

They've been drinking across the road at the Brewery—or the Blurry, as it's known in the later hours. It's the last place to drink on weekends. Norfolk's venue of late resort, the place where young Islanders hang out. It's a tourism no-go zone and no place for anyone not belonging to the island tribe. If you're not wanted at the Brewery, it's spelt out loud and clear. This is the one place the Norfolk police warned me not to go. When I did visit I discovered the famous island hospitality somewhat lacking. 'Go away,' said a large bloke with black curly hair; he was perched on a bar stool which looked moulded to his arse. 'You're scary. Get away from me.'

His eyes were on the door, mine were on the bar, but there's only so long a fish can stay out of water, so after a time I dawdled outside and finished my tinny on the porch of Slick's Butchery. The next time I went to the Brewery I was with Mike King and everything was cordial. We drank large whiskies and everyone was laughing. Norfolk is all about relationships. It is, after all, one big squirming family unit.

On the night of my arrival, Simon suggests we have a drink at the RSL. Lee offers to guide me through the darkness and slips into the passenger seat of my hire car, a three-door Toyota hatch. As I struggle to find the ignition barrel she reaches over and puts a hand on my knee. I feel something drop into my palm.

'Welcome to Norfolk,' she says with a grin.

I fumble for the internal light which casts a crook yellow shadow over my hand. It's enough light to see the silver foil package. I look at Lee who returns my gaze with expectancy. I unfold the foil to see a large furry bud inside. It smells pungent and fresh. Norfolk is well-known for its clear air and sweet-smelling crops. Everything is home-grown, from vegetables to fruit, and marijuana is no different. The aficionados take great care growing their plants, separating seeds and cultivating strands, making full use of the fertile soil and hidden valleys they inherited from their grandparents.

'Thanks,' I say.

We drive out of the car park into a slipstream of darkness so complete it helps illuminate the evening sky. It's like somebody dropped a dome over the ocean and lit it up with Christmas lights. The brilliance of the sky impresses all who visit. Shortly after Janelle arrived in 1999 she wrote home: 'at night there are so many stars you wouldn't believe it, it's like a fairyland'. At ground level this all-natural dimness hangs as heavy as a stage curtain. Sans moon, Norfolk is wrapped in a mantle of pure, unadulterated blackness, leaving the stars to twinkle in harmony above. It thoroughly disorientates me.

There is no light pollution on Norfolk because there is no public lighting. For a long time there was only one street light, suspended by overhead wires near the school. This lone light has now been joined by three others a kilometre away at the island's only roundabout. During the day it produces a traffic snarl, at night it's deserted. The addition of some dotted solar lighting helps but in general, when night falls on Burnt Pine it fades to black, like the rest of the island.

Burnt Pine is the exotic name for the island's commercial shopping strip and through it runs a scarred and potholed road that under the bounce of car headlights appears strangely moonlike. During the day this pockmarked road is stripped of its allure and looks like what it is, a loosely patched and repaired series of potholes, a surface covered with a kind of asphalt acne that stretches over the island's busiest roads.

The drive from the airport to the RSL is a journey of less than two minutes. The RSL is across the road from the first and last places Janelle Patton worked. The South Pacific Resort and the Castaway Hotel. Janelle was also a TEP and she came to Norfolk to escape her life in Sydney. She wanted to start anew and regarded Norfolk as the perfect place to revamp her life. The two hotels sit side by side, although from the main street the Castaway is hidden from view. It was in the hotel dining room of the Castaway that Janelle worked a breakfast shift on 31 March 2002: the day she died.

The entry to the RSL car park is marked by a yacht mast doubling as a flagpole. Slightly warped by wind and weather it flies the Australian flag. The flag the Norfolk diggers fought under. The timber mast is from the New Zealand racing yacht *Rangi*, built in 1902. It came last in the first Trans-Tasman Race of 1931 and twenty years later was victim to Norfolk's sudden wind shifts when blown ashore at Cascade Bay.

I park and follow Lee through the club entrance. There is a painting of the landing at Gallipoli, and the reward notice for the Patton murder: a laminated A5 sheet of yellow paper promising $100 000 for information. It's since been upped to $300 000 but so far there have been no takers. One of Janelle's last gifts to her father, for Christmas 2001, was the book *Gallipoli* by Les Carlyon. It was to help the amateur historian with his research for a screenplay about Colonel John Monash.

The atmosphere inside the RSL is gentle and calm. Cigarette smoke hangs mid-air, dormant, as if it has nowhere better to drift. Like many RSL clubs, this one leapt onto the renovation drive of the late 1990s, but it retains some old-world charms like the gun cabinet, a showcase of weapons stretching from the Boer War to Vietnam. To the right of the bistro counter is a wall covered with black and white photos of departed diggers, a wall in honour of the fallen and the silent. Norfolk Island might squabble over its relationship with Australia but its commitment to King, Queen and Mother Country sent a tremendous number of island men to battle. Seventy-eight went to World War I and eighty to World War II—almost one in ten of the population at the time.

Without asking me, Simon picks up the telephone and rings reception at the South Pacific, where I'm staying across the road. He tells the desk clerk I'm safely deposited at the 'beer bank' and will be checking in later.

As I pull up a stool at the bar and take in the room I notice something amiss. It's to do with the overall sound. There's an absent clatter which niggles at me until the penny drops—there are no poker machines. In place of the most vacuous electronic jingle ever composed is the gruff, soulful melody of human voices, mostly male. Norfolk Island has chased all manner of online gaming projects in the pursuit of financial liberty but it said no to the poker machine. There was no referendum, just common recognition that pokies were a slice of modern life Norfolk didn't want, or need.

Lee slides onto a stool next to me. In one glance she looks amused and bemused. She's been 'on-island', as the locals say, for twelve months, working as a TEP in the usual mix of revolving hospitality jobs. The first time she went to the Brewery she stood with her back to the wall getting propositioned by married men while her boyfriend chatted nearby. She straightens her back and swings her legs from the bar stool.

'Can or stubbie?' Simon asks.

I scan the bar and see all the blokes are drinking cans. Perhaps it's fresher beer, maybe cans come by airfreight and stubbies by boat? Although this doesn't make any sense. Perhaps the can/stubbie divide is a distinction between who is and isn't in the know.

'Stubbie,' I say.

Simon gives me a stubbie holder as well and proceeds to host two conversations at the same time, one with me from the left side of his mouth and one with an Islander from the right side. This impressive ventriloquist act continues for a while until he deems it time for us to meet. On arrival of the second stubbie I shake hands with Laurie

'Bucket' Quintal, direct descendant of Able Seaman Matthew Quintal, who set fire to the bow of the *Bounty* after the mutineers and their Tahitian women arrived on Pitcairn Island in 1790. It's said the men cried as they watched the boat burn, knowing they'd just scuttled their last hope of seeing England again.

Like all Norfolk men of Pitcairn descent, Laurie 'Bucket' Quintal backs up a placid demeanour with the strong build of his Tahitian ancestry. With sunnies perched on his forehead and dressed in rugby league kit of shorts and jersey, he looks like he's come from footy training. He doesn't say much now but months later, at the same bar, we discuss what may have unfolded the day Janelle died.

'Tim's just in from the mainland, he's here for a week's break,' says Simon as we're introduced. Acknowledging the real reason for my visit seems reckless, certainly embarrassing for my acquaintances who, never suggesting otherwise, make it clear that the motive for my visit here shall remain unvoiced around them. I'm here to ask how a girl can disappear in the middle of the day without anyone seeing anything at all. But by default I've lapsed into an unwanted game of charades.

Four drinks and more than an hour later, the front desk of the South Pacific calls the bar, asking if I could check in. It seems the patient employee in his early twenties would like to go home. He thanks me for turning up and rushes me to my room, one of about twenty in a single block. The place looks more army barracks than resort. There is a network of covered walkways connecting the rooms to the reception and dining areas. Dank synthetic grass is carpeted underfoot to prevent guests slipping over and breaking a bone.

Inside, the room is stuffy and hot. It has pink fibro walls, a low ceiling and even lower ceiling fan. On maximum setting it chops through the heavy air like a helicopter blade. I go to bed wondering how many people snip their fingertips during a morning stretch.

I also wonder if Janelle Patton ever cleaned the room.

CHAPTER 2

EASTER SUNDAY 2002

THE DAY Janelle died was hot and muggy, with a nor'easterly blowing across the island. Locals have a low tolerance of humidity so they remember the day well. The heavy, clammy weather didn't break until a terrific rain storm in mid afternoon. By then Janelle was dead, her body partially covered by a sheet of black builders' plastic. This plastic was no shroud to hide the corpse or dignify the body—it was to protect the killer's vehicle from bloodstains—a sheath to stop the flood of clues.

At first the proud Islanders thought it was a bizarre but explainable hit and run accident gone wrong. How else could the term 'death by suspicious circumstances' be explained? Why else would a body be found in a public reserve on an Easter Sunday? Concern over speeding had been voiced for years, and now there was tragic evidence to confirm what Islanders already knew: that people drove too fast on the winding country lanes which crisscross the island.

Those who knew Janelle more intimately suspected suicide. She was sometimes referred to as 'Nutty Nel'. It was said with affection rather than hostility, but it indicated her island friends considered her unstable; a bubbly girl who could blow like the wind. In their eyes death by her own hand was plausible.

The Australian Federal Police took four days to reveal this was no traffic accident or suicide. By then the island suspected foul play. Dem Tull said it was murder. As always, it was first with the news. Dem Tull is Norfolk for 'They Say', meaning the voice of the community. It's the de facto island bush telegraph and slang for news, chatter, gossip, rumour, hearsay, scuttlebutt, slander and infamy. The English language is expansive when it comes to synonyms for gossip; the Norfolk language—or patois, a mixture of eighteenth century English and Tahitian—bundles it all into one saying. Dem Tull was the first Norfolk expression I learnt.

Dem Tull is usually born from a seed of truth but like the age-old game of Chinese Whispers, the more people involved, the looser the truth becomes. In the end it becomes an exotic blend of fact and fiction, a cocktail, if you like, of faction.

This intoxicating drink muddles the reality. And if the story circulates for long enough, it becomes a version of the truth, congealing over time into history, myth, even legend. Like all small communities, Norfolk is built on these stories. And just as the blood of the Islanders is an exotic mix of Polynesian and English, its folklore is an equally exotic blend of truths and untruths, forever married, forever coexisting, forever jostling with one another.

Dem Tull said Janelle was stabbed in the chest, and left for dead. Then it grew. She was murdered by a jealous woman, murdered by a husband and wife, she was about to blow a drug deal, she knew something she shouldn't, she was tortured, she was assassinated by a professional hit man, her body left as a warning to others, she was knocked off by a tourist, even killed by her own parents. Dem Tull is creative and insidious. It rarely discriminates and it moves with great speed, fuelled by free local phone calls and a small-town love of chitchat.

In response to the island's first murder in many years, Tom Lloyd, the veteran editor of the weekly *Norfolk Islander*, reluctantly rolled his front page proofs through his 1960s printing press.

The 73-year-old with wispy white hair and a forehead of sunspots started the paper in 1965 but never dreamed he would record such an 'ugly event'. It hit the community, he wrote, like 'some seismic shock wave'. So too did the rumours over what happened and why. The front page banner said 'Our little Island has been rocked to its foundation.'

The fifth paragraph said: 'In true Norfolk fashion the rumour mill was soon churning out its own version of what had happened and their own warped theories, regardless of the families and individuals who they were pillorying.'

The job of sifting through the spite and finding the killer of Janelle Patton eventually landed in the lap of a Canberra policeman, Detective Sergeant Bob Peters. Since 2003 the detective has led a Canberra Review Team investigating so-called 'cold cases'—unsolved homicides dating from the 1960s. The Patton case was always going to go to the Australian Federal Police because it provides policing on the island. It's a throwback to the 1890s when the island was stripped of the right to police itself by the colony of New South Wales.

The mildly spoken detective, with short cropped, salt and pepper hair has notched up more than twenty-five trips to the island and he still doesn't know why Janelle was murdered, or who killed her. But two of his own, more private questions have been solved. Bob Peters has knocked back retirement to stay on the case until, he says, 'I've got nothing left to offer'. And when the 56-year-old detective does retire, it won't be on Norfolk Island. He's seen enough to know his sunsets will be prettier elsewhere.

———

The Patton murder is unusual because it took place in the middle of the day. As they say in the best thrillers, *in broad daylight*. This not only breaks the statistical pattern for most homicides but is strangely compelling on an island where everyone knows everyone else. Norfolk is an island where people can see without being seen. But in this case nobody saw anything. No witnesses have come forward. No one saw Janelle get into a car, or struggle with an attacker, nor did they see her knifed to death or her body dumped in a public reserve. The disappearance, the attack, the murder, the disposal of the body—every chapter took place with no known witness on an island with no road in or out. And every chapter of this crime took place in daylight. The killer, or killers, carelessly or confidently disregarded the cover of night and struck at midday—with apparent impunity.

Every person entering and leaving Norfolk Island requires a passport, their names recorded by airport immigration. Norfolk doesn't even have a harbour and visiting yachts are rare. The only door in is via customs. It's thanks to Norfolk's immigration regime that police were given their first dynamic lead—a list of every one of the 2700 people who were on the island the day Janelle was murdered. This effectively means the Australian Federal Police know the *name* of Janelle's killer, they just don't know *which* name is the one. In a case about which so few facts are known, this list of names stands out as a beacon of hope and frustration for all involved. The paradox isn't lost on Bob Peters.

From day one, police knew the Patton case would be a process of elimination. This list was cause for early optimism. Nabbing a suspect would be relatively simple. In the weeks following Janelle's murder, Brendan Lindsay, the second policeman on the scene and the man who initially led the investigation, told the *Australian* newspaper: 'We can identify every individual that was on the island that day, it's just a matter of narrowing things down.'

People ask, how hard can it be? As Bob Peters has discovered, locating the truth on Norfolk can be as frustrating as finding the island on the weather map. He hopes it won't prove impossible. The detective even looked to the heavens for an answer but there were no satellite images taken of Norfolk the day Janelle died. He hoped a photograph from space might have given him the break he needs because so far little has gone his way.

Bob Peters and his team have no eyewitnesses, no murder weapon, no identifying forensic or DNA evidence (beyond a few loose hairs) and plenty of suspected motives with no clear winner. The difficulties don't stop there. Police don't know where Janelle was murdered or how she disappeared from a public road. Nor do police know how her body was shifted to Cockpit public reserve where it was found. One of their earliest pieces of evidence was ten latent sets of partial palm prints found on the sheet of plastic covering the body, but the prints were smudged, dense, overlapping and muddled. Like kids' fingers on a chocolate cake, they could belong to any number of hands.

Despite a high profile, time-consuming fingerprinting exercise only one match has been made. The Australian Federal Police recorded the prints of 1311 locals aged between fifteen and seventy years. The process was voluntary and there's nothing the AFP can do about the three hundred or so individuals who refused to come forward. These mysterious prints remain the investigation's most powerful lead because they connect the killer with the body, although the origin of the plastic remains a mystery. Police suspect it was taken from a building site or nicked from someone's property.

After two years of hope and disappointment, bogus leads and sleepless nights, Bob Peters' investigation took a new turn. It was decided a coronial investigation would be held. It took Peters six weeks to write up his team's investigation: its highs and lows, its loose ends and untethered clues. He told the court his summary was a 'combination of established facts, uncorroborated evidence and hearsay'.

The detective then sat in the convict-era courtroom, trapped in a hopelessly tight witness box, and read word for word a 227-page statement. If it were made into a movie, it would be called *Dem Tull Strikes Back*. It took Peters two breathless days to reach his punchline: he didn't have enough 'admissible evidence' to arrest anyone for the crime. But he did name names. And those who weren't named took great interest in those who were. Norfolk Island was both horrified and mesmerised by what unfolded.

Sixteen people were revealed as 'Persons of Interest'. Thirteen lived on the island. They were part of the community and four belonged to the same family. One was a prominent businessman operating the largest tourism enterprise in town. He made his money out of ferrying elderly tourists around the island; now he was included in an infamous list of names which will never be forgotten. The community reaction was predictable: outrage. It felt publicly besmirched. The individuals named claimed defamation. They were now members of a sorry acronym, the PoIs—or, as the joke went, the 'Pissed-off Islanders'.

The court was told, repeatedly, that 'Persons of Interest' were not suspects. There was nothing to link them to the murder. But the police sure liked the look of them—why else would they be on the list? The PoIs were stranded in a sort of judicial limbo, such is the power of this vague quasi-legal term and the Coroners Court. These sixteen would remain under the magnifying glass until a clear suspect appeared, or an arrest and charge were made.

Sixteen people is more than a handful. It's an abundance. And to make sure Bob Peters honoured the Norfolk tradition of keeping it all in the family, he included Janelle's parents, Ron and Carol Patton. They had arrived on the island the day before their daughter was murdered. Some locals thought this fact alone was sufficient to lock them up. Who else would want to kill the girl, they asked, but her parents? They were the first names on Bob Peters' list.

The coronial inquest ran for four days and investigated the circumstances of Janelle's death. Coronial inquests are not trials, nor do they deal with the guilt or innocence of individuals. All they do is air the available evidence regarding the time, place and cause of death. The coroner also has the power to recommend charges be laid if there is sufficient evidence against an individual.

In the Patton case the outcome was already known. There was insufficient evidence to charge anyone for the crime; instead, Norfolk Island was exposed to a spectacular judicial version of show and tell. The inquest was in part an orchestrated media event, aimed at achieving maximum publicity. Here was a real murder mystery and the coroner hoped all the attention might flush out new clues, maybe crack an alibi or unearth a witness. It was also designed to shock the community about how Janelle fought for her life and died. It took twenty minutes for the extent of her injuries to be read into the court record. Janelle Patton wasn't just murdered, she was butchered.

The inquest did produce some fresh information. It spat out a few treasured, hidden truths. It added to Bob Peters' knowledge of those on his list of sixteen. It helped him claw beneath the island's secretive crust, its multi-layered community and brash bravado. But what if the sixteen were all innocent?

Three weeks after the inquest ended an Australian politician who chairs a committee overseeing Norfolk Island made an astonishing claim, a news breaker. He said the police and the island community knew all along who killed Janelle. According to Senator Ross Lightfoot, the evidence pointed to a local male, living on Norfolk. 'People on the island know who murdered Janelle Patton, no question they know,' he told the *Sunday* program on Channel Nine in June 2004.

This was news to Bob Peters. He didn't know who the killer was. He had some ideas, lots of ideas, but he didn't know for sure. And nor did the island community. There has never been any evidence to suggest the island is complicit in a giant cover-up. The idea that Norfolk is protecting one of its own is widely asserted but fanciful. Islanders know a lot about the people they live with—after all, they've been with them since birth—and if there is one constant in the Norfolk community, it's the belief that this level of violence is beyond them. But Senator Ross Lightfoot, a man who thinks Norfolk is a deeply troubled place, had added a political gravitas to a claim that won't go away.

'It's very, very hard to penetrate that husk of silence that surrounds Norfolk Islanders when they want to protect their own,' he said. Lightfoot claimed a policeman had told him of the killer's identity, but he stopped short of saying who this person was.

Senator Lightfoot's comments astonished the island because it implied the coronial inquest had been nothing but a sham. Bob Peters and Coroner Ron Cahill were furious. They had just invested a great deal of time and Commonwealth money into explaining how this island whodunit was a real mystery. And there were lots of people listening, including, of course, the person who killed Janelle.

When Ron Cahill brought the inquest to a close he said he had no doubt 'Janelle Patton was murdered by persons unknown . . . The finding I make is an open one and as far as I'm concerned the coronial investigation continues.'

Now, three weeks later, these words and the inquest which produced them appeared confused. Had the inquest been a charade? Why ask the community for more clues if the killer was known?

Bob Peters was dispatched to interview the cavalier Senator about his claims. To do this he had to get clearance from the President of the Senate. Bob Peters asked for evidence from Lightfoot, the Senator said he'd get back to him. He's still waiting for an answer.

CHAPTER 3

———

NORFOLK BY BUS

FOR MOST first time visitors the wonderful world of Norfolk is revealed through the windows of a bus. There are many half-day island tours and they all promise much the same. Mine offered commentary by a 'descendant of a *Bounty* mutineer', and morning tea at a home built by a 'descendant of a *Bounty* mutineer'. It was a splendid day and no one was returning my phone calls. It wouldn't be the last time I paid to hear a commentary about the island I was trying to understand.

For all the fuss about the *Bounty*, Fletcher Christian and his Polynesian women, people who have never been to Norfolk are usually hazy about the island's link to the infamous mutiny and Pitcairn Island. Once they arrive they can't escape it. The *Bounty* never sailed to Norfolk, nor did any mutineer step ashore there, but the mutiny and those who led it define Norfolk in a way nothing else does. Forty years ago this past was not spoken about publicly; much like Australia's convict heritage, it was treated with silence. Only in recent decades has there been a rejuvenated sense of identity, replacing embarrassment and even disgrace. At the root of this pride is the connection by nearly half of Norfolk's population to Pitcairn Island, where the *Bounty* mutineers did set up home.

In April 1789, when the convict settlement of Norfolk Island was a year old, HMS *Bounty* was 2000 kilometres to the northeast sailing through modern day Tonga. It was off the island of Tofua that 26-year-old Fletcher Christian shouted his immortalised words (as recorded by Bligh): 'That—Captain Bligh—that is the thing—I am in hell—I am in hell.' The opening act of what would become the Pitcairn people's story was full of confusion, panic and desperation. William Bligh and eighteen crew were forced into the ship's small launch and cut adrift. The dispossessed captain had only a quadrant and a compass for instruments; he had no charts and only five days worth of food. In what is one of the great ocean escapes, Bligh sailed 5800 kilometres to Timor with the loss of only one man.

As the new captain of the *Bounty*, Fletcher Christian spent many months trying to find somewhere to live. Nine months later, in January 1790, Fletcher Christian beached the *Bounty* on the rocks of Pitcairn Island. On board were twenty-eight people: the nine mutineers, twelve Polynesian women, six Polynesian men, and a baby girl. From day one, these refugees of the Pacific faced a mathematical problem: there were more men than women and when two of the females died, the violence began.

Christian had done his best to avoid this problem. In the early days of his search for a new homeland he had more females on the *Bounty* but one girl escaped over the side of the ship and swam to safety while six older females were returned to an island in a canoe.

With the exception of the lovers of Christian and his shipmates Quintal and Adams, the remaining nine women were more kidnapped than chaperoned. They had no idea where they were being taken because Fletcher Christian had no clue where he was sailing; the best fix he could get on his compass was oblivion. On the lam from Bligh and the English navy he was a criminal in exile on one of history's great one-way journeys. To survive he needed an unknown and uninhabited island, preferably with no harbour. He needed a place where he could run the *Bounty* ashore and hide from the English forever. Going missing in the Pacific wasn't difficult but finding an island where he and the mutineers could live was. Christian had already tried and failed on several Tahitian islands.

His last chance was Pitcairn Island. He had read about the island on board the *Bounty*. After two months of searching the open sea he discovered the tiny mountainous rock in the far east of the Pacific, beyond French Polynesia. In 1790, Pitcairn Island was misplaced on the maps, making it a perfect home for a man who didn't want to be found. The tiny island is so far in the nowhere of the Pacific it's still tricky to find in the atlas, although the recent sexual assault trials have helped bring into focus the island's geographical isolation and the strange story behind its creation.

One hundred and fifty years ago the people of Pitcairn abandoned their homeland for the larger island of Norfolk. This lineage is what Norfolk Island is all about. Today on Norfolk Island, the seven original Pitcairn family names still dominate.

Four of the seven come directly from the *Bounty*—Christian, Quintal, McCoy and Adams. These are followed by Buffett and Evans, the two Englishmen who were Pitcairn's first immigrants and landed in 1823. The last of the seven are the Nobbs, descended from Reverend George Hunn Nobbs, who came ashore on Pitcairn in 1828. He had a big white beard, considerable talent and ambition. He took over the leadership of the community within a year of his arrival and eventually led the Pitcairners to their new life on Norfolk Island.

Collectively this group is known as the seven families. The phone book prints these names in delightful repetition and only nicknames differentiate one from another. They have lived their entire lives together, for better or worse, for richer or poorer, these families are wed to each other like clumps of dirt. They swear not one of them murdered Janelle Patton.

––––––––

At the travel agency where the bus tour begins, a blackboard sits on the footpath advertising Norfolk's only Murder Mystery Dinner. It's an evening based on the island's second convict settlement of 1825–1856, before the penal colony was closed and the island given to the Pitcairners. It offers a 'three course dinner fit for the commandants', a night 'full of intrigue and history' and a prize for solving the murder mystery. As I got to know Norfolk better I wondered if I should attend the dinner. It was an evening I imagined I could have some fun at, but in the end, I could never bring myself to go. Even during the coronial inquest held two years after Janelle's death, the sign sat on the footpath like a misplaced theatre prop or a particularly cruel joke.

Inside the office a portly woman greets me from behind the desk with a bright smile. She's well dressed in a black chiffon dress with heels. In her mid twenties, she's one of the missing demographic on Norfolk. There are not many people aged twenty to thirty on the island; most are offshore pursuing wide open spaces, careers or a university education. This is why women of this age stand out and are shadowed by long gazes from local men. Most are TEPs, people like Janelle Patton, who come to Norfolk to work for six to twelve months and can stay for up to three years.

I hand over my paper coupon which she passes to a colleague to inspect. He holds the voucher in two hands and tugs at it from the top right corner. It doesn't tear so he yanks it harder, ripping it in half. The woman giggles, he smiles, then he chucks the coupon in the rubbish bin and notes my name in a book. 'That's fine,' he says, 'just wait out the front for the bus.' Without missing a beat, the woman in black asks if my accommodation is suitable. 'There's more than eighty places to stay here, on an island only five kilometres by eight. I'm often surprised it's not sinking!'

Out the front, tourists cluster about the footpath like idle seagulls waiting for hot chips. As always there's a mixed bag of fashion, ranging from white terry towelling sunhats to cream bowling slacks and stubbies with collared shirts. One couple is wearing matching Cancer Council sunglasses, those segmented wraparound shades which look like industrial-grade goggles, suitable for a spot of arc welding while on holiday. I've always thought these sunglasses look slightly demonic, but such a practical approach to glare protection is admirable in a market driven by vanity and glamour. After all, Norfolk Island is the Ibiza of the sixty-plus travel sector.

I lean against a shop window and feel the sun on my face. It's a typical island day, a light breeze and the temperature in the low twenties. Next to me is a woman with a wooden cane and fluffy white hair who looks like she's leapt from bed in fright. She is impatient for the bus and to amplify her mood of urgency keeps checking the gold watch that is carefully strapped over a white tissue wrapped around her wrist. She makes it known she has rushed to get here on time and expected the bus to do the same. Now seeing everything is running late she asks aloud why she didn't stop to collect her hat and camera.

'Island time, that's anytime,' she jibes, tapping her cane like a physical exclamation mark. Her friend, who is giving a verbal commentary on a flurry of ants circling the pavement, taunts back: 'Norfolk time, that's Hilly Time. Tomorrow will do.'

They both laugh until one splutters for air. Like captains seeking land after weeks at sea, they gaze up the road for the tour bus to appear. They clamour to get on the first bus to arrive, which turns out to be the last to leave.

I get on the second bus and move to the back seat. The guide and driver is a short, thin woman with squiggly ringlets of blond hair. Her name is Maxine Christian, a tour guide who has been called in to help handle the excess numbers. As we pull out of Burnt Pine, she reveals her heritage: a sixth generation descendant of mutineers Fletcher and Quintal. 'So I got a double whammy,' she jokes over the bus loudspeakers, 'and I thought it time to thin the blood down, so I married a lovely Australian man and we've had two children.'

As on Pitcairn, Norfolk's population was originally built on inbreeding, a natural consequence of its geographical isolation. But unlike Pitcairn's, Norfolk's population has always flourished with enough outsiders to keep the gene pool rich. Forty-seven per cent of the Islanders are related to the descendants of the *Bounty* Mutineers and their Tahitian wives. This blood is now being progressively thinned through marriage and relationships with outsiders. Many fear that as the blood thins so too does the traditional culture and the historic rights Pitcairners have on the island. It's now rare for two Islanders of Pitcairn descent to marry or have children. Usually one of the ring bearers is from Australia or New Zealand.

Norfolk's historic inbreeding has been as much of interest to anthropologists as to joke-tellers. When police were thinking about DNA testing in the wake of Janelle Patton's murder, the locals claimed that half the tests would come back the same. Another gag of bad taste: 'What is the definition of confusion? Father's Day on Norfolk Island.'

The island is by its nature a cousinly place. During Bounty Day on 8 June, when the locals re-enact the 1856 arrival of the Pitcairners to Norfolk, Laurie 'Bucket' Quintal stood with his arms around Yvon Grube on the convict-built pier at Kingston. She wore a soft sunhat with the words HMS *Bounty* printed on the brim. As I took their photo she turned to him and asked, 'Who am I to you?' He frowned for a moment and did his best to remember: 'Ah, first cousin . . .?'

They both laughed. His answer was good enough.

The closeness of Norfolk's population is what makes the community tick. It's also what makes it special and divisive. By its very nature it excludes outsiders. The Pitcairners, as they're known, are an exclusive club, honoured by birthright. The 'Pitcairners' doesn't refer to the people who live on Pitcairn, it refers to the descendants of those who came from the island in 1856.

The decision to leave Pitcairn was made in 1853 when drought, illness and overcrowding forced the community to abandon its tiny homeland. In 1855 a majority of the Pitcairn community voted to emigrate to Norfolk, which was a big decision given that it's 4830 kilometres away on the other side of the Pacific. They didn't all want to go but in 1856 they did, with the help of the British government. Two years later, homesickness lured seventeen people, mostly from the Young family, back to Pitcairn Island. Another group of Islanders returned to Pitcairn in 1863. It is the descendants of these families who make up the forty-seven people who live on Pitcairn Island today. In October 2004, six local men were found guilty of raping and sexually assaulting children in the British dependent territory. In preparation for the trial a number of prison cells were built by the same men who were later charged. The case has scandalised and divided the island because those found guilty include the Pitcairn mayor Steve Christian (who was found guilty of four counts of rape) and his son, Randy. Both help man the long boats which connect the island to passing ships in the Pacific. Two separate appeals are underway against the convictions, both delving into the history of Pitcairn and testing the jurisdiction of British Law on one of the world's most remote inhabited islands. Until these appeals are heard, the six convicted men continue to live within the small community.

Norfolk and Pitcairn Islands might be at opposite ends of the Pacific but they're connected by blood, mutiny and isolation. Because of this shared history, Pitcairn Islanders can skip Norfolk's tough quota system when it comes to immigration permits and apply under a 'special relationship' provision within the Act—which is designed to protect Norfolk's Pitcairn lineage.

On Norfolk everyone knows each other's bloodline and that of their collective offspring. It means Islanders can place each other. Through this elastic gene pool comes a sense of family. This unbreakable shackle bonds and unifies the Islander community as one and it does so in a unique way. This is why Norfolk and Pitcairn Islanders have such a thin skin for criticism: to criticise one is to criticise many. Just as a family will defend one member's honour, the island as a whole will close ranks to defend itself against outsiders. And just as in any family, the harshest criticism is reserved for only those within the circle. Telling strangers of a scandal derogatory to another Islander is said to have been an offence under old Pitcairn law. The old Norfolk ethos says that in any dispute between an Islander and an outsider, the Islander is always right. The origin of this can be traced back to Fletcher Christian and William Bligh. When the script was written for the Norfolk version of *Mutiny on the Bounty*, which plays to tourists two nights a week under the stars on a reconstructed ship, the scriptwriter was told to ensure Bligh appeared the tyrant. The actors, some of them descendants of those they play, lip synch to a pre-recorded dialogue. To compensate for a lack of vocal engagement in their performance the actors' physical gestures are wildly overblown, so the performance ends up looking like a tired English pantomime. When I went to the show, which is interminably long and skips the violent behaviour of the mutineers once they'd settled on Pitcairn Island, a fairy tern swooped low and shat on my forehead. Not surprisingly, I never met an Islander who would defend William Bligh.

This is why island families worry about the origin of Janelle Patton's killer and why, from day one, there's been great debate about whether the killer is a 'local'. If it is ultimately revealed to be one of kin, then it's easy to imagine the domino effect of shame and disappointment as it ripples through the island's tangled family tree. The desire for the offender to be an outsider, a TEP, a tourist or a mainlander is a natural reaction by any family wanting to protect its honour. The possibility that such a vicious, violent, hate-driven crime was committed within an established island clan is, for many, a burden too great to shoulder.

On Norfolk Island the link between an individual and an entire family is often dangerously blurred and locals aren't immune from making the classic mistake that outsiders are prone to: bitching about a third party only to discover, to their horror, that he or she is the brother, sister, aunt or uncle of someone closely related to the person they're bitching to. These revelations can emerge at any time, regardless of how much they know about the island's genetic jigsaw puzzle.

In the early twentieth century, anthropologists were fascinated with the blood of the Pitcairners because it mixed English and Tahitian bloodlines—in its day two fairly divergent groups. The Pitcairn descendants were perfect as subjects for a study of the effects of marriage and offspring within a closed genetic pool. The history of Norfolk is littered with unfavourable commentary regarding intermarriage and its effect on the physical and mental capacity of its people as a whole. In the 1880s, it was suggested intermarriage was the reason for a 'declining physique' and loss of energy.

In 1885, James J Spruson, the assistant registrar of copyright in New South Wales, published a history of Norfolk. It contains errors and contradictions and it's never clear if the copy is his or somebody else's, which makes his job title a concern. The book includes a paragraph which has often been quoted and is worth repeating because it supported the then argument that Norfolk's bloodline was the seed of its damnation. The Pitcairn families, Spruson wrote, 'are too closely allied by intermarriage to thrive well. Therefore nothing can save the stock now from utter deterioration but the free admixture of new blood. Vested interests, strong prejudices and the peculiar circumstances of the island, however, stand in the way of applying needful reform, so that the prospects of this once promising little community are really sad to contemplate.'

In 1892 the Bishop of Tasmania, HH Montgomery, said that intermarriage on Norfolk 'has had a serious effect already in the deterioration of the race, physically and mentally'.

The belief that the Islanders were so inbred as to produce a state of eternal apathy was scientifically rebutted by Harry Shapiro, an anthropologist who visited Norfolk in 1923, 'to study their inheritance, society and the effects of inbreeding'. I found a copy of his paper in Norfolk's small library, a slim A5 document squeezed amongst a bundle of other reports. His self-confessed interest in Norfolk Islanders was due to 'at least five generations of inbreeding'. His report is full of the ethnological jargon of the day—exotic terms like 'hybrids' and 'parent stock'.

It also includes measurements of the Islanders' ears, foreheads, noses and chins. He includes black and white photographs of his subjects, taken with the subtlety and grace of police mug shots. The Islanders appear morbid in the photos, almost dead, as if they are being secretly held upright by steel wires. They are either sitting or slouching against whitewashed walls. They are all expressionless, dishevelled, barefooted and shy. Pitcairners were never keen on having their photos taken. Colleen McCullough's husband, Ric Robinson, once said to me, 'I've still got enough coconut in me not to like cameras pointing at my face.'

How the anthropologist Harry Shapiro managed to get so many Islanders to sit for a photo session shows they had no clue what he was up to. His conclusions, however, were more favourable than his apparent methods. He found the Islanders to be in good shape. They possessed, he said, 'a physical vigour and exuberance which equals if not surpasses either parent stock'. He concluded the 'close interbreeding' on Norfolk had 'not led to physical deterioration'.

What did cause Harry Shapiro great concern were the Islanders' teeth. He couldn't, no matter how many jaws he prised open, find a complete set: 'The hybrids are subject to a very early loss of their teeth which is complete while still comparatively young', he wrote. Shapiro couldn't locate a particular cause for this deficiency and noted that by the age of fifty, the 'hybrids' no longer had any teeth at all. Eighty years on, modern dentistry has fixed rotten teeth and the 'hybrids' prefer to be known as Norfolk Islanders, but Shapiro's observations of island society remain telling.

Shapiro noted the Islanders appeared 'more English than Tahitian' and he observed the 'social solidarity of the group' meant it was rare for an Islander to 'inform a stranger of any scandal or gossip which is derogatory to a fellow islander'. Under the heading 'Mental and Moral Traits' he touched on the many levels of getting to know a Norfolk Islander. Despite their 'apparent openness of manner', he wrote, it was 'impossible to gain their entire confidence, that a reserve is felt even after a long acquaintance'.

Harry Shapiro's words remain pertinent; this reserve is a defence mechanism to a history of arrivals and departures. As for all humanity, relationships on Norfolk are about investment and return: unless people are willing to commit to the island, there's only so much an Islander is willing to reveal. It didn't bode well for my journey, which was why I was on the bus tour.

———

After Maxine's opening statement about family bloodlines, she drives out of Burnt Pine. Norfolk is an island of roller-coaster roads, of tucks and folds, hidden valleys and rolling green hills, covered with the thick-rooted kikuyu grass. It's more English than Pacific. There are no palm-fringed reefs or pearl-string beaches, there are no beachside bars or thumping beats—instead there is silence, interrupted by the murmur of elderly tourists and passing cars. All around are tall, straight pines which dot the landscape like soldiers in formation.

Norfolk Island is too far south for coconuts but warm enough for tropical fish, turtles, coral reefs and a sensational turquoise sea, the kind of azure, aqua hue found in a summery, gin-based cocktail. Even the freshwater ducks have taken to paddling at the beach. Inland, wild guavas grow, yellow and red. Bush lemons and woody avocado trees hang heavy with their burden. Feral fowl are constantly on the move, gruff hens and crazy roosters that torture tourists with their off-pitch crow. Norfolk's cash cow is now tourism, but its self-sufficient agricultural ways still blossom. It's a reflection of the island's isolation and a reality of the economy because imported fruit and vegetables are banned except for potatoes and garlic.

Maxine slows the bus and beeps the horn at some obstinate cattle. Buxom and lazy, the free-roaming herds graze the asphalt fringes and side gullies of Norfolk's twisting roads. The pastoral rights are an island heritage, passed down through families. The cattle have right of way over traffic. Visitors are reminded of this quaint road rule when they land at the airport. But it's no joke. The cattle are a formidable obstacle and larger than the small hire cars on offer. The beasts are liable to show up around any corner, bang in the middle of the road, swishing their tails and in no hurry to move. It's even worse at night. These living, breathing speed humps are far more effective at reducing speed levels than the three police officers. It's a criminal offence to hit one, but like all single-vehicle accidents on Norfolk, they're rarely reported. People find the cattle a menace and the miles of fences which grid the island are to keep the cattle out, not in.

Eight kilometres long and five kilometres wide, the island is not as small as it sounds, simply because it's so very hilly. An undulating landscape offering escape and privacy. If Norfolk were flat it would be insufferable, but its beauty lies in its ceaseless ripples, like swell lines on the horizon. Locals find solitude and silence in the creases and folds, which is why Colleen McCullough moved to Norfolk in 1980.

Maxine pauses in front of a neat front yard dotted with kentia palms. 'This is where one of our most famous residents lives,' she announces. 'You don't see her often, she's very reclusive and rarer than the boobook owl.'

Everyone looks out the bus window expecting to see something, but there's nothing there except a long driveway disappearing into a tunnel of pruned shrubs. It's the property 'Out Yenna', home to the Australian author and her husband Ric Robinson. Ric and Colleen are two of the most politicised people on the island. They argue Norfolk is a distinct and separate place from Australia, which is denied independence by Canberra.

Colleen McCullough may be a physical recluse, now suffering from an eye disease which is sending her slowly blind, but her voice in support of Norfolk is omnipresent. As she's got older the occasional quotes she provides about the state of Norfolk have got darker. In response to the Pitcairn sex trials of 2004, and promoting yet another book, the author said of the six men convicted: 'They are as much Polynesian as anything else. It's Polynesian to break your girls in at twelve.' Colleen McCullough has always been the ambassador the island never employed.

For some years, Pitcairners on Norfolk have been revising their Polynesian history. For some it's a bandwagon, for others a neglected part of their history. For more than a century, Islanders regarded themselves as English; now some want to be Polynesian.

Sitting across from me at the back of the bus are two women who, by the way they're acting, must be siblings or very close friends. There's the parallel giggle when no one else is laughing, or the pulling of hair from behind the seat. They're in their mid forties and can hardly keep still. One has a narrow face with a drawn look, the other is rosier and rounder. Both are spicing up Maxine's tour with a self-deprecating, backseat commentary of their own. We leave Colleen McCullough's property in the rear-vision mirror and head to one of the island churches. One of the sisters has been travelling in Europe and is showing signs of monument fatigue. When we pull up in front of St Barnabas, the island's oldest chapel, an ornate sandstone built in 1880, she declares she can do no more ABCs: 'Another Bloody Cathedral'.

St Barnabas Chapel was originally built for the Melanesian Mission, whose school was based on the island from 1866, ten years after the Pitcairners arrived. The mission is notable because it was the first land deal made with outsiders and angered Islanders who were led to believe they had all the island real estate to themselves. When the mission moved its headquarters to Honiara in 1920, the chapel was handed back. It's now used for Church of England services.

The chapel is impressive and traditional. The polished kauri pews face one another and at each end are inlaid with pearl-shell decorations. When Janelle Patton drove past with her parents the day before she was murdered, she told her mum the pews were the sort where 'everyone can check on who has come to church and who hasn't'. The small cushioned kneelers are in colourful psychedelic swirls and patterns, each dedicated to a family or former parishioner. The kauri pews give way to sandstone walls and a wonderful timber roof, designed in the shape of a ship's keel. The floor is marble, quarried from Devonshire in England.

But what's really fun about the chapel—and where the two women from the back of the bus race to after the inside tour—is what grows behind it. It's a tree, an epic tree, like a caricature from a children's book. It is all limbs and branches; majestic, burly and menacing at the same time. Its roots form a series of cubbyholes and trenches and the whole thing erupts from the lawn like a spew of lava. The tree is a Sri Lankan fig and its branches hang, in part, over a small cemetery. The middle of the trunk is so fat it's big enough for a handful of people to stand in. To get up, there is a cut timber log leaning at a 45-degree angle to a low-hanging branch. The two sisters clamber up, pulling themselves along with the rope handle. Others from the bus make their way to the tree as well. It's got greater gravitational pull than the altar.

A woman in a lime green linen suit, pleated pants and white canvas shoes with *Softboy* written on the heels, toddles down the grassy field towards me.

'It's awful when you can't climb anymore. I'd like to get up there, but I just can't manage it.' I smile as we watch our bus companions exploring the tree like kids in a playground. Approaching the plank is her friend, a wiry man with a charcoal goatee and hesitant gait. He looks hell-bent on stepping up the timber plank to join the others. Exasperated and no doubt jealous, she sighs, 'There he goes. Well, don't fall, you silly old goat.' She turns away and smiles, not bothering to see if he makes it. I watch him carefully clasp the rope with both hands and haul himself up, one step at a time. A short, determined journey in care.

The woman pulls out a handkerchief to mop her brow. Her name is Judy. 'My friends said why go to Norfolk? There's nothing to do, you'll be bored, but I'm loving it here, it's great fun. It's certainly a change from Melbourne.' She pauses and looks down the hill. 'I'm not going in there though,' and she points towards the Parish Centre next to the chapel, where a friendship and companion service for elderly residents is underway. The group is called the White Oaks and we can hear them singing their theme song to a childish piano melody. The lyrics are written on a blackboard and easel where a young woman taps each line with a metre-long ruler. Judy grins at me and I understand her joke. For visitors like Judy there is a thin line between the twilight years and the final years. Everywhere I go on Norfolk I feel the shadow of mortality, a presence driven by the vibrant, almost wicked energy from Norfolk's tourists, seventy per cent of whom are over fifty. A quarter of all visitors are over the age of seventy.

When we stop for morning tea at the home built by a '*Bounty* descendant', Maxine tells us the property had been in the Christian family forever until one of the children inherited it and broke all the rules by putting it on the market. The extended family had to buy it back.

The home is a simple, roomy place built from Norfolk pine, with large verandas. Handing out biscuits on the front porch is the woman in black from the tour shop. She stands on the top step and announces more tour options, starting with the 'progressive dinners'. These are mobile dinner parties where tourists enjoy the hospitality of Islanders in their own homes. Each course is held at a different residence and visitors get to hear stories of the old days from the locals. Also on offer is a 'Pitcairners 1856 theme dinner and show', scenic flights, 4WD tours and the murder mystery dinner. After taking a few bookings from happy-to-try visitors the girl in black takes me aside and suggests I come to the Friday night fish fry, where there's some 'Tahitian dancing and people more your age'.

As the bus heads towards Kingston, we pass the old sawmill which turned the giant pines of a century ago into the timber of today's island homes. The bus drives down Rooty Hill Road towards Kingston. This is the now infamous road from which Janelle Patton disappeared on Easter Sunday 2002. There's no mention of this on the tour and as we stop for a photo op at Queen Elizabeth lookout, the destination of Janelle's last, fatal walk, I stay in my seat and wonder how many years it will take before the story of Janelle makes it into the tourist brochures. How long does it take a murder to become a yarn suitable for visitors— ten, thirty, fifty years? It'll be a brave person to use the story of Janelle as a commercial lure for tourism.

Down on the flat land of Kingston we pass the convict buildings which attract so many visitors. As we approach the convict pier and main access to the ocean, a parked car blocks our passage. 'That's a funny place to park,' says Maxine, more to herself than to us. As she shifts the bus into reverse and the automatic chime rings out, she says, 'Oh well, you can get away with anything on Norfolk Island.' I write that down in my notebook as the two sisters look at me suspiciously.

At the end of our tour, Maxine places the step box at the door of the bus one last time and helps the passengers clamber down, thanking them one by one. Judy from Melbourne, still looking bouncy in her lime green linen suit, corners Maxine and asks the question I didn't expect to hear. 'What happened to the young girl who was killed?'

Intrigued, with ears burning, a few people gather in a tight scrum to hear the reply. I do the same. Maxine says, 'Everyone thought she had been killed in a car accident. We were horrified when the police announced she had been murdered, here on this little place.'

CHAPTER 4

BACK FOOT FORWARD

ON THE surface, Norfolk Island is an unlikely place for a crime as hateful as murder. But all communities have sinister undercurrents—there's no reason why Norfolk shouldn't. In the end it was the willingness of locals to imply the opposite that suggested there must be plenty going on. In this respect it was not unlike Pitcairn Island.

The idea that human evil didn't stalk Norfolk, or was repelled by its Christian faith and honest values, was contradicted by a visit to the local court registry. In ramshackle order in an old vault were boxes of documents and transcripts that whispered the obliquely sinister and completely normal face of modern day life.

There was the case of 69-year-old Stephen Nobbs, the Seventh Day Adventist church deacon and first man in island history to be convicted of sex crimes against children. He was charged with three counts of indecent assault and four acts of indecency. The charges spanned three decades. Two of the girls were Christians and one a Nobbs (and two were daughters of close relatives). On appeal to the Norfolk Supreme Court in 2001, Nobbs was convicted on four of the charges. Because there was no 'penetration' the assaults were classified at the lower end of the sexual assault scale. Justice Wilcox found Stephen Nobbs was a man 'used to getting his way', that 'no remorse has been shown', and the judge was unable to 'regard him as a reliable witness'. He was sentenced to forty-eight weekends of periodic detention.

To many on Norfolk the sentence was too lenient. They thought the deacon, who the court found tried to get the girls to 'keep their mouths shut' so that everything would be 'rosy', should have gone to jail rather than the police lock-up. As special dispensation for his faith Nobbs had Saturday mornings free to go to church and didn't start detention until eight o'clock on Saturday evenings. Custodial sentences have to be served off the island and this is a major issue for magistrates and judges when sentencing. It's also an issue for the island's tight budget because jail isn't cheap. The prosecution pushed for a full-time imprisonment but Justice Wilcox agreed with the magistrate that such a sentence should not apply and said, 'the fact it would have to be served in Australia rather than on the island itself is a very big factor'. The finance minister of the day must have breathed a silent sigh of relief. The average cost of housing an inmate in a New South Wales prison in 2003/4 was $63 000 a year or $173 a day. The cost is higher for remand prisoners and maximum security, where anyone convicted for Janelle Patton's murder would serve their time. Here it rises to $189 a day, or $69 000 a year. This is the prospective bill the Island would be charged if the Norfolk Supreme Court hands down a custodial sentence. Over the period of a fifteen- to twenty-year sentence it's easy to see how this ongoing cost would become a burden for an island already struggling to pay its way, and is why to date, judges have shied away from sending people to jail.

Also in the court files were assault charges, apprehended violence orders, two rape cases, and an arson case involving someone trying to burn down the RSL while people were drinking inside. All were acquitted by island juries.

There were quirky cases too, people arguing over the status of Norfolk Island or trying to prevent deportation. There was rumoured to be a case of bestiality from the nineteenth century, when a man was caught fucking a cow amongst the pines. I never saw the file but according to retired judge and resident Adrian Cook QC, it exists. Cook and his mate, Owen Walsh, started digging up some of these older cases but stopped because it was too sensitive for living relatives.

In 2003, a month before my first visit to Norfolk Island, a brand-new, five-bedroom mansion was burnt to the ground. Before it went up in flames, the house looked like it came straight out of the Hollywood Hills. It was plonked on a spectacular site and there were rumblings in the community about how this land had been purchased. It belonged to a resident of only twenty months, a so-called investment manager called Grant Cardno, who sometimes gave himself the title of Sir Cardno. Grant Cardno declined to talk to me about why his house was torched under the cover of darkness. He said he would rebuild, and perhaps at a later stage could explain more. So far he's done neither. Two years on there is still to be an inquest into the fire and the blackened concrete pillars stand as a reminder of what went before. Under Norfolk Island law, arson carries a life sentence, but no one can ever recall anyone ever being convicted for this kind of crime.

Nor do domestic violence cases come before the courts. There is no mandatory reporting on Norfolk and, as in any remote community, the figures are unknown because it's rarely reported. A former Church of England reverend who lived on Norfolk for four years was surprised at what he believed was the incidence of domestic violence within his parish. So too are some of the doctors who have worked at the island hospital.

In 1994 the Australian Law Reform Commission went to the island to investigate the extent of domestic violence in the community. The commission found violence and intimidation through beatings, stalking, crank phone calls, burglary, trespassing and sexual harassment. For my original story on Norfolk Island I spoke with former commissioner, Chris Sidoti. He spoke of the fear women had of talking to the commission when it visited, but only during the day:

'They were extremely busy at night, as women beat a path to their door during the evenings to talk to them under cover of darkness, where they couldn't be recognised or seen by their neighbours. The story these women told was one of quite widespread domestic violence in Norfolk Island that was largely swept under the carpet, that wasn't being acknowledged, and anybody who raised any problems about the issue was either shunned by the local community if the troublemaker, so-called, was seen as a local, or if not a local, was basically driven off the island. And there were even some locals who were driven off the island because of their opposition, their stand at what was going on.'

'Those levels of fear that you talk about, had you experienced those in terms of the commission's work anywhere else in Australia?' I asked.

'No I hadn't. I certainly hadn't experienced the enormous nervousness of isolation, of being ostracised within the community, or even of being forced out of the community, by law and by social control, as I did on Norfolk Island.'

The Law Reform Commission report carries edited quotes from anonymous women. While these comments are now a decade old, the sentiment remains unchanged.

> I've yet to know what the laws are on the Island . . . Inevitably people convicted of offences just get a rap over the knuckles . . . They don't send them off the Island, because it's expensive to lock them up. In a way, the locals laugh about what they can get away with . . . There is no fear of the law . . . They have this disregard for the law . . . because nobody seems to know what it is.
>
> There is a distant reluctance on the part of the police . . . to get embroiled in what they consider to be disputes of an essentially civil character. They tend to regard anything to do with family law as being of that ilk.

As much as Norfolk sells itself as an idyllic acardia, a safer and worthier place than the rest of Australia, or the world, it knew in its heart it was, sadly, very much the same. 'Still, it's a great place to live,' everyone said after discussing the bad bits, and Norfolk apparently is, provided you follow the rules.

Norfolk Island is a community of sanction and payback. All societies have social mores and the smaller the community, the more significant and implicit they become. I was told repeatedly of an underground on Norfolk which uses social pressure to force people to leave if they're creating problems. It involves late-night visits, a tap on the shoulder, silence at the pub. The focus is on 'blow-ins', usually TEPs or the next category up, GEPs—people on General Entry Permits whose time on Norfolk is dependent on owning a local business. These people can never be more than outsiders. Their acceptance or otherwise rests on their participation in the community.

One of the major businessmen on Norfolk is Geoff Bennett. He owns the only supermarket. Originally from New Zealand he's most erudite about Norfolk's ways but refused to say much. When I asked him the naive question: 'How does a new resident become an Islander?' he said, 'The same way a cat becomes a dog.'

Two Islanders who know about the rules are 73-year-old Tom Lloyd and his wife Tim (her father wanted a boy so she got the name anyway). Since 1965 they've published the *Norfolk Islander*. Arson gutted their printery and office in 1980. Tom says somebody took umbrage with his coverage of Norfolk's testy relationship with Canberra, although he's vague about the details. To this day Tom Lloyd doesn't know who lit the match or why. In his small, paper-strewn office he agrees it still bothers him: 'I believe it was a Norfolk Islander who did it. That somebody could do it to one of their own . . .' He frowns from behind his desk. 'I'd like to give them the benefit of the doubt by maybe hiding my head in the sand and saying they had bellies full of beer when they did it.'

'Do you try not to be critical in the newspaper?'

'Well, not to be too critical, but at times to be critical. It's had its ups and downs and the community has reacted against that criticism.'

'Because it doesn't handle criticism well, does it?'

'No, this community no. In certain areas it doesn't.'

'Is that because it's seen as an attack on the island as a whole?'

'I think it is. I honestly do.' Tom pauses and looks down at his fingernails. 'I sometimes feel there is an inherent inferiority complex in a lot of people on the island. They try and cover this up with a bit of bravado. It's not unusual but it is more noticeable here. A lot of people can't stand criticism.'

'But they themselves are critical?'

'Oh yes, it's alright for them to criticise anybody else but God help you if you try and criticise them back. You're liable to wear a fistful of knuckles, you know.'

————

For me, everything about Norfolk Island flashed amber. It was obvious it was best to tread carefully. From the police to long-time residents, this was the most common piece of advice I was given. When my friends asked what Norfolk was like I'd say, 'The back foot is the best foot forward.' I knew enough to know one early mistake and the doors would bang shut, one by one, leaving me out in the cold. That's why it is important to understand the rules of Norfolk. I use the word 'rules' in its broadest sense, of knowing what is, and isn't, a smart thing to do— and understanding why. These sorts of rules exist in all hermetic societies, it's not unusual. What is unusual is to carelessly disregard or fail to respect them. Perhaps this is what Janelle Patton inadvertently did. Had she stepped on too many toes and made enemies? Norfolk Island can be a lonely place in which to be disliked, especially if the grudge is held by entrenched Norfolk families.

There is little room on Norfolk for a 'lack of tact'. Living on Norfolk, as on any remote island, is governed by an innate law of diplomacy. Living without creating too much fuss is the lifeline Islanders embrace. It's a self-preservation order as much as anything else. This was a way of life that didn't fit with Janelle Patton's nature or background, and it's not one city-dwellers like myself easily accept or understand. Many TEPs have come to grief by not realising this lesson early enough.

The quickest way to disturb the waters of Norfolk is to prod and probe, or stick your nose into other people's affairs. Rocking the boat on Norfolk is not sustainable behaviour for outsiders, especially TEPs, who are expected to bite their tongue on all manner of issues. Complaining about wages, hours or work conditions is a sure way to have their temporary permit revoked by their employer. But Janelle Patton didn't let that change her ways. Janelle didn't follow the rules of Norfolk Island. She did as she wished with a confidence that said 'to hell with the consequences'. For this she ultimately paid with her life. This isn't to say Janelle was killed *because* of her actions. We still don't know. But her actions may have contributed to her death. There is an important difference between the two.

––––––

The first rule I was told was a blokey one: 'Don't fuck a local,' they said. I wasn't planning on it but now I was intrigued as to why I shouldn't. 'Because you don't know who you're fucking with.'

This conversation was taking place in the RSL. The person I was speaking with was a recently admitted, bona fide resident who'd done his five-year apprenticeship as a Temporary Entry Permit holder and now, finding his voice as a ridgy-didge resident, felt confident in imparting some wisdom about Norfolk's bedtime politics. I was intrigued with his comments because he *was* fucking a local, although in a nice way—he'd just married her. 'I've worked up to that, matey,' he said, 'but if you're just off the jet, stay away.'

It's no secret Norfolk Island is awash with adultery. For all its pandering to God's ways, the need for fresh flesh is keenly felt by both genders. It's a natural by-product of isolation and endless familiarity.

'There's a fair bit of fence jumping,' said local author Peter Clarke, great, great grand nephew of author Marcus Clarke, when I mentioned the incessant talk of who was sleeping with who. 'But,' he added, 'it's all neighbourly.'

Could it be any other way, I wondered.

Peter had already implied all sorts of group adventures had once taken place on nearby Phillip Island, of which he has a fabulous view from his living room. I'd gone to see Peter about David Lewis, the primary schoolteacher who threw Norfolk's only modern day coup d'état on Bastille Day, 1983. Lewis was so taken with Norfolk he didn't want to leave. When his school posting ended and the immigration office said it was time to go, he tried to take over the island and declare total independence from Australia. Unlike some locals who talk about such action, David Lewis actually did it. He must be the only revolutionary who armed himself with feral rabbits and a bit of gunpowder. Rabbits are banned on Norfolk but were allowed to run free on nearby Phillip Island for decades. The latter is now a barren wasteland and a daily reminder of what rabbits can do to vegetation. In 1983 rabbits were yet to be exterminated on Phillip Island and it's from here that David Lewis made his catch. On the day of the coup he delivered a tape-recorded message to the local radio station threatening ecological devastation by releasing several bunnies around the island: 'I am the only person who can stop the cages opening this evening and releasing the rest of the rabbits.'

The tape made numerous political demands and was given to the station announcer Max Hobbins, who alerted police. Max now drives tour buses and when I rang him to ask his take on this momentous day in Norfolk's history he said, 'David Lewis was a fuckwit,' and hung-up the phone. It was another expansive conversation with a Norfolk native and it made me laugh with despair. Apparently the tape recording is a hoot to listen to but I could only find a transcript. The tape never went to air and police found the schoolteacher crouched on the Kingston foreshore trying to set off bombs made of gunpowder.

David Lewis clearly broke all the rules and the island considered him mad. After a lengthy and amusing legal battle where he beat charges of 'sedition' then attempted to argue Norfolk was not part of Australia, he was deported for his troubles (with Mike King escorting him to the plane as the then immigration officer). On arrival at Sydney airport David Lewis set up a one-man protest in the terminal for several days. He walked around in bare feet with a placard denouncing Norfolk's system as undemocratic and advocating the island's independence. Lewis isn't the first person to become obsessed with the constitutionality of Norfolk Island and the laws it operates under.

David Lewis, who now lives in Queensland, is still pissed off with how the Norfolk Island government pursued him to recover its deportation costs, but like everyone else who has experienced strange happenings on Norfolk, he refuses to talk about it. The island has a stunning capacity to make people go mute, even its revolutionaries. To this day Lewis remains on Norfolk's list of prohibited and dangerous persons—forever banned from entering the territory.

'A brilliant mind and a great chess player,' said Peter Clarke about his old mate David Lewis, 'but there was something not quite right.' As I left his spectacular house Peter Clarke said, 'If you quote me I want to see it first. I have to live here, you don't.'

———

It made sense on an island with no road in or out that 'fence jumping' had to happen close to home. The corollary of this was, of course, where the warning lay. The island was also awash with ex-wives, husbands, partners, lovers and people with a past unbeknown to newcomers. There was a good chance if you did get lucky you would be taking more than just one person to bed and these 'invisible extras' might not be so desirable. Not knowing 'who you're fucking with' meant you didn't know who you might be fucking over. I didn't really have cause to contemplate this, until I was in a position to do so.

It was another night, at another place which sold a lot of beer: the Leagues Club. There at the table was the larrikin Minister for Lands, Toon Buffett. It was March 2004. He was pissed and happy as a pig in mud. His wife Shelley was there too, as were a group of other people I didn't know, including a middle-aged woman sitting opposite me.

'Da men on Norfuk are hopeless,' she moaned in a mild island lilt. Her eyes were bloodshot, but animated. 'They're truly useless.'

It was clear she wanted to see if I was useless as well. And as I looked around the table I could hear the warning bells. I didn't know where she fitted in, who she had arrived with or who she might be with. In fact I couldn't even remember her name. I also knew I didn't want to go back with this raging group of 45-year-old-plus drinkers for a late-hour session on a Wednesday night. One of them was at the bar securing takeaways and I'd already been busted trying to avoid drinking the extra schooner in front of me. I'd foolishly thought that third-party monitoring of other people's beer intake was a thing of the past, but here on 'Norfuk' eyes were sharply aware of the movements of others. And that's what reminded me of the need to exit. The extrapolation of this first, rather practical tip, is the basis of many more social by-laws.

The nature of Norfolk's size and isolation brings together an eclectic group of individuals of vastly different education levels, skills, outlooks and ages who otherwise may not have cause to meet. Norfolk enjoys a sort of social socialism, the one unifying theme being the island. Together these diverse lives intersect, bypass and cut back on each other like a freeway system. The only way to get off is to leave the island. That Norfolk Island is *not* the city is most apparent. It is not a fragmented mass of individuals where personal behaviour is diluted by population, it's an extended family unit. Norfolk is an island where the Butterfly Effect is tangible and the sooner people realise their anonymity no longer exists the sooner they understand their personal actions and behaviour will be noted and discussed. Where people go, who they associate with, what they say and who they take home will be registered in a collective consciousness. If it's intriguing enough it will be broadcast via Dem Tull.

The by-product of isolation is a fascination with other people's lives. It helps alleviate the boredom of one's own. In this respect

Norfolk is like any other remote place but its location in the Pacific, its steep cliffs and extended family bloodlines, make it more intense and a lot trickier to navigate than an average outback town.

I was surprised at the extent of divisions on an island so successful at selling itself as a friendly, hospitable and loving place; a proud and honest people showing tourists a world they honestly believed to be more functional than others. Yet beneath this easygoing public façade lay an intense society whose members knew far too much about one another.

When I told people what I was doing on Norfolk I was met with suspicion and reticence. Some suggested I come over and work as a TEP and silently take notes while serving beer. 'Write it all down and then run for the hills,' some joked. It reminded me of British writer Dea Birkett, whose book *Serpent in Paradise* scandalised Pitcairn long before it scandalised itself with revelations of systemic sexual assault.

People have to be invited onto Pitcairn Island. There is no airstrip or boat service. It's not a place one drops in for a cup of tea—it's an odyssey. Dea Birkett got sponsorship from the British Royal Mail after proposing a story on the importance of a postal service to this far-flung community. She lived on the remote rock for four months and then five years later wrote a book outing the seething undercarriage of the island life of fewer than fifty people. She included her affair with a married man called Nigger. She revealed it all but never revealed to the islanders her profession or true intent. I didn't think it was fair; it was sneaky. She later said her book was 'a tale of a big city person's failure to fit into a tiny community', one she hoped 'was an honest account of a difficult time, and an explanation'. Pitcairners didn't see it that way; they felt duped by an outsider, a constant fear on Norfolk as well. No wonder the only Pitcairn-born person in Britain said they wanted to see Dea Birkett hanged.

I preferred to be upfront about my mission. Everyone knew who I was anyway. My anonymity was long blown. There are few secrets on Norfolk, except for who killed Janelle Patton. There was no point trying to be covert, so I was overt. I was never treated badly, I was just treated with offhanded courtesy, a bit like an unwanted guest at a wedding.

Every time I returned to Norfolk Island people said, 'You've come back?' Because I'd loiter about Kingston a lot, trying to nab people inside their offices, locals would see me and say, 'When are you leaving?' It was said in a nice way, as a genuine inquiry, but it made me nervous. They couldn't believe I was hanging around longer than a week, which is the usual benchmark for most visitors. At one stage this became, 'You're leaving Wednesday.' I wasn't but some locals like to play a sort of 'we know what you are up to' mind game.

I knew I was pushing my welcome when I went for a beer one day and blokes walked away from me with their finger to their lips, saying, 'Shush,' to me, and each other. Others would stop talking and stare into space, making their disquiet known. This would leave me either with no mates, or with a few who were happy to take me as I was, like Toon Buffett or Mike King, who would tease those going mute by tugging at their shirt tails and saying, 'What have you got to hide?' This in turn made them even more flighty but Mike'd get a great laugh out of it.

For the most part the famed Norfolk hospitality didn't extend to a journalist who openly stated they were writing a contemporary book about the place. I wasn't a tourist and I wasn't writing a travel article. Nor was I sponsored by the tourism board. But I did want to try and understand what made the place tick. It made me wonder if Norfolk Island really wanted to be understood. No one ever said jump in my truck or boat and I'll show you what's important to me. No one offered to show me their island, their world, the one they so desperately wanted to protect and honour. I was never invited to anything by an elected representative of an island which claims to be misunderstood, misrepresented and maligned by mainland media and politicians. I got the feeling it enjoyed its ambiguity, it helped cloud everything over. 'It takes time to understand this island,' locals kept saying, which wasn't surprising because so few were willing to explain it. Perhaps people were tired of all the division and niggling. Like one family member who no longer talks to another, explaining why was too complicated.

In general, Islanders preferred it if I just went away. 'We just want to be left alone,' is the political and social catchcry of Norfolk Island, while it simultaneously chases more and more tourists. Hypocrisy is the grease of life. Norfolk was no different. 'To understand Norfolk is to understand its people,' I was told. But if there was no consensus, or willingness, could there be any comprehension?

It's this multifarious and awkward world that Detective Sergeant Bob Peters stumbled into when he started his investigation into the death of Janelle Patton.

CHAPTER 5

WALKING AND TALKING

On the evening of Easter Sunday, 31 March 2002, 56-year-old Bob Peters received a call which changed his life, postponed his retirement and sent him to Norfolk Island for the first time.

It was his granddaughter's first birthday party. 'Everyone was nearly asleep,' he says, 'except the birthday girl.' His boss told him he was needed in the External Territory. The details were sketchy; a young woman, multiple injuries, suspected 'foul play'. It had all the signs of murder.

A private charter flight from Sydney's Bankstown airport left on the Tuesday—two days after the murder. It flew to Norfolk via Lord Howe Island. Priority was given to forensic pathologist Dr Allan Cala, two crime scene investigators and their equipment. There was no room for the man who was to eventually lead the investigation. Bob Peters had to wait for the first commercial flight, which didn't leave Sydney until the following day. He also had to renew his passport.

Bob Peters and fellow detective Tony Edmondson touched down on Wednesday afternoon, three days after Janelle Patton's murder. They never saw her body in situ, instead having to rely on colour snapshots and video footage taken by their colleagues. There were no professional crime scene photographers to document the scene with an eagle eye. As always on Norfolk, the police behaved like the locals and made do with what they had.

Bob Peters' initial brief was to 'provide assistance and support' to the Norfolk Island police. He stayed for ten days before returning temporarily to Canberra. Both Peters and Edmondson were back within weeks, this time with more clothes. On his first trip Bob Peters put his suit in for drycleaning but baulked when told it would take five days and have to go to Auckland.

One month after the murder Bob Peters was put in charge of the investigation. It was now clear this murder case was not as simple as its island location suggested. There was no quick arrest or ready-made suspect. Instead the police couldn't see the forest for the trees. There was lots of information but no eyewitnesses. The Australian Federal Police (AFP) realised the investigation—named Operation Dunedin— was 'likely to become protracted' and handed the brief over to Bob Peters, who was given the assistance of two other detectives: his initial colleague, Detective Senior Constable Tony Edmondson from the Australian Capital Territory investigations group, and Federal Agent Mark Elvin, from the National Investigations Unit. Two intelligence analysts were also engaged. The delay in appointing a lead detective is criticised by two reviews of the Patton case, one by the Australian Federal Police and one by a New South Wales Police review panel. Both are 'protected documents', and cannot be seen.

Bob Peters' passport is cluttered with the same stamp. When he clears Norfolk customs, locals say, 'Welcome back'; others are cheekier and say, 'Welcome home.' He smiles at their lark and reminds himself, this isn't my home—I don't live here, I come here for work. When Peters returns to Sydney he plays out a small ritual as a personal reward for his time away. He buys a milkshake and a newspaper: 'not yesterday's, or the day before yesterday's, but today's newspaper'. Then, as he waits for his connecting flight to Canberra, he sits in solitude, flicking through the newsprint and slurping on a straw. There are no Islanders greeting him with impossible questions like, 'Making progress?' 'Getting close?' Instead, it's just Bob Peters, alone on a chair in a departure lounge overlooking the tarmac and surrounded by all the flow and motion of a busy airport. Nobody knows who he is and nobody disturbs his treasured peace. He has returned to the city, returned to his cloak of anonymity. In that moment, he is at ease.

There's nothing brash about Bob Peters. Like an old Holden with a manual throttle, he takes time to warm up. He doesn't care for the limelight and has little time for the media game required of a lead detective in a high profile murder mystery. He's friendly, humble and disarmingly unassuming. He speaks quietly and often mumbles. When he talks about the case, he weighs his words with care; like placing bait on a hook, he doesn't want to snare himself. He entered the police force in 1975, in part, he says, because 'I don't like crims. I don't like people getting away with doing things to other people. It wasn't any great crusade of protecting the community.'

I first met Detective Sergeant Bob Peters eleven months after Janelle Patton's murder. I interviewed him at the Winchester Police Centre in Belconnen, Canberra, where External Territory policing is based. The Australian Federal Police provide one sergeant and two constables to Norfolk Island, rotated on two-year postings.

Policing on Norfolk was once seen as a good opportunity to kick back, earn tax-free dollars and keep the peace. The past few years have seen the gloss of the position removed following two murders and a double fatal car accident which killed two teenage girls instantly when a car in which they were passengers hit a telegraph pole. The sergeant who had to deal with all four of these deaths was Brendan Lindsay. He suggested the girls may have survived if they'd been wearing seatbelts, which are not compulsory on Norfolk. Brendan Lindsay finished his term on the island in October 2004.

The Winchester Police Centre is more a bunker than an office block. It sits between a string of squat office towers and the local fruit market where Bob Peters goes for a decent coffee, except on Mondays when it is shut. Surrounding the bunker is the sort of barbwire fence they put around detention centres.

The Winchester Police Centre is named after former AFP Assistant Commissioner Colin Winchester, himself a victim of homicide. He was shot in his driveway one January evening in 1989, as he got out of his car. I remember driving to my weekend job the next morning and passing police combing the roadside scrub. Colin Winchester is the highest-ranking police officer to be murdered in Australia and a large photograph of him hangs on the wall in the entrance to the building. It's the good cop portrait, shot at a slight angle. His police cap is perched so high on his head it would topple at the hint of a joke. He wears a proud smile, happily unaware of his eventual fate.

During this initial interview, Bob Peters made it clear for the first time that he considered sections of the Norfolk Island community to be holding back information. He was rubbished for his effort, as was I for broadcasting it on the ABC. Not by all Islanders, but from vocal sections who took this suggestion as a slur on the community. As an outsider, the second lesson on Norfolk is *thou shall not comment, nor criticise.* Criticism is a privilege to be earned, not a right.

This is what Bob Peters told me in February 2003: 'The only way we can solve this case, unless there's a forensic breakthrough, will be with the assistance of the Norfolk Island population.'

'Do you believe there are people on the island who possibly have information and haven't come forward?' I asked.

'I strongly suspect that, yes.'

'And do you believe that information could be crucial to providing a breakthrough?'

'Yes.'

'And do you believe it's fear that's keeping them quiet?'

'If they have that knowledge and they're hiding it and keeping it to themselves, there could be a variety of motivations for that, from fear, loyalty, disinterest.'

Bob Peters still holds this view. He's discovered nothing new to sway his opinion. His final words always struck me as insightful. 'Fear, loyalty, disinterest.' This is the base for many island views, not only regarding murder.

'Our primary aim is to give Janelle and her family justice, and the Norfolk Island community justice,' Peters told me. 'Somewhere along the line, someone viciously killed a young woman who had every reason to live. You can't just close the door on that.'

There is no greater responsibility than being charged with the job of solving the murder of another human being. Homicide detectives see themselves as an elite part of the police force. Bob Peters' name is now linked to the Patton case, and the first murder on Norfolk Island in a hundred years. This is, as they say, his moment. And it's going very slowly.

Like any detective his age, 56-year-old Bob Peters wears a modest suit, the kind of cut of a policeman who started his career before there was such thing as an 'Academy'. Bob Peters wears the same clothes on Norfolk Island and cops a fair amount of flack for sticking to city formalities. Twice he mentions the need to 'keep up appearances' during his visits. There's no question he sticks out when he strolls through Burnt Pine. Norfolk is a place where a suit's best friend is a coathanger, not a pair of shoulders. But true to his job, Peters won't swap his collar and tie for the breezy island kit of shorts and short-sleeved shirt. Comfy Casual is a look he'll leave for the locals. He's on the island to investigate a murder, not to play golf or look at the coral. He hopes his more formal appearance will remind locals why he's in their midst. This is his job—trying to cut through the gossip surrounding a woman's murder.

He tells me: 'In an investigation like this where you've got no eyewitnesses, where you've got no firm motive and where you've got no firm forensic evidence that's going to positively identify the offender, it's a matter of patience and persistence as much as anything else.' Bob then gives me a line which still rings in my ears: 'It's an old police adage from way back that you "walk, walk, walk, and talk, talk, talk".'

If Peters wasn't a dogged detective before he arrived on Norfolk, then he is now. His refrain may well be his epitaph. 'We deal in facts, not suspicion. We have to be one hundred and ten per cent sure.' This is no easy task on a place like Norfolk Island. Bob Peters likes his job—it was the grisly side of homicide which first attracted him to the profession—but this case irks him. A constant gnawing of the unconscious. It interferes with his sleep and interrupts his weekends. He finds it hard to switch off. He is resigned to slogging it out and for more than two years he has been doing the 'walk' and listening to the 'talk'. Like everyone else, he's still to make sense of what happened to Janelle Patton and why. I can't help wondering what happens when the talking stops and the walking ends. Flashing before me is a vision of Peters standing alone on the island roundabout, his tie fluttering in the Pacific breeze.

'I was thinking very strongly about retirement,' admits Bob Peters. 'I wanted to retire, but you can't just walk out halfway through. It might come to a stage where I just can't do anything more and if it hasn't been solved I'll hand it over to somebody else, but I mean, I'll be taking that pretty personally. We've got kids the same age as what Janelle was so I couldn't just walk out.'

I ask about the Norfolk community and its remarkable level of interrelations. 'Does it make this investigation more difficult?'

'Yeah, not knowing straight up who the person you might be interviewing might be related to and not knowing their family histories, or any animosities, or any bonds there might be. With a lot of information we received you just can't accept it at face value. A lot in the community said, "Well, we told you something, why didn't you just go and arrest them straight away?"

'Well, suspicions are one thing, facts are another. I suppose in some regards if you're going to make inquiries in a suburb of Canberra for Joe Bloggs, then you'd look up the records to see if there were neighbourhood disputes, or who their associates are, or if they have a record, but you just can't do that here because so much of it is anecdotal. There are so many petty, minor and major disputes never reported to anyone.'

It seemed to me that the interrelationship jigsaw on the island might be a problem for Bob Peters and his investigation team, who would have to research all public information to ensure it's not a deliberate attempt to slander old enemies or particular families. 'Was there a lot of misinformation or malicious information in the early days about other people?' I ask.

'I've got my suspicions that some of it was not to hinder us but to cause distress to the other parties. We've established that two groups have been at loggerheads for some time; the problem is, it doesn't mean the information isn't right, it just changes how you handle it and that is one of the things which has slowed us down to some extent, because every piece of information we've received we've had to look at all the motivations or possible motivations behind it and a heck of a lot of information is anonymous.'

The reality of heading an investigation from 2000 kilometres away in Canberra has also caused problems. Bob Peters is always having to do 'things by long distance': 'If someone rings you up about something, you've got to wait until you get to Norfolk to follow it up. And when I'm here something comes up in Canberra—it's always staggered. You don't have the luxury of working in the city, where if someone says you should look at this car or object then you ring the forensic crew to take a look. Here you have to have a week's notice and make sure it's a worthwhile exercise and not pie in the sky, given the expense.'

One of the most widely used and efficient tools for collecting evidence against a suspect is the phone intercept. This allows police to tap a phone line and monitor conversations. On Norfolk there are no phone intercepts—the legislation to allow the practice doesn't exist. It's no surprise Norfolk police struggle to charge and convict anyone for anything more serious than speeding or drink-driving; what does go to trial is before a hometown jury which, like all hometown juries, is reluctant to convict.

————

In the weeks following the murder Bob Peters and his team struggled against time to get a fix on who was where on the day of the murder. The Australian Federal Police decided one way to speed this process up would be to issue a survey to the 690 tourists and 2081 others living and working on Norfolk Island that day. The three-page document was designed to assist police in establishing, as best they could, the movements of every person on the island on Easter Sunday. The survey was voluntary. It included a time sheet of quarter-hour blocks starting at 11 am and finishing at 6 pm. People were asked to explain where they were, whether they had seen Janelle, what they were doing and who they were with. It took four weeks for the questionnaire to be released to the community. Islanders are critical of the delay. Many could no longer remember where they had been or what they did on Easter Sunday.

Identical surveys were sent to the 690 tourists. As a group it showed considerable interest in solving the crime. Eighty-four per cent of tourists completed the survey. Two of these people were the parents of the deceased. But police were disappointed with the local response. Only fifty-six per cent of people living on Norfolk on Easter Sunday 2002 bothered to return a survey. Bob Peters said, 'I have heard, anecdotally, a variety of reasons for this disappointing response, ranging from "you took too long to send it out", to "I know I wasn't involved so why should I fill it out?".'

The final page of the community survey was left blank for 'additional comments'. On that page Carol Patton wrote the following:

We came to Norfolk Island determined that we would not try to organise Janelle—rather that we would allow her to organise us

& show us her territory & life. We knew that she really loved her independence on the island & wanted to enjoy a hassle-free week with her—that is one reason why we did not jump in the car at 2 o'clock & drive up to her place. We decided not to invade her privacy & let her do things in her own time.

Many Islanders believe Bob Peters and his team stuffed up the murder investigation from the start. It's a criticism he has heard often. 'There's eighteen hundred detectives on this island,' Bob once mused to me over a cigarette at the front of the Island police station. Many locals claim not enough was done in the initial days following the murder to lock down the island and search its thousands of vehicles. Islanders say they would have been happy to help, a community effort to snare the killer and deliver swift justice. The legality of such a process eludes the community. So does the technical capacity to swab, test and analyse so many cars.

It is widely said on Norfolk that police will never solve this crime. It's part aspersion and part honest belief. A contributing factor is a deep distrust of police—they are outsiders and Bob Peters is from Canberra. Any person of authority from Canberra is seen in a somewhat dim light. Colleen McCullough called Peters' team the 'Keystone Cops' and played on the common sentiment that police from Canberra can't investigate murders because Canberra doesn't have many murders to investigate. I often heard how the New South Wales Homicide Squad would have cracked the case in no time simply because New South Wales is the murder capital of Australian states.

If a similar murder happened in Canberra, Bob Peters says, 'there would have been ten detectives put on the job straight away. The reality was we just couldn't do that, so a lot of things that should have been done in the first few weeks didn't get done, and I don't know if we've lost anything out of that or not. I may find out later on down the track.' Otherwise he shrugs at this criticism. He says for all he cares the 'WA police can come over and investigate the case', but he reminds me it's the Australian Federal Police who provide law enforcement on Norfolk. Not only that, the Commonwealth of Australia is paying the majority of the investigation costs. In response to this one local said to me, 'So they should—the girl was from Australia.' Many locals are like this when it comes to Australia. They've got a healthy chip on their shoulder about the big island to the west.

———

Norfolk Islanders also have little experience of murder investigations. From day one the Patton murder has been reported as Norfolk's first homicide in one hundred and fifty years. The first in its post-penal history which began when the last of the convicts shed their shackles and left in 1856. It sounds good, and fits with the notion of the Island of Saints. An image the island's spiritual leader at the time, George Hunn Nobbs, successfully sold to the outside world. The problem is, it's not true. A few Islanders know this, even more suspect it, but many wouldn't know at all because Norfolk is a community of families and it's human nature for the dark moments to be interned by decades of silence.

For the media, the theme of Norfolk being in the midst of its first homicide was sensational. Journalists loved it. Time and time again it served up a snappy lead for their copy. It helped elevate the Patton murder into something more than just a crime. It suggested a 'loss of innocence, the loss of paradise'. The idea that Norfolk had never known murder in all its years was as treasured by the media as it was by the community. It was neat and tidy. It was integral to the story. Murder in paradise was a sure sign the Norfolk community was sliding towards the soiled values of Australia and the rest of the world. Everyone was happy to go with the yarn. It took many months to track down documents to prove otherwise.

There was at least one earlier murder on Norfolk Island, a well-documented and recorded case, complete with a verdict by a jury of island elders. It happened in August 1893, when a local woman threw her newly born daughter down a well. It caused the New South Wales Governor of the day, Sir Robert Duff, 'much perplexity' in how to deal with it because the island's laws didn't extend to murder. The crime was off the books.

It can be argued this long-since buried case of infanticide changed the political course of Norfolk and helped end forty years of self-determination by the Islanders. It led the Colonial Office to question what it saw as the 'unsatisfactory state of island laws', not only in criminal matters but also in the recovery of debts. It accelerated the push to have the island governed by the colony of New South Wales. The British government had been pressing for a revamp of the island's laws and administration since an unflattering report in 1884. By 1896, three years after the murder, Norfolk's future was tied to that of New South Wales and, in 1914, the Commonwealth of Australia.

The murder of 1893 took place in the dead of a winter's night. On 26 August a young woman called Greena Christian gave birth in shame and darkness, half standing, half squatting. Greena was single, her baby illegitimate. She claimed it died seconds after birth. An island jury found otherwise.

Embarrassed about being knocked up by an anonymous Islander, Greena Christian hid her pregnancy to term. She even concealed it from her mother, who lived in the same house. Alone in her bedroom at two in the morning she delivered the child. Unable to see on account of the darkness, Greena Christian struck a match. In those few, flickering seconds, she held the child and thought it dead. 'It did not cry', when she shook it 'but seemed limp and helpless'. She pronounced the child dead, wrapped it in an old skirt, carried the baby to a disused well and dropped it down the hole.

The next day the local surgeon, Dr Peter Metcalfe, was summoned from the cricket ground by Greena's mother to investigate. Under questioning by the English doctor, Greena Christian changed her story several times before finally admitting to the birth.

The body of the baby girl was salvaged from the well and sent to Dr Metcalfe for an autopsy. His findings cast doubt on Greena Christian's claims. He found the baby to be a 'full-grown, well developed healthy-looking female child'. There were no signs of strangulation and the lungs appeared to be in working order. There was no discolouring on the body except for severe bruises on the cranium as a result of the fall down the well.

The island's chief magistrate, Stephen Christian, held an inquiry before a jury of seven island elders, including three fellow Christians, a Nobbs, a Quintal and an Evans. There were no eyewitnesses to the crime. No one saw the birth, death or dumping of the body. The guilty verdict was based largely on Dr Metcalfe's post-mortem evidence.

In 1893, Norfolk Island had no jurisdiction to handle a crime of this magnitude. The power of a jury only extended to theft, aggravated assault and disputes over property. Despite the island jury and its guilty verdict, it amounted to no more than a crude committal. Greena Christian hadn't been cross-examined and had no legal representation. The scales of justice rested with His Excellency, New South Wales Governor Robert Duff, who by extension was Governor of Norfolk Island.

Stephen Christian, no doubt a relative of the accused, asked for 'merciful consideration'. He pleaded extenuating circumstances, saying the girl, 'while not half-witted', was not in 'full possession of all her faculties'. In colourful prose he asked the governor to consider the woman's experience: 'In the agony of that dreadful night, alone in a darkened room, suffering the pangs of labour, with no one to cheer or help her in the slightest, in her terror and shame [she] could not have been conscious of what she was doing.'

Governor Duff was worried. He might hold the scales of justice but he didn't have any idea how to balance them. He turned to the Colonial Office, outlining his concerns. 'The case seems to illustrate the unsatisfactory state of the law and the difficulty of administering it under existing conditions', he wrote. To add to the pressure he was told criminal abortion had been practised on the island before.

The Greena Christian case is fascinating for its inclusion of the opinion of Edmund Barton, the New South Wales Attorney General of the day and the man who, seven years later, became Australia's first prime minister. Edmund Barton found the case 'entirely novel'. What intrigued him was the absence of any legal jurisdiction to deal with the crime. This extended to an appropriate court to hear the charges and the logistical problem of a jail—there wasn't one. 'I can see no escape from this difficulty', wrote Edmund Barton in a long letter to Governor Duff about Norfolk's lack of 'appointed gaol or house of correction'. He concluded Greena Christian must be 'tried on the charge of having murdered the infant'. The question was how. The obvious solution was to hold the trial in New South Wales but for this Governor Duff needed two hundred and fifty pounds to send a 'man-of-war' to bring the defendant to Sydney. The British treasury refused—it might have been its colony once, but it didn't care for Norfolk now.

Governor Duff then discovered another legal hole: he had no power 'to transport convicts into New South Wales from any part of the world'. His hands were tied; the trial of Greena Christian had to take place on the island. The only way a trial could occur was in a court summoned and constituted by the governor himself.

In the end, Greena Christian was convicted of 'concealment of birth'. Technically it was a misdemeanour. She was sentenced to nine months' hard labour. It was the lowest charge available to Judge Docker after murder and manslaughter. With no jail on the island, Greena Christian was confined to a private household. Her hard labour was to be employed by day and locked up in her bedroom by night.

The only newspaper reference I could find to the case was in the *Truth* newspaper of 1 July 1894. True to its individual style of the day, the paper slapped a poem bang in the middle of its front page with no editorial reference to what it was about. I spent many weeks searching for Greena Christian's fate, so here are the final three stanzas of what the *Truth* called 'An Idyll of Norfolk Island'.

Call Ann Charlotte Emily Christian,
Who's charged with a-killing her kid;
Down a well, quite a deep and a misty 'un,
She owned that she'd put it, she did;
But says 'twas a dead and a twisty 'un
Each juryman looked at his neighbour.
And they found it was worth but 'concealment of birth,'
'Nine months' says the Judge, 'with hard labour.'

But a hitch here arose, quite a nailer,
That sent all their reason awhirl,
'We've a gaol, it is true, but no gaoler;
Oh! what shall we do with the girl?'
Law's subtlety! Where art thou failer?
And this the result of their dodging—
'At Brown's she shall bed, for the nine months we said,
And we'll pay for her board and her lodging!'

Oh! Grant me, kind Fate, with the shell on,
(And grant it, as well, unto more folk),
When I graduate as a felon,
Nine years, and not months, keep the spell on
And gratitude will I accord,
Since the duns couldn't down such a ward of 'the Crown'
Which would pay for my lodgings and board!

The confusion over what to do with Greena Christian was caused by inconsistent and incomplete laws between Norfolk and New South Wales, problems which remain today. Commonwealth legislation does not apply to Norfolk unless expressly requested. More than one hundred and ten years after Greena Christian threw her baby girl down a well, incompatible or nonexistent legislation poses problems for Bob Peters and his team investigating the murder of Janelle Patton.

The Greena Christian case led to a renewed push for the island to be annexed to New South Wales and all its laws revamped. When Robert Duff died suddenly in March 1895, Governor-designate Viscount Hampden set his sights on bringing Norfolk into line, just as some politicians today are using the Patton murder for a similar end. Hampden considered the experiment from 1856 of allowing the Pitcairners to govern themselves as having failed. He declared it time for new rules and new settlers.

Two years later, in 1897, new laws were in place. The Pitcairners were stripped of any say in electing their chief magistrate. It became a government appointment made in, and by, Sydney. These decisions didn't necessarily produce better leadership—in fact the first chief magistrate appointed by New South Wales was a disaster and had to be removed from office. The point is, the island's difficulty in dealing with murder led the mainland powers to reshape Norfolk's administration. It kicked off endless inquiries and special reports into island affairs. It led Australian and British politicians of the day to wonder what the hell was going on in the place locals call paradise.

When I eventually showed Bob Peters the 1893 murder file he didn't bat an eyelid. After reading the case in his office he raised his head and said, 'I don't think much has changed.'

CHAPTER 6

THE LONG DAY'S WAIT

RON AND Carol Patton first went to Norfolk Island on their honey-moon. As a graduate in history, Ron was keen to check out the crumbling convict ruins before the locals nicked all the sandstone for their houses. It was August 1968 and the island was in its early years of tourism. It was unkempt and rugged. Ron was twenty-three and remembers fewer houses and people, and little in the way of organised tours: 'We walked all over this island, there were no fences to block our way. Now they're everywhere.'

Carol, a year younger than her husband, smiles about the honey-moon, as if no one has asked about it for a long time. She was just out of teachers' college and shows me a black and white photograph of herself. She is standing on 'Bloody Bridge' in a floral sixties dress, one month shy of twenty-two. She is gazing towards the ocean. She tells me: 'We met another couple here who were also on their honeymoon and we spent most of the time picnicking with them and that's why, as Ron said, we explored every inch of the island. We had a good couple of weeks with them, we just went up hills and down dales, all over the place. I just remember the funny little red car we had to squeeze in and out of, and all the old ruins which are nothing like what they are now because they've been restored.'

'It was a Fiat Bambino,' Ron chimes in. Carol rolls her eyes—she wouldn't have a clue what sort of car it was. She says, 'It was a nice place, but it was more than thirty-odd years ago. It's a long time.'

Carol doesn't believe their honeymoon on Norfolk had much influence on Janelle's decision to go and live there. This was no homage to her parents, rather a desire to break free from her life in Sydney—an overdue sea change for a woman in her late twenties who had never left home and had never travelled.

In 1999, Janelle was desperately low, if not depressed. She was still living at home with her younger brother, Mark. She was still sleeping in the same bedroom she had been brought up in, staring at the only ceiling she had ever known. Ron and Carol had suggested numerous times that she should leave. She agreed, but found change difficult. She wasn't lazy, she lacked confidence. If she was going to move out it would have been with a boyfriend, but her intimate relationships hadn't got to the stage of shopping for homewares. At twenty-seven she was pushing the boundaries of hospitality by staying in the family home.

Her job as a leasing administrator at IBM held no great attraction and she was enduring another personal setback: Todd, her boyfriend at the time, had called things off a few months earlier. He wanted time out after months of tension and argument over life's modern dilemma—when to commit to a personal relationship and to whom. He told Janelle he wasn't ready to take her on and suggested she should go away and sort herself out. Perhaps later they could get together again. It was a decision she couldn't accept and one he now feels, in the wake of her murder, desperate about.

Carol recalls her conversation with Janelle in September 1999: 'She said, "I want to do something different for a while, Mum, I might go and work on an island." I said, "Oh for goodness sake, Janelle, what on earth would you be doing on an island? What island?" I asked. "Oh I don't know, I'll get on the internet." So she got on to this place called Island Employment and printed off some pages—we had Dunk Island, Lizard Island and all these other Queensland islands, then she came up with Norfolk and asked, "Isn't that where you went for your honeymoon?" We said yes and she said, "I might go there, there's a job going at South Pacific Resort".'

Carol pauses. 'I said, "Janelle, I think it would be very quiet, you know, there's cows all over the place. I don't think it would be quite your scene. I don't know if you'd fit in."' Carol laughs, then continues: 'She said, "Oh I don't know, Mum, it might be just what I need." So she rang up and got a phone interview and about a week later said she was going. It all happened very quickly. We were away on a long weekend with friends and Janelle called and said, "I've got to be gone by late October." I said, "That doesn't give you very long," and she said, "No, it's a bit scary. I can't believe I'm really doing this".'

Carol sits back in her chair: 'She didn't have a passport, she had nothing. This was Janelle! She had to get the passport rushed through. So that's how she came to Norfolk. I don't think our honeymoon was a factor in her decision, but she did ask us about it.'

'That gives you a bit of an insight into her temperament,' says Ron. 'She actually said to Carol she couldn't believe she was doing it, coming to Norfolk Island, because she was a person of routine, and this was so spontaneous, this was a change.'

On 23 October 1999, Janelle took her first international flight and left mainland Australia for Norfolk Island. She was twenty-seven. The first stamp in her first passport was Norfolk Island customs. The next day she started her job as a room attendant at the South Pacific Resort, a position she was overqualified but underskilled for. After living a sheltered life at home Janelle was not big on doing any cleaning herself—she preferred to let her mum take care of the domestic chores. Later in a letter home she enthusiastically joked with Carol about how she had cleaned her 'first toilet': 'You wouldn't know me now—I can make beds, wash up, vacuum, clean windows and even hang curtains. A bit of a change, eh?'

As I discovered, the South Pacific Resort sounds more glamorous than it is. The sprawling complex is popular because it is cheaper than much of the overpriced island accommodation. On-island it is referred to as the 'South Pac' or the 'South Pathetic'. It houses many elderly travellers on package tours. Its basic rooms are small, with low ceilings and poor ventilation. They are hot in the afternoon and cold during the night, the idea of insulation appearing to have been an afterthought. Painted on the wall in the bar is a giant map of the *Bounty*'s confused journey in 1789. This was the first place Janelle Patton worked but she didn't stay long.

Leaving Sydney was a change Janelle desperately needed, even if it meant downgrading her career to cleaning rooms for eight dollars an hour, tax-free. Norfolk offered the chance of a new start, to escape the lows she couldn't beat in Sydney. In his statement to the coronial inquest, Bob Peters noted the need for Janelle to break free from the city: 'She had developed a very low level of self-esteem and had begun drinking heavily and taking anti-depressant medication and her physical health was suffering. She decided to move away from Sydney and make a fresh start.'

In the two and a half years Janelle lived on Norfolk Island, she returned to Sydney four times. Her final trip home was for a fortnight in November 2001. For some time she had encouraged her parents to return to Norfolk and see a slice of the island life she was now enjoying. Plans were made for a seven-day holiday over the Easter break. That year the school holidays didn't coincide with Easter so Carol applied for a week's leave from Granville High School where she teaches maths. It was the Pattons' first holiday in two years and, technically, their first overseas trip since their honeymoon in 1968, thirty-four years earlier.

————

The Pattons arrived late morning on Easter Saturday, 30 March 2002. 'Everybody said to us she was just so excited about us coming,' says Carol, who noted how healthy and happy her only daughter looked when they arrived.

Janelle bundled her parents into her car and drove them to Panorama Apartments where they checked in. She told the manager her parents were smokers so she could get them the 'ocean room' with balcony. Carol was shocked: 'How dare you tell lies,' she said to Janelle, who shrugged, then smiled. 'It doesn't matter,' she said. Ron laughs at the memory. 'As things turned out, it was very useful.'

The day was hot and the Pattons changed into shorts and shirts. Janelle then drove the couple of kilometres to her self-contained flat at the back of Ruth and Foxy McCoy's house in Allendale Drive. Janelle made piles of sandwiches and ran through the plan for their seven-day holiday. After lunch, Janelle took her parents on a drive around the island. These few hours are special to Ron and Carol because it's the last time they spent alone with their daughter.

On the way to some of her favourite island spots Janelle drove via Headstone Tip. Here garbage is thrown over the side of the cliff and into the ocean below, where a brown whirling cesspool heaves it against the rocks. The tip is now closed and has been replaced by a recycling centre, but in 2002 Carol couldn't believe Headstone Tip was still functioning. She remembered being fascinated by this method of garbage disposal during her honeymoon. 'My goodness,' she said to Janelle, 'they aren't still throwing garbage down there. I've got to get a photo.'

The photo shows a healthy, happy and tanned Janelle, with dark strands of hair blowing across her face. She's in summery clothes: a yellow singlet top, sunglasses and long baggy board shorts. There's nothing to indicate what was to unfold the next day. There's no stress in her face. She looks rested and content. Her pose is that of a rugby player about to pass the ball, except in her hands is a box of empty Carlton Cold stubbies, her favourite beer. Moments after the photo was taken she tossed the bottles down the metal chute and into the sea below.

Carol Patton doesn't drink alcohol and when she told Janelle how disgusting all those empty beer bottles were, Janelle provoked her further and said, 'Yeah, Mum, just one night's issue.'

They continued north and stopped at Anson Bay, a small, isolated beach on the island's northwestern tip. Here the Pattons snapped more photos with their new camera. This roll of film is the last visual record of Janelle alive and was studied by the forensic lab in Canberra in the hope the sunglasses worn by Janelle in the images would match the pair later found on Rooty Hill Road.

One of the prettiest photos was taken by Carol. It's of Ron and Janelle sitting on the steep cliffs of Anson Bay with the twinkling water far below. Anson Bay was one of Janelle's favourite spots. Taken twenty hours before Janelle's murder, these photographs are an insight into the stress caused by grief. Both Ron and Carol are fuller in the face, without the weariness which now strains their eyes. Carol isn't as grey. Ron has since lost weight.

Because of Janelle's split shifts she couldn't spend all Saturday afternoon with her parents. She had to start work in the dining room of the Castaway Hotel at four o'clock. For the second day in a row she realised she wouldn't have time for her regular walk. On the drive back she said, 'I've got to go for my walk. I haven't been for a walk for a couple of days.'

Janelle had hoped to squeeze in a walk before starting work that afternoon but the island drive had taken longer than expected. 'Because she'd come out to pick us up from the airport, she missed her walk,' says Ron.

Janelle was dogmatic about exercise. She tried to take a forty to eighty minute walk every day and was hard on herself if she got lax. Carol says Janelle was 'fanatical about exercise, making sure she didn't get fat and all the rest of it'. Janelle was also fanatical about her diet, always consuming low calorie foodstuffs, except for beer, which she consumed with pleasure and haste.

Janelle decided she would take her walk the next day, Easter Sunday, following the breakfast shift. She then turned her attention to getting her mum and dad to come to the Castaway restaurant that evening. 'Come up for dinner, come up for dinner. I want you to come to dinner,' Janelle said to her parents as they got out of the car in front of their apartment block. 'We were so tired after the flight,' says Carol, who was happy to skip the meal and stay in the apartment, but Janelle wouldn't take no for an answer: 'You've got to come,' she said, 'you've got to come to dinner for the fish fry.'

Faced with Janelle's insatiable insistence Ron and Carol agreed to a seven o'clock dinner at the Castaway Hotel. It was a fortuitous decision. If not for Janelle's typical eagerness to make people do what she felt was in their best interests, Ron and Carol would not have seen their daughter again. This would be their last evening with Janelle, and the last time they would see her alive.

The hotel bar at the Castaway was once a rowdy place; now it is a genteel dining room with chandelier lighting and a blue and white colour scheme. It's a pleasant space with the feel of a colonial sports club, complete with low slung chairs and glass doors opening to a deck covered with synthetic grass. Outside, kentia palms rub against each other in the wind, creaking amongst the murmur of elderly diners.

Before dinner Ron and Carol rested in their apartment. At 6.15 pm they received a phone message that Janelle was waiting for them to arrive. Even though dinner was not until seven o'clock, Janelle was impatient to wine and dine her parents, even if she herself was working the floor.

What happened next was typical of Janelle's relentless spirit. Ron says, 'We went up to the restaurant and she was so excited she sort of stopped everybody and introduced us, saying here's my mum and dad.' Carol laughs and interrupts Ron. 'She just said "Stop! Attention!" And the whole dining room stopped—as you do when Janelle tells you to do something. We had just walked in the door and we looked really stupid. She said this is my mum and dad and everybody clapped. The people she worked with at Castaway have said, "She drove us mad, she was just so excited you were coming", and all her friends and Ruth her landlady have said the same. All they heard about for weeks before was the fact we were coming over and what Janelle was going to do with us.'

Janelle didn't have time to sit with her parents so she hovered around their table while she worked the room as a waitress. Ron drank a beer, Carol a soft drink. After a meal of fish and chips they called it a night. Around nine o'clock they kissed Janelle goodbye.

Her last words were, 'I love you, thanks for coming, see you tomorrow.'

Carol remembers this farewell as 'a little unusual'. She says it wasn't a touchy-feely sort of situation. 'I interpret it as Janelle being grateful we had come over,' says Carol. She had a whole week planned for us. She said she would stay at the restaurant for a while because a large tour group from South Australia were on their final night and were planning on partying.'

Ron and Carol arranged to meet Janelle between one and two o'clock the next day. Janelle planned to work the breakfast shift, go for her walk and then swing by their apartment. If the weather was good they would go to Emily Bay. Janelle said she would cook some Mexican for dinner.

As Ron and Carol navigated the darkness on their drive home they were impressed with what they had seen. Janelle seemed genuinely happy and healthy. As settled and comfortable in her new life as they had ever seen her. For the first time in many years Janelle looked at ease with who she was and where she was heading. Ron mentioned she was even looking 'a bit fatter in the face' and Carol laughed because on her lap were two extra bowls of dessert which Janelle had nicked from the kitchen. She might deny herself food, but she was always overloading friends and family. Later that week the Pattons had to toss out the uneaten dessert and sheepishly returned the bowls to the restaurant's owner.

When the Pattons told me this, I thought, how many people would bother to return a couple of bowls after the trauma of their daughter's murder? This simple story says a lot about the values and honesty of Ron and Carol Patton.

Happiness is what most parents desire for their children. It's the simplest of aspirations. It supersedes wealth, career or celebrity. In Ron's mind his daughter *was* happy. Ron likes to say Norfolk was a 'maturing experience' for Janelle. Many times I heard him say, 'She was spreading her wings, she was growing up and managing on her own.' For that, Ron Patton thanks Norfolk Island. What pains him is how this process was cut short. His daughter's maturity never blossomed, her wings never carried her away in safety. Instead, something went wrong.

When the Pattons went to bed that night they were looking forward to the next six days of their holiday—to sparking memories of their own honeymoon when, like Janelle, they also hung out on Norfolk in their twenties.

––––––

Janelle finished her shift at the Castaway at 11.15 pm and drove straight home. Fifteen minutes later, at 11.32, her telephone rang. It was a call from her lover in waiting, 37-year-old nightclub manager Brent Wilson. He was now living in Auckland but the two had recently met on Norfolk Island where he had lived for nine years. Brent Wilson met Janelle through his friend Terence Jope at Mariah's restaurant and bar. He was in the final stages of divorce proceedings and the next day visited Janelle at her flat. The pair saw each other for the next 'four to six weeks' until his departure for New Zealand ten days before her murder.

Phone records show Janelle and Brent Wilson talked for forty-nine minutes and forty seconds on the night before her murder. The conversation took place over a series of calls, and although the rates were off-peak, it was costing more than a $1.20 a minute. (Brent Wilson was one of the few people called to give evidence at the coronial inquest. He did this over speaker-phone from Auckland.)

Janelle talked about visiting Auckland and life on Norfolk. She was 'excited' about her parents' visit and Brent Wilson recalled the conversation as 'a happy one'. There was nothing to indicate trouble ahead and many of the relationship issues Janelle had previously complained about were not brought up. He said Janelle 'seemed to be mellowing out and, you know, sort of putting everything behind her and moving on'.

But Brent Wilson's police statement contains a more sinister claim: 'Janelle told me that someone was prowling around her house at night. She started locking her doors in response to this. She never actually saw anybody. However she did say that someone had been through her underwear drawer and messed her bed up.'

Janelle never revealed the underwear story to her mother. Maybe because Carol, as she said herself, would 'go berserk with worry'. In a phone call with her several weeks before Easter, Janelle did hint at an intruder.

Carol asked, 'Are you sure?'

Janelle replied, 'Yes, I know they have.'

For Carol this news was alarming: 'I don't know how Janelle knew that, she said something about the door and I asked if she had reported it to the police, which she hadn't. "Well get a lock on your door and report it to the police," I told her. "You can't have people coming into your house." She said, "It's alright, I think I know who it was. I think it was Bucket just trying to scare me." That is *all* she said to me.' For the record, Bucket denies ever having entered Janelle's flat without her, or going through her belongings.

Two hours after speaking to Brent Wilson, Janelle's phone rang again. By now it was 2.20 am on Sunday morning and Janelle was most likely asleep. She was certainly at home. If not, then somebody was because the phone was answered. The call duration was one minute and forty-seven seconds. Police don't know who made the call, and nor can it be traced. Norfolk Telecom can only track the origin of local calls. Those made from offshore carry no subscriber details except for the duration. This is due to the complicated way telephone calls are routed to Norfolk Island. It means police are sure of only one fact—that it came from overseas.

Was this phone call a threat? A warning? Or a wrong number? Police have no idea who rang Janelle at 2.20 in the morning or why. The logical explanation is that it was Brent Wilson again, but he can't remember. He said it would have been odd to speak to Janelle for such a brief time. The coroner then asked Brent Wilson if he could inquire with his provider as to whether he made the second call. At the time I thought the Commonwealth of Australia would have more resources than an Auckland nightclub manager. Brent Wilson said his mobile phone was a pre-paid account and there were no records to check.

This late-night phone call, made twelve hours before Janelle's murder, remains a mystery.

———

By seven o'clock Sunday morning, Janelle was back at the Castaway Hotel working the breakfast shift. The island was running at capacity, 690 tourists in a total population of 2771 people, every one of them recorded by Norfolk Island customs. Easter Sunday church services were set to commence and the weather was balmy. By nine o'clock it was twenty-four degrees. The front page of Saturday's *Norfolk Islander* carried an Easter message. The banner said 'Love So Amazing' and included the line, 'thoughtfulness adds a special kind of beauty'. Inside was an ad for a wet-T-shirt competition at the Brewery.

Janelle's four co-workers on Sunday morning say she appeared in good spirits and was excited about her parents' visit. There was no hint of what was to come. Only one person suggests otherwise, a male guest of the hotel who told police he believed Janelle 'appeared distracted and preoccupied . . . as if she had received some disturbing news'. This is the only contrary view to the general perception that nothing was troubling Janelle.

Ron and Carol Patton woke about seven that morning. Ron got out of bed and turned on the jug but there was no power. Without electricity there was no water pump, and no water. They ate breakfast on the balcony without a cup of tea and drove to the island markets where Ron bought a key ring.

Next was a drive up Mt Pitt, Norfolk's highest point at three hundred metres, but the summit road was being rebuilt and it was closed to traffic. The Pattons took a walk through the small botanical gardens instead. Ron and Carol are no bushwalkers and to Carol's disappointment the gardens, nestled in remnant rainforest, displayed no pretty flowers. She says it was 'more like a jungle walk'. They then stopped at the green parrot enclosure and tried to spot one of the endangered birds inside.

Shortly before midday they drove to a café in Burnt Pine where Ron ordered a milkshake which he recalls 'took a long time to come'.

It's about now, around midday, that Janelle disappeared from Rooty Hill Road. It was only a couple of kilometres away from where Ron and Carol Patton were sitting and the intimate distance between parents and daughter makes the mystery of what unfolded even more painful to contemplate.

About 12.30 pm the Pattons drove back to their apartment for a sandwich and a rest. Their most pressing thought was going to the beach at Emily Bay for a swim and to lie in the sun. By now it was nudging twenty-six degrees which is hot for Norfolk Island. The only thing delaying them from the feel of the ocean was Janelle's arrival, but she was expected shortly.

When Janelle failed to show by two o'clock Ron wondered where she could be. Half an hour later he decided to call her flat. The phone rang out without being answered. Police confirm a call was made from the Panorama Apartments, where the Pattons were staying, to Janelle's flat at 2.33 pm.

As is often the case with Norfolk's quaint accommodation, rooms don't always have their own telephone—it's the sort of extra which must be requested. It's odd in today's world to ask if a room comes with a telephone but on Norfolk the communication needs of visitors aren't a priority. In these cases access to a telephone is sometimes from the laundry, common room or reception, and calls can easily be over-heard. In this case Ron made the call upstairs, next to the manager's office.

After waiting another ten minutes Ron and Carol decided Janelle must have made other plans, or was held up and running late. Not wanting to waste more of their day they stuck a note on the front door of their room saying they had gone to the beach. As they drove down the winding hills to Emily Bay they were half looking for Janelle and half taking in the scenery.

Carol admits 'a bit of annoyance' was creeping in: 'We had talked about the possibilities of going to the beach anyway, we didn't think Janelle would go without us but we thought we'd check.'

The Pattons parked their car overlooking the beach at Emily Bay but didn't venture out. They watched people swimming and snorkelling and enjoying their holiday. Ron noticed the turquoise water fall into shadow, then the occasional splat of rain on the windscreen. It was getting close to three o'clock and Carol suggested they drive to Janelle's flat to see if she was home, but faced with a series of similar looking driveways, they weren't sure which one led to her place.

The day was still warm but more clouds were billowing overhead and the sky had darkened—the rainstorm which was to prove such a heartbreak for the investigation team was brewing.

Just as Ron and Carol returned to Panorama Apartments the sky opened. It was past three o'clock and the heavy rain gave them hope Janelle would surface. In this weather, they thought, she will seek shelter and return home. Until now, Ron and Carol were assuming Janelle's plans hadn't changed—she was just running late. They believed her timing was askew, not her intentions. They didn't for a minute consider she was at risk.

As the rain dashed the windows and blurred the view, Ron watched sport on TV. After forty minutes the worst of the rainstorm had blown out to sea. The gutters poured and the roads gushed but the sky above was clearing. The Pattons were keen to claim the remains of the day but where was their daughter? Almost three hours had passed since they were due to meet Janelle.

Ron decided to make a second phone call to Janelle's flat. Again the phone rang out. Janelle didn't have an answering machine. By now it was 4.13 pm and Janelle Patton was dead, her body lying on the sodden grass of Cockpit reserve. The image of Ron listening to the ringing of Janelle's unanswered telephone as she lay under a sheet of builders' plastic a few kilometres away is as alien and incongruous as it sounds. Norfolk is many things to many people—much of it good, some of it terrible—but in no one's visual snapshot is there room for the image of a father trying to telephone his daughter as she lies abandoned, alone and lifeless nearby. 'Never on Norfolk,' they say. 'Never on Norfolk,' they said.

Ron returned to the apartment with his hands in his pockets and looked at Carol. They decided to go back to Janelle's street. This time they found the driveway and saw Janelle's car. Its windows were down and the seats were wet. This suggested it had been parked there before the rainstorm. Ron walked to the back door of the flat where a flooded ashtray overflowed with wet cigarette butts. The door to Janelle's flat was swinging open and a curtain blew in and out of the doorway.

When Carol saw this scene she thought Janelle must have been at home: 'We were a bit annoyed, she was supposed to be meeting us. Because no one locks doors we just walked into the flat and called out and there was no sign of her. All these groceries, her purse and handbag, it was all on the table. I said to Ron, it's a bit strange, and we noticed that her sneakers were gone because all the shoes were lined up near the door and we said, she must be gone for a walk, but she must have gone a lot later than planned. There's obviously been some delay. So we thought, oh well, we'll wait here until she comes back. And then minutes later one of her work mates called in, or called out, and I said to her, "Janelle's not here. Have you seen her?" She said, "Didn't she meet up with you guys, she was supposed to meet you today", and I said, "No."'

The work mate was Caytie Nobbs. She confirmed Janelle finished work on time and her plans hadn't changed.

Caytie's arrival on the scene still remains a mystery to the Pattons. Caytie said she was meeting Janelle to go to the Brewery but the time of her arrival was about five o'clock. It makes the Pattons wonder, even now, if Janelle actually was going to cook them dinner at all.

Caytie Nobbs picked up the phone and called the Castaway Hotel to see if Janelle was there. The call was made at 6.02 pm. Caytie told the Pattons she knew where Janelle walked and went for a short drive to see if she could find her. She returned ten minutes later and explained the route to the Pattons so they could take a look themselves.

Carol wrote another note for her daughter and left it on the dining room table. The Pattons then drove the same path Janelle had walked six hours earlier, although they were still in the dark about when Janelle had left her flat. They had every reason to believe she might still have been on her walk, even at twenty past six.

————

Having been in Janelle's flat the Pattons had established four key facts. They knew Janelle had gone to the supermarket, returned home, changed her clothes and put on her sneakers. All these actions were consistent with her plans outlined the night before. Nothing had changed except the timing. Everything was running late—quite late, but on Norfolk, time is elastic. After living on the island for more than two years, maybe Janelle was running to local time. What else could explain her apparent disappearance?

Of Janelle, Carol says. 'She was very much a creature of routine and the fact that she had to work in the morning on the Sunday, then she had to go for her walk, then she was going to meet us and then she was going to cook us dinner. It wouldn't have changed, it was just a routine, it was almost an excessive routine.'

Ron: 'She had left her cigarettes and her purse and everything.'

Carol: 'She left everything.'

Ron: 'She was coming back to where she lived, she wasn't going off with anyone. She'd been organising all the details of our trip in the weeks beforehand, there's just no way she would have gone off with somebody willingly.'

At Queen Elizabeth lookout Ron and Carol decided to drive via their apartment one last time, just in case Janelle had walked over to visit them. When they arrived Ron saw some people talking out the front and asked if anyone had seen his daughter. A local woman who knew Janelle went inside and made some phone calls but none of Janelle's friends had seen her all day.

It was now heading towards seven o'clock and by anyone's reckoning Janelle was five hours late in meeting her parents. Her wallet, bag, keys and car were all at her flat. For the first time that afternoon Ron and Carol were worried. It was dusk and nothing was adding up.

Ron and Carol were also hungry. Whatever plans Janelle had for dinner would have to wait for another night. They stopped at the Ocean Blue Café at Middlegate and ordered fish and chips. As Ron waited for their takeaway Carol stayed in the car. She recalls feeling 'a bit creepy, sitting in the car, alone in the dark.'

They then drove back to Janelle's flat for the third and final time that day. By now Carol was resolute. She told Ron, 'We're just going to sit here now and wait until she comes. She's got to come back.' Ron says, 'We were in a quandary in the sense that—right, you come from Sydney, you come from New South Wales, Australia and your daughter's twenty-nine, she's meant to meet you between one and two and we tried to ring her. We thought she might have been down at

Emily Bay, so we went down there and that's about the time it started raining. So then we came back and it pelted down rain, and we're saying, well, what should we do? As I said to Carol, I said, look, if you approach the police after an hour or two that someone's meant to meet you, in New South Wales they'd say wait twenty-four hours. Therefore, you're on an island that you don't really know that well . . .'

Carol: 'No mobile phones . . .'

Ron: 'Right. You don't know exactly where Janelle is, or what she's doing. She could have gone somewhere. May not have; but could have. So we thought, well . . .'

Carol: 'We'll wait and she'll come back.'

As they entered the flat, Janelle's landlords came out to meet them. Ruth and Baker 'Foxy' McCoy are long-term islanders aged in their seventies. Their house is adjacent to the self-contained flat Janelle had been renting for twelve months. Ruth and Foxy had heard all about Ron and Carol's visit and were keen to meet them.

As the two couples exchanged greetings Carol lost her appetite. It was what Ruth said that tested Carol's composure and made her stomach lurch. She revealed she had seen Janelle leave for her walk hours earlier.

'What time was that?' asked Carol. 'Was that late?'

'No,' said Ruth, 'before midday, around eleven thirty. As we were coming home we saw her at the end of the street going for a walk.'

Carol had every reason to be worried. She knew enough about her daughter to be uncomfortable with the news. Even as she relays the story now, Carol runs her words together in a rush: 'I said, "Oh my goodness, should we be worried here, at what stage do we push the panic button on Norfolk Island? Do we ring police, do we ring police or what? Her car's here, her bag's here, she's not here, we haven't heard from her."

'Ruth said, "You're her parents, so it's up to you, but if you weren't here, I think I would phone the police because Janelle was very much a routine person and it would seem that something must have happened to her." I don't think any of us in our wildest dreams imagined what. But you know, maybe just an accident of some sort.'

The Pattons were now convinced something had happened to Janelle. They followed the McCoys into the main house and Foxy dialled 22222 for the Norfolk Island police. He handed the receiver to Ron.

According to police this call was made at 7.50 pm. The Pattons are sure it was much earlier and wonder if there isn't a missing hour somewhere. They claim the call to the police was made around seven o'clock.

Carol recounts the conversation which took place: 'Ron said to the policeman, "My daughter is missing and I wonder if there is a report of an accident or anything like that?" The police asked Ron what Janelle was last wearing. Well, we didn't know, so Ron gave the phone back to Foxy and they spoke in their little local language and we picked up a few words.

'When Foxy got off the phone he said they wanted us to go down to the police station and put in a report. They went in their car and we followed them. When we got down to the police station, as I remember, they said, "We believe your daughter's missing?" We told them what she looked like. This tall, long dark hair, thin. Brendan Lindsay, the policeman, asked if she ever wore her hair in a plait, or a ponytail. I said if she was out walking, yes, she would, because that's how she would have always worn it. Then he stopped and said, "Look, before I go any further I have to tell you there's been an incident, a body of a young woman's not long been found. Before we go any further we need to identify whether it's your daughter or not." Well, as soon as they said that, I thought it would have to be because I thought two young women in one day on Norfolk Island? I don't think so. So they asked Ruth or Foxy to go and have a look. Ruth volunteered to do it, she's a former nursing sister and she came back, I have no idea how much later and said, yes, it was Janelle.

'We said, what's happened? And they said, "It looks like she's been murdered", and I thought, oh my goodness. I honestly don't know what happened after that.'

Ever since, Ron and Carol have thought *could we have acted earlier?* The notion that by some action, or movement, the alarm could have been raised sooner has crossed their minds countless times.

'When you look back at this,' says Ron, 'you sort of say to yourself—oh, if, but! In our case there is no if or but. The time limit is so short, the reality of it is we couldn't have got to the police any earlier in a sense and had any positive response from them. It was only after

Janelle's body was found that they realised there was a problem, or the police would have then connected us with her, which happened.'

Janelle's body was discovered at 6.15 pm by two New Zealand tourists out for a walk. They rang the police station at 6.33. Ten minutes later Constable Michael Julius nudged the wheels of the police wagon onto the muddy tracks of Cockpit reserve. The surface was as slippery as ice. He parked and made a short search on foot, finding Janelle Patton's body just as the tourists had described—lying near two steel rubbish drums and partially covered by a piece of flapping plastic. Constable Julius touched the right leg and felt it was cold. He then sought a pulse from the wrist and noted the arm was 'cold to touch and stiff'.

He radioed Sergeant Brendan Lindsay who took command of the crime scene just after seven o'clock. A call was made to the Volunteer Emergency Squad for lights and a generator. Constable Julius left Cockpit to collect local doctor Lloyd Fletcher. Additional calls for help were made to Norfolk's Special Constables—local Islanders who help the police in times of need.

Shortly before eight o'clock Dr Fletcher was escorted into Cockpit reserve to view the body. By the time Ron Patton reported Janelle missing, police knew the prognosis was bleak. There are only six minutes separating Ron Patton's phone call to the station and Dr Fletcher's medical pronouncement of death at 7.56 pm.

It was up to Sergeant Brendan Lindsay, on his second secondment to Norfolk Island, to break the news. It was awkward because first the body had to be confirmed as that of Janelle Patton. While Ruth went to look everyone sat about in a terrible silence.

At nine o'clock Brendan Lindsay and Ruth McCoy entered Cockpit reserve. They ducked under the tape barrier and walked to the steel rubbish bins. Ruth didn't need long to identify the body—she could see the back of Janelle's head and her ponytail sticking out from beneath the plastic sheeting.

Only ten hours earlier she had seen Janelle outside the supermarket, full of energy and life. She had thrust a basket of Easter eggs in Ruth's hand and kissed her on the cheek. Brendan Lindsay and Ruth McCoy drove back in the darkness to officially inform the Pattons of their daughter's murder.

Ron and Carol were driven to the island hospital and given sleeping tablets and a hospital room. They stayed for several days. 'You needed something,' says Ron of his blurred memories. 'We were starting to float, but reality was having an effect.'

CHAPTER 7

WHO WAS JANELLE?

I NEVER knew Janelle Patton. My sense of who she was can only ever be second and third hand. Janelle, born 30 June 1972, was two years younger than me. If we had been at school together she would have been in the year behind. She went to Pennant Hills High in Sydney and finished Year 12 in 1989. She worked as a foreign exchange clerk, a customer services officer for Westpac and a leasing administrator with IBM.

In photographs she comes across as a pretty brunette, with long, straight, dark hair and brown eyes. 'Outgoing' and 'intelligent' are two of the first adjectives used by people to describe her. They say her mannerisms came from her mum, her love of talking from her dad. She was thin, feisty, fit and organised. She preferred structure to chaos but so many of her actions left a trail of wreckage she could neither see, nor cared to see. At Janelle's core was an obsessive and intense personality that left her boyfriends reeling and, at times, her family staggered. 'If she walked into this pub right now people would take notice,' says Cath Allen, Janelle's closest girlfriend since high school. 'She had presence.'

In photos Janelle is slim. In her early twenties she wore braces on her teeth. Like so many girls, she was emotionally and physically scarred by a struggle with an eating disorder in her late teenage years. From slim she turned pencil thin, beginning in Year 12. Janelle was never medically diagnosed with anorexia nervosa or bulimia but she fought against many of the symptoms.

So many sides of Janelle's character come up repeatedly in the literature about eating disorders. From an early age she was preoccupied with perfection in everything she did. As she battled with food she developed two more obsessions: exercise, especially walking, and counting calories.

Friends say Janelle was 'fastidious in appearance, reliable and conscientious'. She was also argumentative, opinionated and defiant; this sent her into the ring with her mother time and time again.

'We had our blues,' admits Carol. 'We had some big blues.' Cath Allen calls the mother–daughter relationship 'stormy but close'. Effectively the clash was between two headstrong women who often didn't see eye to eye but who, underneath it all, shared a mutual love.

On the outside Janelle was 'bright, bubbly, friendly and confident'. An exterior of happiness which, say her family, masked an insecurity within. Carol believes there was a link between her low self-esteem, her struggle with food and her outlook on relationships. There are many women today like Janelle Patton. I went to school with them, I sat in university lectures with them. They're go-getters; strong willed and driven. They're aggressive in body and mind and don't wish to be relegated to second place. Their actions are grounded in a personal righteousness, a generational confidence verging on arrogance. At the core is the belief that their way is the one way. Janelle shared many of these traits. When she drank it made things a whole lot harder. Alcohol was Janelle's poison—she turned tempestuous and unmanageable.

Several times Ron and Carol were called by friends or boyfriends to come and sort out the pieces after a night's drinking. It was an act of concern by those who didn't know what else to do, but it sent Janelle even further off the handle. 'Alcohol was a way of dealing with a lack in self-esteem,' says Carol. 'But when she had too much to drink she became nasty, aggressive, opinionated and argumentative. I said to Janelle, "You really need to see what happens when you drink too much; this is what happens."'

I've spoken with many people who knew Janelle, some of them well. I've listened to them defend and denounce her, sometimes in the same conversation. Everyone has an opinion: who she was, why she was, what she wanted and how she behaved. This isn't surprising—she had an opinion on everyone else, and would have expected nothing less. Janelle had the talent to motivate and tire those around her. She was a great organiser of other people. 'An over-organiser,' says Carol. 'She tried to organise not only herself, but everyone else around her. It did drive people to distraction. But she was a very caring person, a deep-down caring person.' It is this side of Janelle, her loyalty to and love for family and friends which, says Cath Allen, 'makes her so much more than what has been written in the media'.

This need to organise the world and those around her was regarded by many as domineering. Her younger brother Mark admits people saw this as 'controlling'; he felt it at times as well but he believes her motive was only to make others happy—although it was a happiness she was the judge of.

'She was always in your face,' say her Islander lovers, the sum of which was too much to take. This is one reason why they ended their relationships—they couldn't hack her personality. There was too much fire. She was too full-on for the slow-paced men of Norfolk Island.

'She was like a heat-seeking missile, an Exocet missile,' says long-time surfer Steve Borg, who was visiting Auckland when Janelle was murdered. 'Borgie', as he's known, is a former TEP turned resident who had a fling with Janelle. 'Once she locked onto something,' Steve says, continuing his missile analogy, 'there was no stopping her.'

It seems this explosive tenacity needed to be harnessed, otherwise it was liable to be misdirected. One of the problems on Norfolk was the limited scope for someone with Janelle's frenetic energy. Steve Borg decided to get her involved with the island's board-riders club. He roped her into the role of club secretary which she took up in her usual stride. 'She was brilliant,' he says. 'She went out and hassled everyone for cash.' Janelle raised unprecedented funds: $1200 to send four local surfers to the Oceanic Cup in Tonga.

'I gave Janelle her first pair of Ockanoie board shorts,' Steve Borg says as he thinks of the woman who upset so many on the island, 'but, man, once she knew your make-up, she could push your buttons.' Being able to 'push your buttons' is a common refrain from men who knew Janelle. Once she figured someone out, she seems to have taken delight in being able to provoke reactions.

Steve Borg calls himself a close friend of Janelle's and the first time

I saw him in a small office on the main street of Burnt Pine he turned away in anger and grief at what had happened to her. 'I hope they catch that fucker and put them in a cage above the roundabout, where people can drive past and spit on them.' His tone of voice carried as much venom as the statement. In the corner of his eye was a tear as he spun his chair to a filing cabinet and pulled out a photo of him and Janelle. But Steve Borg wasn't immune to her talent for irritating people. No one was. After one surf-riders' meeting in early 2002, Janelle turned on him for not pulling his weight in an organisation he helped establish. He drove home in a furious state, telling his girlfriend in jest and anger, 'One day someone will kill that girl.'

When Steve Borg first said this line over a beer at the RSL I let it pass. When he repeated it, this time with particular emphasis, I asked if he wanted to be quoted. He looked at me and said, 'I know you'll quote me, mate.'

———

Ron Patton agrees with Steve Borg's description of his daughter as a 'heat-seeking missile'. He reckons the analogy is spot-on. Janelle wasn't for fence sitting or prevaricating, and she would never have fitted into the local Island Assembly. She was a two-tone person—black and white. When I first met Ron and Carol and asked them what came to mind when they thought of their daughter, they said in perfect unison: 'Strong willed!' Ron went on: 'She was very determined. She basically had more guts than most men have. She was a person who was prepared to do things. If she had a job to do, she did it thoroughly and everyone we've come across has mentioned that in her working career. She was an organiser, she was a doer.'

During the first hours of the coronial inquest, Bob Peters established two key aspects of Janelle's character that caused her difficulty on Norfolk. Firstly, Peters stated, 'she had strong personal opinions on a variety of subjects' and was never afraid to voice them, 'albeit sometimes with a lack of diplomacy or tact'. Secondly, Janelle refused to acknowledge personal rejection. Peters said this 'inability to accept the end of a relationship was to carry over to her life on Norfolk Island'.

Carol agrees Janelle's obsessive personality posed challenges. 'Everything had to be right, even when she was a little thing at school.

I think that obsessiveness manifested itself in a lot of different ways. It would have been a very difficult personality to cope with.'

Janelle's track record in ending relationships was terrible. Janelle's behaviour with former lovers bordered on stalking. Her response to rejection was to pester and protest and do all she could to repair the split. It didn't make for smooth break-ups. Carol says Janelle suffered from 'fatal attractions'. It was a constant in her life which took a heavy toll on her health and state of mind. It also took a toll on all those around her. Janelle's close friend Cath Allen says Janelle hated 'things ending badly and didn't like negatives in her life, she didn't want them hanging around'. The failure of a relationship was a big negative and would force Janelle to look inward and wonder why. Like most people, introspection wasn't Janelle's idea of a fun time.

On Norfolk her tendency for 'fatal attractions' played out most in her relationship with Paul 'Jap' Menghetti, but her other Island lovers also experienced a tsunami of drama in breaking up with her. Janelle was a square peg in a round hole. Her personality didn't fit the island. To me, the two appear incompatible: the brash, upfront and busy nature of Janelle Patton, combined with her love of drama, argument and interest in other people's lives, clashed with the unspoken rhythms and rules of island life. On the surface this Pacific lifestyle is laidback and straightforward but underneath it's complex, claustrophobic and tense. Janelle would have been better off going to New York or London, where her personality would have been swallowed by the crowds.

Would Janelle have been murdered as viciously and callously if she had been a Norfolk resident? I doubt it. Would she have been murdered if she was a born-and-bred Islander? I don't think so. Janelle's landlady, Ruth McCoy, has no doubt Janelle was targeted. If this is the case I believe she was targeted, in part, because she was a female and because she was a TEP who chose not to understand the world she was living in. I wonder if the person who killed her saw her as 'disposable', because in the throes of death she was handled no better than a piece of garbage.

But if Janelle had been an Islander she would have behaved differently. She would have been a part of the established community which brings us back to the rules, to knowing one's place and position in island society. Understanding what voice this affords a person is perhaps the most important rule of all.

While it's clear Janelle didn't follow the rules as they applied to life on Norfolk, it's fair to point out that she didn't follow many rules, no matter where she was. Janelle just wasn't that sort of character. Janelle was Janelle and that was it. When it came to relationships in general, be they sexual or platonic, she pushed the boundaries. On Norfolk everything was magnified. 'She was aware of the rules, of course she was,' says Greg Magri, 'but she was a free spirit. It was in her to do it, it was in her nature. People would tell her no, don't go there, Nel, but she would. She would go there every time.'

Greg Magri was the final name on Bob Peters' list of sixteen Persons of Interest. He was nominated by one of his in-laws as having driven his black Honda Civic on Rooty Hill Road on the day of Janelle's murder. It's a claim he denies and says he was nowhere near the road that day. Greg Magri is horrified he is a person of interest and he still can't fathom why he made the list. Three years her senior, Greg met Janelle within weeks of her arrival in 1999. His is one of Janelle's few friendships that went the distance. Greg says he played the role of confidant and close personal friend. Janelle liked to air her grievances with Greg, which he tolerated but got tired of. He says their relationship was platonic and based on him being someone she could 'download and bitch to' about all and sundry. When he first met Janelle he concluded she was 'half pie mad'. Mad Nel is what he called her, although with his Norfolk accent it sounds more like 'Mard Nul'.

Greg Magri had a close insight into Janelle's character and the relationships that caused her so much angst. He agrees with the impression shared by her island lovers that she was 'manipulative'. He says bluntly, 'She used and abused men.'

'Did she know what she was doing?'

Yes, he tells me, without a doubt. He doesn't agree Janelle was insecure. He believes she was 'very strong and confident within herself'. He liked Janelle for her energy and hard-headed approach to life. He enjoyed ribbing her about the way she handled her personal affairs. She in turn would bitch and snipe about whatever was on her mind until he looked her in the eye and said, 'There, you feel better now?'

Greg says Janelle was a woman fuelled by drama; 'she was always in an argument with someone, not always in a bad way'. But there was always 'friction'—a niggle with someone over something. It was one of the constants in her life. She was also very possessive of her friends. 'She didn't have a lot of friends,' he says, 'but those she did have she was possessive of.'

'What was she looking for?' I ask.

'She was looking for a long-term relationship and she didn't care who it was with.'

The role Greg played in Janelle's life was one he initiated. It began with Janelle's first island relationship, with a Canadian TEP called Larry Perrett. Greg met Janelle at Foodlands Supermarket where he was working as a checkout operator. He invited Janelle and Larry to his house to help them sort out their rapidly escalating domestic issues, which by this stage he was hearing all about. Janelle and Larry were living together in Dead Rat Lane, a small, potholed road near the Leagues club in Burnt Pine. This street is popular with TEPs because it's home to a block of flats and short-term accommodation. This was Janelle's first experience of living full-time with a boyfriend and it wasn't going well.

Like any good mediator Greg kept the two parties apart. He sat Janelle at one end of his dining room table and Larry at the other. 'What's the problem?' he asked, taking on the role of self-appointed go-between. The issues, said Greg, were petty and domestic. 'It was narrow-minded, simple shit, like if the dishes were washed and so on, and they blew up to be so big, bigger than they were.'

Domestic disharmony is inevitably triggered by greater problems. Janelle's drinking, which had been a problem in Sydney, contributed to the worsening relationship with Larry Perrett. She also took issue with Larry smoking marijuana. It was a drug she had no time for and to make her point she ripped up his marijuana plants from the backyard and destroyed them. It seemed Janelle knew exactly how to piss people off. The two broke up shortly after. Larry Perrett returned to Canada a few months later where, in 2003, he died of cancer.

After separating with Larry Perrett, Janelle maintained her friendship with Greg Magri. Janelle would often come round for dinner. Given her history with food it's not surprising when Greg says she was 'impossible' to cook for. 'Once we were cooking chicken and, no joking, she must have peeled every piece of fat off the chook. When she went to the toilet I had to rub it with butter just to get it burning.'

Janelle went to Greg's house for dinner on the Wednesday four days before her death. He told police she appeared a little 'upset' about Steve Borg's new girlfriend but couldn't elaborate on why she was concerned. Nor could he 'determine if Janelle was jealous'. Another concern voiced over dinner was with her landlady Ruth McCoy. This was due to Janelle's burgeoning relationship with Brent Wilson. Ruth McCoy was close friends with Wilson's ex-wife Jeanne and, according to Magri, had given Janelle an ultimatum that if she continued her relationship with Brent Wilson she would have to move out. This was despite Brent Wilson now living in Auckland. Yet again, Janelle was having to navigate the trip-wires of Norfolk's tangled and interrelated community.

Greg Magri told police the last time he saw Janelle alive was the following night when he went to the RSL Club after the Easter Carnival. He says he had 'a conversation with her and she appeared happy'. They agreed to meet up once her parents arrived.

When Greg learnt of Janelle Patton's death and the whispers of 'suspicious circumstances', that scurried from people's lips, his first thought wasn't murder, it was suicide. Two days after the discovery of Janelle's body he went to visit Ron and Carol at the hospital where they were still staying. According to Greg the first question they asked was how well he knew Janelle. He said, 'Not wanting to be talking out of turn here but I wouldn't be surprised if she had hung herself because that's the sort of girl she was.'

'Oh,' said the Pattons, consumed by grief and confusion, 'you did know her well.'

Although Janelle had never attempted suicide before, Ron and Carol had seen how lost and unstable she could become. In mid 1999, in the months before leaving for Norfolk Island, Janelle was at her worst point. She was depressed over the break-up with her Sydney boyfriend Todd. She had wanted to get married, he wanted out. He encouraged her to see a psychologist which she agreed to but she stopped going after a couple of sessions. Todd offered moral support and accompanied Janelle on her few visits. She interpreted this as a sign that he still wished to be with her when, in Ron's words, he was simply 'trying to help'.

By now Carol was 'very worried' about Janelle: 'She was on anti-depression tablets and coming home from work with her tablets and shutting herself in the room, with her music and drinking. A couple of nights I went in there; if she wasn't unconscious she was close to it. She would get up in the morning and go to work, but she was depressed. She wasn't as particular about her appearance as she usually was. At one stage there was a note about how she was just a nuisance to everyone, that sort of thing. Now whether it was serious or not I don't know. I did say to someone at the time if she doesn't get away or do something, I really think she will die. Whether she would have consciously killed herself, or if it had happened by just knocking herself out with this mix of what she was taking, I don't know.'

As Carol tells me this her demeanour is reflective, her shoulders hunched. We're sitting in the Pattons' new kitchen in their Pennant Hills home—it was built by Todd, the ex-boyfriend, who remains in close contact and feels guilty for pushing Janelle away. As a sign of how protective they are of Janelle's Sydney friends, the Pattons say Todd doesn't want to talk to me. I don't push it beyond making two requests, but I wonder if they ever asked him.

The Pattons' three-bedroom house isn't large and Janelle's bedroom is just off the lounge room. I say it must 'have been hell' for them to deal with Janelle in this destructive and distressing state.

'It was,' says Carol.

Ron: 'The thing is, we always supported her.'

Carol: 'Yeah, but it was a real concern and that's why I was so glad she was going to up herself and go and do something. It gave her a new lease of life and all of a sudden she was a different person. She was planning something. She had the motivation to do something.'

'Is this why it was crucial Janelle left Sydney?' I ask.

'Yes,' says Carol.

'But not to Norfolk Island,' adds Ron, shaking his head.

This is what causes the Pattons such anguish. The move to Norfolk was a lifeline for Janelle. A positive shift from a life and lifestyle suffocating her verve. At twenty-seven, leaving her parents and childhood surroundings was overdue. Janelle hoped a fresh start would break the melancholy and her growing sense of dejection. Ron says on Norfolk 'Janelle was maturing and she needed that'. Finding the right road to happiness is something he can relate to; to have his daughter's chance of success taken from her breaks his heart.

The one relationship in Janelle's past which she confessed caused great damage was with former Navy Seaman Dale Richard Battersby, or Rick as he prefers to be known. Rick and Janelle met at a Kings Cross nightclub in early 1994. She was twenty-two, he was twenty-four. Some months later they were engaged. The relationship lasted little more than twelve months and was volatile. Like many young sailors when they hit land, Rick was a heavy drinker. The relationship ended in Sydney's Waverley Court in May 1995, when he was charged with assaulting Janelle.

As with all domestic violence matters, police automatically filed an Apprehended Violence Order, preventing Battersby from approaching his ex-fiancée. The Pattons believe Janelle was so 'emotionally and physically scarred by this relationship she never fully recovered'. They say her self-esteem and sense of pride were crushed. When I put this to Battersby he says, 'Fair enough,' and understands why Carol and Ron side with Janelle. But he says they forget the 'emotional and physical scars' their daughter left on her ex-lovers. Him included.

Rick Battersby was unnamed during the coronial inquest because, like all of Janelle's mainland relationships, police do not believe any person she was involved with before coming to the island had anything to do with her murder. But their relationship was mentioned in relation to the assault charge. Bob Peters told the hearing that Janelle 'finally decided to stand up to this man and he was charged with assaulting her . . . He had also allegedly broken her jaw in November 1994, but at the time she told her parents she had fallen on the dance floor at a nightclub and other people had fallen on her.'

When Rick Battersby heard Janelle Patton had been murdered he wasn't surprised. He believes her character and 'lack of respect for others' marked her for violence. He followed the inquest from his Adelaide home and decided to out himself because he wanted to tell his side of the story. He rang Sydney's *Daily Telegraph*, who shunted him back to the Adelaide *Advertiser*. His message was clear; the real victims were Janelle Patton's lovers. He said Janelle was a 'vindictive and abusive person' who made many enemies. He wanted this in print. He wanted the record straight. He didn't care to see Janelle depicted as a person who wasn't to blame. She was dead. He was getting even.

The Pattons call the story a fabrication. Rick Battersby admits he's 'more than bitter' about the assault charge, which scuttled his chance of joining the police force. 'So you can understand why for nine years I've been fighting my own battles of depression because of what happened.' Ric says his father and brother are policemen. He freely admits one of his motivations for speaking out is the hope that he can get the charge overturned.

In a brutally frank conversation about his time with Janelle, Rick Battersby said he needed to see a 'hypnotist' to get over the anger she left him with. 'It wasn't just me who mentally tormented her, she was quite disturbed in herself. She was an intelligent girl. She knew what she was doing. From what I could tell, her only real physiological problem was from her eating disorder and it was all about her being the victim.'

Before the assault charge was heard Janelle Patton tried to get the charges dropped, something Battersby was actively encouraging her to do (to the point of pretending to still desire her). The Pattons say this indicates the hold he had over her. Janelle's attempts to do this failed. In domestic violence cases only police can withdraw the charge, not the victim. Rick Battersby pleaded guilty to assault and was fined $500 and $50 court costs.

According to the charge sheet, the assault took place around 1 am after the pair had been drinking in Kings Cross with two friends. During the taxi ride home they argued over Janelle 'dancing with other men at a nightclub'. As the two got out of the taxi, Battersby pushed Janelle in the back and she fell 'heavily to the bitumen'. He then 'further assaulted the victim by striking her several times to her head, by punching her and striking her with his open palm'. Injuries listed include 'grazes' to her elbow and palms, as well as bruising to her 'middle three fingers' and 'soreness to her head and neck'.

The assault was witnessed by their friends in the taxi. Janelle then went into the unit in which the group were staying, where another 'altercation took place'. Rick Battersby wanted Janelle out and asked her to leave. When she refused, he pushed her out of the hallway and into the stairwell corridor. He then tossed out her belongings and slammed the door shut. The fact sheet says Janelle then 'became hysterical and began banging on the door and shouting'. She also 'kicked' and 'head butted' the door which resulted in 'her sustaining bruises, lumps and grazing to her forehead and face'. By this stage neighbours had called the police.

Rick Battersby says Janelle's reaction wasn't only caused by him throwing her out of the unit but also because he called her mother to ask for someone to come and collect her. The Pattons remember the call, but say it was Janelle ringing 'in hysterics'. They drove the long distance from the Hills district to Sydney's eastern suburbs where Ron found blood on the door of the unit and nobody around. He was too late. The police had already arrived to find Janelle in tears in the stairwell. After Battersby made 'full admissions' he was arrested and everyone was taken to Maroubra police station where Ron and Carol finally found their daughter.

Battersby also admits to breaking Janelle's jaw but claims it was an accident after she beat him with a phone receiver following his refusal to have sex with her because he 'was too drunk and tired'. He also claims Janelle then rang his mother in Adelaide to bitch about Rick. It's another story of excessive alcohol, rage and fury on both sides. It can't be verified because no charge was laid. The Apprehended Violence Order which accompanied the assault charge is not a document signed by Battersby as a true statement, the facts are as given only by Janelle. The AVO sheet refers to this incident as being 'punched in the jaw'. Rick Battersby denies the punch and says she 'fell off the bed' after he tried to get her off him.

Whatever took place, Battersby sticks to his claim that Janelle was also violent. Certainly his stories of Janelle's character and actions while she was with him tally with what other ex-lovers have told me. And it's this side of her personality that Rick Battersby points to when he says he wasn't surprised to hear she had been murdered.

'People can be murdered by being in the wrong place at the wrong time. Janelle wasn't the type of person who would put herself in the wrong place. I believe she basically put herself in a place where eventually someone was going to cause her harm. And I'm glad in a way it wasn't me because that's where I was heading with her, if I'd stayed with it.'

When I ask Rick to clarify what he is saying, he repeats his assertion that Janelle's capacity 'to rage' and 'to keep fighting' drove him to the edge of violence and beyond.

'Are you saying she deserved it?' I ask.

'No,' he says, but Janelle 'being found dead was no surprise'.

Rick Battersby is not the only person I've heard say this about Janelle, he just says it with grimacing honesty. He readily admits he was no saint in the relationship, although that's not his point. The facts confirm this. His claim is Janelle was no saint either. 'For the normal person, you go somewhere, you try and fit in, you have to adapt to an environment, like I did in the navy,' says Battersby. 'Janelle wouldn't understand that sort of context because she would have thought, I've been here a week, now I'm a local. And you're going to have to accept me.'

The turmoil which led to the 1995 assault charge wasn't the last time Janelle was involved in a matter before the courts. It was repeated on Norfolk, except this time the assault involved a woman, not a man, and again it ended with an Apprehended Violence Order.

All through Janelle's life she made friends with aplomb and the same was true of her experience with Sue Fieldes. It started with promise but ended in tears after a minor scuffle at the bar of the Sports and Workers Club. Sue Fieldes was charged with common assault and the two former friends took out restraining orders against each other, which on tiny Norfolk is a drastic and nearly unworkable measure.

The story of Susan Fieldes is also a story about Janelle's knack of getting involved in other people's business. No matter how many times people told her to back off or stay out of it, she persisted, each time to her own detriment. There should have been lessons from this troubled relationship but Janelle was never one for turning the other cheek, or modifying her behaviour.

In December 1999, Janelle resigned her post as room maid at the South Pacific Resort and shifted her island career up the road to Food-lands Supermarket, where she was employed as a general attendant. There, the 28-year-old became friends with Sue Fieldes, who was thirteen years older. When Fieldes learnt of Janelle's break-up with Larry Perrett and her claim he was 'mistreating' her, she and her husband offered to help. She organised a room for Janelle in her neighbour's house, owned by Charles Henri Menghetti, whose nickname is 'Spindles'.

Janelle accepted the offer, even though Spindles is the same age as

Ron, her father. She moved into the house as a boarder in early 2000. But she wasn't there for long. Janelle soon became aware of what Dem Tull alleged, and according to police evidence she confronted Sue Fieldes about what 'she believed was an improper relationship' between Fieldes and Charles Menghetti. (Both parties staunchly deny such a relationship existed.) Janelle and Sue's friendship unravelled and their ongoing contact, according to Bob Peters, 'became bitter'. As a result, Sue Fieldes left Foodlands and Charles Menghetti asked Janelle to pack her stuff and get out. The bar-room scuffle which confirmed the depth of bitterness between the former friends took place on a Sunday afternoon in July 2000. According to the two-page court record, the two women bumped into each other at the bar of the Sports and Workers Club. While ordering drinks they became 'embroiled in a verbal altercation' which involved a healthy dose of personal abuse and swearing. Soon the pair were in a physical fight and had to be restrained by fellow drinkers. The barman on duty told police that Sue Fieldes was the 'instigator' of the abuse and the first to strike. But there were no eyewitnesses as to whether the strike was a 'punch' or a 'slap'.

According to Janelle's evidence, she was hit with a 'punch to the nose by Fieldes' right clenched fist'. Sue Fieldes disputed this and said Janelle started 'the conversation and the verbal abuse'. She also denied punching Janelle but admitted hitting her with a 'slap to the side of the face with the back of an open left hand'.

The truth behind the punch or slap claim was never tested in court, instead Sue Fieldes pleaded guilty to the offence of common assault and no conviction was entered. A restraining order was then taken out between the two parties. Shortly after, Sue Fieldes took her young son and left the island and her husband for eight months.

As usual there was a slow build-up to what took place. In May, Sue Fieldes left Foodlands because she no longer wanted to work near Janelle. Her husband, Brian Fieldes, had told Janelle 'to leave his wife alone'. Janelle didn't reply, instead she went and reported it to the police. Then Larry Perrett, the boyfriend whose apartment Janelle had moved out from in the first place, abused Brian Fieldes at the Bowls Club bistro about what he had said to Janelle. An 'altercation' took place but never made it to court.

From all accounts it was a messy affair and Janelle hadn't yet been on the island for twelve months. The animosity between the two ensured that Sue Fieldes made the list of sixteen Persons of Interest.

As to Janelle's lodging with Charles 'Spindles' Menghetti, it didn't last long. He says Janelle rented a room in his house for only one week. In that time, according to his police statement, Janelle 'lectured' him about eating red meat, played loud music in her bedroom and 'would sometimes sit on the back veranda drinking until 3 am'. Charles Menghetti also said she complained about early morning telephone calls and 'on one occasion found she had taken the telephone off the hook'. According to Menghetti Janelle had 'personality problems and needed some help or counselling'. It was because of this behaviour, he told police, that he asked her to leave.

What's surprising is Janelle left one Menghetti house for another. It's unclear if the two brothers ever talked about the logic of this shift, or Charles' observation of Janelle's behaviour as a boarder, but she moved to the house of Paul 'Jap' Menghetti, the younger brother of Charles 'Spindles' Menghetti and, at the time, a widower with four kids. Eventually Janelle moved into the main bedroom.

For his entire life Jap Menghetti has worked in the same job, as a mechanic for the Norfolk Island Administration. His property, called 100 Acre Farm, is on a magnificent corner of the island near Headstone. This was the start of Janelle's longest and, in her mind, happiest relationship on Norfolk. It lasted fifteen months, from May 2000 until August 2001. 'I do love it here,' wrote Janelle in an email home. 'I love being around Jap and the kids (even though they do shit me at times). I'm doing things that I never thought I'd be ever doing in my life. I cut firewood with an axe so that we have hot-water for showers. I've been orange picking by myself and got chased by three cows (all they wanted was an orange but I thought they were coming to ram me). I'm experimenting with cooking (and yes my scones actually rise now!!) and I love gardening!'

Now in his early fifties, Jap Menghetti was twenty-one years older than Janelle. He is a thin, gently spoken, reserved character with a bright cackle and a dry wit when it comes to island observations. He doesn't drink, which on Norfolk is an anomaly of sizable proportions. He says grace before his evening meal and, like all Islanders his age, is a jack of all trades. He was brought up in the 'hard days, not good days' of Norfolk, when its isolation meant a raw life based on ingenuity and physical activity. Social life revolved around family, cards and music, not television or booze. He is a born and bred Islander of Italian and Norfolk heritage. His speech is peppered with the original Norfolk lilt, a melodic accent which hasn't passed down to younger generations and so is rapidly disappearing.

Janelle saw Jap's position, family, large timber house and property as the embodiment of everything she was seeking. She was smitten. Despite the age difference, Janelle was keen on a more permanent relationship. Jap Menghetti wasn't.

It didn't take long for friction to arise between 28-year-old Janelle and Jap's eldest daughter, Dana Menghetti, who was nineteen. Bob Peters says Dana had trouble accepting her father's relationship and Janelle's 'possessive nature'. According to Dana the two never got on from the start and the dislike arose 'from statements Janelle made about her late mother'. Janelle made her feelings for Dana obvious throughout her 2001 diary.

[Tuesday 20.2.01] Really humid. Went for a swim straight from work. Jap came over & left when I questioned him about Dana calling me 'Crazy Janelle!' Spoke to Mum—wants me home.

[Sunday 2.9.01] Father's Day. Did a bottle run. Popped in a small present to Jap. Dana a stupid fucking cow!

[Friday 7.9.01] Went to the RSL for lunch with Kel. Dinner at Bucket's. Met Jap at the pier for a chat. Went to RSL and Brewery—Dana a fucking bitch. Crashed at Shano's.

[Friday 9.11.01] Went to Steve's then down to the beach. Caught up with Larrin & Harvey. Then to Brewery (Dana—bitch there) & to Compound. Smashed.

———

After nine months at the Menghetti homestead Janelle moved out, leaving in February 2001. The relationship continued for six months, albeit on a somewhat downgraded basis. Jap Menghetti made it clear his family, not Janelle, would take priority. He told police he mainly visited Janelle on Wednesday, Friday and Saturday nights.

Janelle continued to stay involved with the broader Menghetti family, buying presents for Jap's children and visiting his elderly father who lived alone in Burnt Pine. In her diary for 13 June 2001, Janelle wrote: '. . . was tired & decided to sleep for the arvo. Jap over for tea—told me a few home truths about where I fit in.' Five days later was the entry: 'Jap down for tea & spat on me.'

By early August 2001 Janelle's dairy entries refer to moves to end the relationship: 'Jap and I went for a drive—tried to break-up as we are going nowhere . . . Jap came down to work at lunch—smart arse (can't help but love him) . . . Jap down for tea—argued.' The entry for Friday 24 August says: 'Not a word from Jap. Went for a walk after work. Jap went to Toon's farewell. Went out to his [place] pissed (for an argue)—Didn't want to know me. Left me on the veranda after I fell.'

By the end of August and first weeks of September 2001, Bob Peters says Janelle's diary 'regularly referred to periods of crying and being emotionally upset'. Her diary entry for Friday 19 October reads: 'Spoke to Jap (fuckwit). Found out he's been rooting Robyn & has been since Kurt's b'day or thereabouts. Told me he's my first enemy on Norfolk.'

Despite spending fifteen months with Janelle, including a trip to Sydney where he dined with Janelle and her parents in their family home, Jap Menghetti has nothing to say about their time together. The best I could get from him was that Janelle was 'ultimately harmless' and he had 'no idea who would want to kill her'. From his statement to police, he described Janelle as a 'clinical and clingy sort of person' who he encouraged to return to Australia because he believed she was just 'beating time' on Norfolk.

After Jap Menghetti ended the relationship in August 2001, Janelle followed a pattern of behaviour which most people would call harassment. She would turn up at Jap's house in the early hours of the morning 'uninvited and unwelcomed' and sometimes drunk. She would telephone insistently, calls which Jap Menghetti would try not to answer. There were also other incidents, including an argument so heated Jap threatened to call the police but couldn't because Janelle ripped the phone out of the socket.

When Janelle found out Jap had started a relationship with Robyn Murdoch, then CEO of the island public service, Janelle went to her house on Quality Row at least three times, 'banging' and 'rattling the door'. Once Robyn Murdoch sent out a visiting friend who made it clear, with a deftness of language Janelle often used on others, that she should leave immediately. When Jap Menghetti found out Janelle was seeing Laurie Quintal he says he was 'thrilled'. He thought it might give him 'some relief from the harassment', and it did, but Janelle never gave up hope that their relationship might be rekindled one day.

Jap Menghetti's police statement said he regarded her behaviour as more of a nuisance than anything too serious. But the friction between Janelle Patton and the Menghetti family was well known and established. Janelle partly blamed Dana Menghetti for the breakdown of the relationship. Jap Menghetti went on to marry Robyn Murdoch and the pair, along with Dana Menghetti and Charles 'Spindles' Menghetti, were all named as Persons of Interest during the coronial inquest.

The relationship with Jap Menghetti now over, Janelle met Shane Warmington, a TEP from Sydney who was managing the bar at the RSL. He says he was interested in casual sex; Janelle wanted to move in. Shane started to avoid Janelle and their relationship was brief, lasting no more than two or three weeks. He says Janelle tried to play him off against Jap in a failed effort to get the two men to fight over her. Shane Warmington told police Janelle was 'very good at aggravating an emotional reaction from people'. He believed 'she always seemed to be playing mental games' with people involved in her life. But he didn't 'believe this behaviour was serious enough to have caused someone to kill her'. Shane Warmington says the day after they first slept together Janelle got up early and, without asking, drove his car around town. On an island where everyone knows everyone else's car, he regarded it as an impertinent public display of sexual prowess.

It is Shane Warmington who introduced Janelle to his mate Laurie 'Bucket' Quintal, and after a while the two became involved. But Janelle remained obsessed with Jap Menghetti. According to Laurie Quintal, Janelle was at his house cooking dinner one day when she suddenly disappeared. Laurie had left Janelle in the kitchen to take a shower; when he came out Janelle was gone and didn't return until '2 am the next morning'. Janelle had ditched dinner to go and harass Jap Menghetti and his new girlfriend, Robyn Murdoch, instead.

Laurie and Janelle were together for about four months, although he says six—as always on Norfolk, people's perceptions of time are rarely consistent, a problem Bob Peters and his team realised from day one of their investigation. Laurie says he instigated the break-up with Janelle in January 2002 because, once again it would seem, she wanted a more serious relationship than he was after. Bob Peters agrees, pointing to evidence in Janelle's diary, but Ron Patton says Janelle left Quintal, not the other way around. He points to this note, found in Janelle's flat after her death, as proof that she was moving on: 'Look Bucket, I'm sore. I'm bruised big time. I'm devastated by everything you said and did to me last night. On top of that you'd been also bitching behind my back and I never thought a friend would do that. You made it clear your opinion of me, so let's just leave it at that. I have to go now. Sorry.'

This note is not dated. It was found in Janelle's flat five days after her death. If someone was looking to point a suspicious finger at Laurie Quintal, then they succeeded. The Pattons confirm the note is in Janelle's handwriting. Laurie Quintal agrees the note is about him and confirms a physical fight took place when he forced Janelle out of his house on Valentine's Day, 2002. The situation was so tense that their mutual friend, Steve Borg, was called to come and collect her.

Bob Peters believes there was a second 'physical altercation' between the pair, one which the above note relates to. By crosschecking Janelle's diary he believes an earlier argument took place on 22 January after Janelle confronted him about comments he allegedly made to others. Janelle wrote in her diary that Laurie Quintal apologised the next day and she refers to bruises on her neck, chest and arms.

Janelle mentioned to at least one other person that 'Bucket' had been 'physically violent' towards her. Laurie Quintal admits having to manhandle Janelle out of his house. Like other men, Laurie Quintal told me Janelle's rage could be unstoppable and 'a man's got a right to protect his body and property'. But he disagrees with Bob Peters and claims there was only one time he physically shoved her from his home.

Despite Janelle's claims there is no doubt Laurie Quintal was fond of her. Of all her former island lovers, he speaks most endearingly and willingly about her. He believed Janelle was wasting her life and talents by remaining on Norfolk and, like Jap Menghetti, told her to return to Australia. 'She was such a bubbly little thing,' says Laurie, who lives on a portion of land dating back to the original 1856 grant to the Quintal family. He shows me a photo of Janelle sitting on his knee in a bar. She looks so tiny compared to his muscular build. He wears a toothy grin, as big as a half-moon. Janelle's face shines with a wide, open laugh, caught half gasp by the camera flash. In her hand rests a beer. It's another night out in the relaxed evening air of Norfolk Island. These are Laurie's memories, the good ones; even after he was rocked by evidence against him and being named a person of interest, he's still clinging to the good memories. And so too are the Pattons.

Norfolk may have taken their only daughter, but the Pattons refuse to be bitter about Janelle's time there. Out of the coronial inquest spewed a barrage of negatives involving Janelle and the way she lived her life. Through it all the Patton family held fast. It stoically weathered the storm as Bob Peters traced his magnifying glass across Janelle's life in pursuit of a motive. Why would someone want to murder this woman? Who harbours this raw violence? Did she give cause to her fate?

As in life, but now in death, it was left to the Patton family to defend Janelle. This it did when Carol read an impact statement to the court:

> We have endured a public dissection of the negative aspects of our daughter's life with little reference to her positive attributes of which there were many. We have heard nothing of her warm and loving nature, her sense of fun and humour, her genuine concern for others and the ability to overcome many difficulties she encountered in her life . . . Nothing was 90% to Janelle, she went at 100% into everything she was involved in, or she didn't go at all . . . there is one irrefutable fact about Janelle. She had an impact on everyone she ever knew for longer than five minutes.

The Patton family is proud of the way Janelle fought, of how she defended herself against her attacker. They're proud she was an individual: a woman who had the 'courage to voice her opinions, the courage to stand her ground'.

Janelle's nature was uncompromising. So too was her approach to relationships. They were made up of big, bold themes. Of passion, drama, drinking, happiness, anger, and highs and lows. Primary emotions of fire and ice. Her desire for long-term, honest commitment is the one constant in them all. For the most part this desire wasn't reciprocated, especially on the part of the Norfolk men who saw Janelle as just another female TEP passing through. They either didn't want to commit, or chose not to commit after sensing her difficult nature. Either way, all of Janelle's Norfolk relationships were with men who were single and willing. She was not, as has been claimed, stealing husbands or sleeping with half the island.

————

Norfolk Island is a soundscape of stillness; of wind and birds and ocean and livestock. Within this sound comes Carol's voice, at the end of a 45-minute interview in a holiday unit, on their first return to Norfolk since Janelle's murder.

'People would be very surprised if we said that underneath, Janelle lacked confidence,' says Carol. 'I mean, on the surface she always came over as being confident, very sure of herself, and I think being here on Norfolk, it was becoming more of her real way. A couple of personal ups and downs in her life contributed to that and she just saw "why would anyone want to employ me, why would anyone want to do this?" She was really down on herself. I think coming to Norfolk helped her think, "I can do it, I am my own person". This she would not have achieved at home. Even though she was murdered here, the two and a half years she spent here were good for her. They were good for her; being happy.'

These last words are said in a faint, distant voice. They are thin and fragile and trail away from the microphone. They're not said with volume but they are said with conviction.

Ron looks at his wife, then at me, and nods in agreement.

CHAPTER 8

BLOODLESS GENOCIDE

NORFOLK ISLAND is led by a merry band of revolving politicians who run for office with mixed emotions. Of the nine elected, five are back-benchers and four are ministers. This means the executive can be overruled at any time. Here was the first speed hump in decision making. Frustration with the slow process of government and the absence of ministerial solidarity has scorched the enthusiasm of many a player, let alone contender. Most who have done their time at Kingston swear never to return. They've been soured by the experience. Battle weary, they retreat and wait for the euphoric sensation of Norfolk life to return, because most say it eluded them when they held office in Kingston.

These political refugees then watch with passing interest as the current members of the Assembly wrestle with, or unwind, the policies they introduced. Either way they've done their community service, like working on a road gang: they're now liberated. It's not much of an advertisement for the younger Islanders who dare to dream they could make a difference. The root of the problem is the small size of the elec-torate. In the 2004 election there were 1332 people on the electoral roll. When it's made up of your immediate family and friends it's a miracle anyone ventures near the political arena. One unpopular decision could incur the wrath of mates, lover, spouse, son or daughter. The list is always long on Norfolk. A decision will hold until someone says, 'What about Grandma?'

For a culture which fought long and hard for its political autonomy Islanders deride their Assembly, calling it the Goon Show. They're proud of the concept of governing themselves, but that doesn't mean they admire those they elect, even if they are, inevitably, their relatives. Only the brave, foolhardy or naive accept the challenge of island politics.

For reasons no one could ever explain to me there are no political parties on Norfolk. Elected members are political freestylers untethered to any party doctrine or policy. Where they stand on any given issue is unknown until they vote in the Assembly. It makes government decision making as accurate as predicting the lotto.

The closest Norfolk has to a political party is the Society of Pitcairn Descendants. At least it has a set of aims. Its chief firebrand is Ric Robinson, the gardener who married the best-selling author, Colleen McCullough. They live on a well-tended estate and are one of the island's largest private employers. The wealthy and prolific writer supports Ric's fight against Australia and whispers him his best political lines. McCullough says of her adopted homeland: 'Canberra is pulling the wings off the world's last specimen of a particular butterfly.' Together they coined the term 'bloodless genocide' to define what they accuse the Australian government of doing to the Pitcairn descendants.

The day I visit 'Out Yenna', the sixteen-acre property the couple call home, Ric is sitting alone in the conservatory reading the *Companion Guide to the High Court* and taking judicious notes. As I'm led in by one of his staff Ric takes his glasses off and welcomes me in a deep, slow voice: 'I saw you at the back of the Assembly meeting yesterday. I'm surprised you stayed so long.'

Ric Robinson has just re-entered politics through the revolving door of the local Assembly, this time on an unopposed by-election. The by-election was notable for being the first in island memory to attract only one candidate. Unopposed, Ric Robinson was back on the back-bench, a part-time position paying $11 000 per annum. There was no need for a vote. 'It just goes to show there aren't that many masochists around these days,' he jokes as I take a seat on a chair covered in a zebra print velvet.

All around are ferns and hanging plants and mirrors and large ornate Roman vases. It's a cross between Africa and ancient Rome. We sit at a solid quartz table which I later read is made of 'Mexican agate'.

Ric is wearing a pair of sleeveless overalls but apart from his dress, he appears like a lay lawyer, for it is here, in this peaceful room, where Ric Robinson researches his argument that Norfolk is not a part of Australia.

'Free association is the goal,' he says in reply to my question about his political vision. 'And getting the feds off our backs.'

Ric asks if he can smoke a cigarette and after a thoughtful drag continues on the topic which occupies most of his time—political freedom from Australia. 'Pitcairners prefer full independence,' he says. 'I think it could work, but the majority of people wouldn't go along with it, so we take the middle course and go for free association, which is basically independence, with Australia looking after foreign affairs and defence.'

Membership of the Society of Pitcairn Descendants is reserved for those with Pitcairn ancestry—anyone who can trace their blood back to the settlers of 1856. The society aims to 'promote the knowledge of the Pitcairn race' and claims Pitcairners are indigenous to Norfolk Island. 'It's not a claim,' says Ric in response to the use of the 'c' word. 'It's a fact. We were the first people as a whole people to settle on Norfolk Island as a permanent homeland—now if you want a definition of indigenous that's it, isn't it?'

The society was born in 1977 and played a key role in resisting the Nimmo Royal Commission, which a year earlier had recommended Norfolk be integrated into Australia. Despite the victory of self-government and the many powers which have since flowed, the Society of Descendants argues the people of Norfolk are 'not free' and accuses Australia of denying Norfolk the right to self-determination.

Ric asks: 'How can it be self-government when every law that is passed by the Norfolk government can be overturned by Australia? How can that be self-government?' What Ric actually means is how can Norfolk be a sovereign state when the Commonwealth has the power through section 122 of the Constitution to veto all Norfolk legislation; a power which allows the federal government to prevent Norfolk doing things it doesn't like, such as turning the island into an offshore financial centre like the Cayman Islands. The answer to Ric's question is that Norfolk can't be sovereign, because it isn't. And this is what he and others mean when they say the people of Norfolk 'are not free'. Refusal to accept Australia's rule over Norfolk is what Ric and the society have been doing, with some enjoyment, since its inception.

One of the island's long-cherished beliefs is that Queen Victoria gave Norfolk Island to the Pitcairn settlers who arrived in 1856. Most arguments used by Ric Robinson and other descendants questioning Australia's legal status in relation to Norfolk as an external territory are based on this claim. As yet, the society is still to prove its case is anything but wishful thinking and historic misinterpretation.

Time and time again formal inquiries convened by governments have stated there is no legal evidence to support the belief that Norfolk was ceded to the Pitcairn settlers. There is, however, genuine confusion and misunderstanding. The settlers who arrived on Norfolk in 1856 claimed the move from Pitcairn was predicated on the condition of unqualified cession and title to the entire island. This belief has filtered through successive generations.

Even a book commissioned by the Society of Descendants and written by Raymond Nobbs, a direct relative of Norfolk's great patriarch, George Hunn Nobbs—the spiritual leader of the community who made the historic journey from Pitcairn to Norfolk in 1856—dismisses the claim as 'untenable in law'. But Raymond Nobbs does provide some historic context. He makes the point that while on Pitcairn, the Islanders enjoyed sole occupation of the island and developed their own self-governing community. This led them 'to assume that Pitcairn was indeed their own island, and in a de facto, rather than legal sense, it was. The transfer of these assumptions to Norfolk allowed them to think of their new home as their island even though their claim was untenable in law.'

Ric is not the only Islander who steadfastly refuses to accept the weight of evidence against them; past and present members of the Norfolk Island Assembly hold similar views. Refusal to accept what Canberra says follows a long tradition, so it's no surprise it is the case when it comes to the most basic of all questions—who does Norfolk Island belong to? Thus the constitutional issue remains very much alive and beats like a rogue heart in the community, pumping oxygen into a debate which runs more on stubborn pride than available fact.

To me the debate over Norfolk's position with Australia is like asking who provoked the mutiny on the *Bounty*. Was it Bligh or

Christian? Did Christian overreact and lose his cool or was Bligh a tyrant who deserved to lose the trust of his first mate? The answer depends on who you talk to and can be supported, to a degree, by different historical records. Most locals consider the constitutional issue a fanciful distraction from the main game of keeping the island financially afloat.

'Is there an easy answer to this riddle?' I ask.

'Of course there is,' Ric says. 'Ask the people, give us the choice—isn't that the fairest, simplest solution? Independence, free association or integration.'

'A simple referendum on the future position of Norfolk?'

'Yes.'

For Norfolk to win the right to self-determination and a referendum on its political destiny it needs to be sponsored by a UN member. Attempts at this have so far failed and Ric sees no point in going to the High Court of Australia for any legal clarification because he doesn't trust it. When it comes to Australia's policy and Ric's homeland, the world is bleak and conspiratorial. Colleen McCullough shares these views and sums up Canberra's actions as 'unilateral authoritarianism and thoughtless tunnel vision'.

Even if Ric and the Society of Descendants beat all the odds and win their UN referendum, a favourable result is no sure thing. Ric agrees most Norfolk Islanders don't want to disassociate themselves from Australia and says the number who want to be integrated into the Australian system, including the taxation system, is increasing. He puts this shift down to the promises of cash in the shape of social welfare and benefits. This, he says, is due to 'the insidious stacking of the population', which is code for Australian newcomers to Norfolk Island.

'When I was Minister for Immigration, every application the board and I turned down was overturned by going to Canberra. It's going to get worse if they can stack it with six month part-timers, and eventually they hope to stack it so much that when we do finally get a referendum, whoops, the Pitcairners are only a minority in the end.'

Like those who believe the invasion of Iraq was all about oil, Ric Robinson says oil is also the key to Canberra's motives for Norfolk, although he says much of the information about oil near Norfolk is censored: 'I think it's the oil and perhaps defence, the strategic position of the place. They didn't give a hoot about Norfolk Island until the

1970s when they discovered huge hydrocarbon deposits in our waters. I'll get you a satellite seepage graph, it's self-explanatory. They found the biggest gas-hydrate deposits up to our northwest. It might not be commercially viable at the moment, but Black Bank is, because it is oil shale, there is oil here and that's the only reason they wanted it. Until terrorism came along they wanted a base in the Pacific as well. I have no doubt whatsoever it is to do with the hydrocarbons in our waters. They are not very honourable.'

I suggest it sounds like everything coming from Canberra is a conspiracy to get the island. Ric stares at me as if I've been in la-la land myself and says, 'It is. It is.'

At this point the woman Ric calls his 'missus' appears in the doorway to the greenhouse, a woman one Islander whispered to me 'loves and hates with equal passion'. Colleen McCullough Robinson; Ric introduces me to his famous wife, who moved to Norfolk in 1980. Ric was Colleen's gardener. Four years later they were married. 'Tim's writing a book about Norfolk Island,' Ric says by way of introducing me. The big, bold author with short spiky hair speaks in a dreamy little voice and says her 'mind is somewhere else'. She dangles a limp hand before me to shake, which I do, ever so gently.

When I first went to Norfolk for the ABC and broadcast a documentary about the island and the murder of Janelle Patton, Colleen McCullough roasted me and those I interviewed in an angry, rambling and at times comical letter to the *Norfolk Islander*: 'We are being set up, folks, as violent, criminal, hideous persons living in a seething stew of secrecy sadism and sex.' I was accused of producing a propaganda report. McCullough said her name was 'mentioned in a rather sneering way', and I was responsible for leading the 'bumbling' and 'ineffectual' Detective Sergeant Bob Peters up the proverbial garden path, forcing him to suggest, 'Norfolk Island is a mafia-like community that exists under the Sicilian law of *omerta*—that is, silence.' She dubbed the investigation team 'the Keystone Cops' and upset the Patton family by referring to Janelle's murder as a 'horrible, regrettable incident'. Colleen accused me of being under pressure from Canberra and in a letter to the *Norfolk Islander* instructed me personally to: 'Try living here for a couple of decades plus and you might just begin to scrape the surface of this wonderful, intriguing, absolutely unique place.'

I didn't have time to live on Norfolk for a couple of decades. I was happy to talk to those who had, but after the briefest of moments hovering in the doorway, Colleen McCullough floated upstairs to continue writing—apparently a whodunit, but not of the Norfolk kind.

'She's in America,' Ric says.

'Oh,' I reply, not quite understanding. 'She's travelling to America?'

'No, for her next book,' and to clarify he taps his forehead. 'Up here.'

'I was hoping she might join us. I have some questions, especially one about you, Ric.' He looks at me inquisitively. I continue: 'After Colleen married you she is quoted, some years back, as saying she "committed a social solecism by marrying an Islander of Pitcairn descent". I was wondering what that actually means.' Ric looks at me blankly; he has no more of an idea than me.

While Ric and Colleen form a unified team in protest against their 'colonial overlords' they write individual submissions to the endless number of parliamentary inquiries into the inner workings of the pine needle paradise. Colleen reserved her most colourful comments for the latest inquiry into Norfolk Island governance. She predicted a bad outcome and was right. Her four page submission is emotive, brash and burns with a red hot patriotism and lack of modesty the late nineteenth century Norfolk patriarch George Hunn Nobbs would have delighted in. In part, she wrote:

> When I sign books in Helsinki, the queue goes around the block. You cannot dismiss me as a yokel. And, after my death, this and other letters will be published to a worldwide audience. Therefore you cannot dismiss me as unimportant. But what Canberra (not the Australian people) has done and continues to do to Norfolk Island shames me as a loyal Australian. The only way this isolated little place can survive is by keeping its own identity . . . We of Norfolk Island are treated by Canberra with arrogance, lack of compassion, wilful misunderstanding, top lofty superiority and a degree of hardheartedness tantamount to cruelty.

Before I leave, Ric finds a printout of an 'oil seepage graph' showing big black marks all around Norfolk Island. He notes my phone number and walks me to the door where I was asked to leave my shoes.

He looks like he's about to pat me on the back but stops himself.

He follows me out the door and, with his hands thrust in his overalls, marches off towards a large garden shed.

Two days later in the small fibro house I was renting the phone rang. It was early morning and I was still asleep, struggling with a dream and the crows of a troubled rooster next door.

I picked up the receiver and did my best to sound awake, a tactic which never works. From the other end came a deep, slow voice which sounded like it had been humming since the crack of dawn.

'It's Ric Robinson,' said the voice.

'Hi, Ric.'

'I'm just ringing to let you know that Norfolk *isn't* a part of Australia. You are clear on that, aren't you?'

———

My time with Ric had been amicable. I liked him for speaking his mind. He answered my questions and I appreciated his candid nature and stubborn conviction. His view on Norfolk was not in line with most on the island, but at least he had a view. His desire to keep Canberra at bay resonated with many Pitcairn descendants and mainland exiles who had no interest in seeing the dead hand of Australian taxation infiltrate their lives. I liked Ric because he advocated a position. He didn't sit on the fence or, like others, trim his sails for a given audience.

Four weeks later, though, Ric wrote a letter to the *Norfolk Islander*. The subtext was that I had tricked him, somehow got under his radar. The letter was an early warning to his constituents that he had spoken with the enemy and was sorry for having done so:

Sir,

Around March of last year an ABC Propaganda announcer named Tim Latham broadcast an anti-Norfolk piece that incensed a lot of locals. Well be warned, there's more coming. Probably because there is now someone called Latham running the Labour [*sic*] Party I failed to recognise the name when he interviewed me for a book he is doing on Norfolk Island. Now that his name has clicked in my mind and given the questions he asked me, I have no doubt that the book will be full of carefully edited quotes and generalisations that larded his radio programme. It seems that our Colonial Overlords have more 'agents of influence' operating against the people of Norfolk Island than we initially thought. Australia must be running out of oil.

Yours etc.
Ric N I Robinson.

CHAPTER 9

THE NORFUK WIEH

OF ALL the thankless jobs in island politics the grandest of them must be Minister for Finance. I was told it was the 'poisoned chalice', the office of the most impossible of tasks—trying to balance the books on an island where nobody wanted to contribute and few kept financial records. The island's GDP in 2004 wasn't even known although it is estimated to be $120–140 million.

Nobody wants to be the finance minister for long. The juggle of keeping friends and doing what's right for the island is a bigger challenge than running a surplus. The trick to keeping all the balls in the air is, in a way, to do nothing. The second trick is to gnaw away at public expenditure. Raping the capital works budget is a popular and practical tactic with proven results, handed down from treasurer to treasurer. This is one reason why the island can't afford to maintain its key asset— the airport runway—and needs to ask Canberra for financial help. Who, I wondered, would accept this difficult job, and why?

The answer in 2004 was Graeme Donaldson. On top of being finance minister, Graeme Donaldson had another twelve portfolios to look after, although pulling the purse strings was top priority. Graeme's mantra of 'living within our means' really meant keeping the community out of the cookie jar. Booze and telephones were two of his tidy earners and both made hay, night and day. These two monopolies, along with a tax on all imports, basically fund the island's carefree lifestyle.

Graeme Donaldson looked just how an accountant should look. Thin and slightly dour, his sense of humour hidden beneath years of maths. I was told he was the first professionally trained accountant to hold the finance portfolio.

'It is difficult,' he said, as we sat in his office beneath a portrait of a young Queen Elizabeth, 'there are lot of tasks. We've got three tiers of government here, local, state—health and education—and Commonwealth matters like welfare, customs, immigration and postal services . . .' He turned over a sheet that listed more policy responsibilities. I asked him to sum up the much talked about financial crisis on the island.

'In a word it's challenging but manageable. I mean, you can still buy a bottle of whisky here for fifteen dollars. I think there's room to move without hurting anybody's lifestyle.'

'Is it too harsh to say the island's on the verge of bankruptcy?'

'Oh yes,' he said, looking at me across his desk with the first sign of a heartbeat, 'Far too harsh. There's quite a bit in untaxed resources on Norfolk Island. You're probably aware we don't have any income tax. We've got no rates or taxes on land. We don't have a GST, we raise most of our revenue from customs duty which is about four million a year and we raise other revenue from departure tax. We've got some healthy dividends from business undertakings as well. Both Telecom and the Liquor Bond generate about $1.3 million each. We've always opted for a simple way of collecting our taxes and when I say simple I mean administratively simple. We just put a levy on petrol or a levy on goods coming into the island or a levy on people coming and going from the island. We don't expect people to lodge an income tax return, or GST returns, or business activity statements. That's a luxury; not having to attend to those sort of matters.'

In a world where tax is a four letter word, Norfolk Islanders glided above it all, blissfully ignorant of the tenacious take of the taxman. Norfolk's peculiar tax-free status has existed since Australian Federation and Islanders have fought hard to maintain its residential tax haven. Residents, companies and trusts are all exempt from Australian taxation, except on income derived from the mainland.

This tax-free cash economy was Norfolk Island's modern day Bounty, one tourists shouldered by paying a host of indirect taxes, including a $30 departure fee, which was producing more than one million dollars a year.

Direct income tax was what Norfolk wished to avoid, at all costs. And why not? Everyone else would too if they had half a chance, or were lucky enough to bed an Islander and apply for residency.

'One of the luxuries here,' Graeme added, 'is not having to deal with those sort of things. One of the luxuries here is that your money is your own. If you have a second job you don't have to worry about paying a second rate of tax on that. The money you earn goes into your pocket and you're not accountable to anybody. That's one of the ways of life on Norfolk Island and I wouldn't like to see that change.'

In 1997, an extensive report on Norfolk's economy was produced by the Commonwealth Grants Commission. This is a federal body which writes lots of reports which the Australian government rarely pays attention to. It labelled the island's taxation system 'regressive'; it didn't tax wealth and the resulting burden fell disproportionately on tourists. The report claimed Norfolk had a revenue raising capacity sixty per cent greater than what it was achieving. I asked Graeme if this figure concerned him, if the island shouldn't be making more of a contribution to funding itself. His response was in line with the island's philosophy on taxation: 'I think that is something to be proud of. If we can keep it at that level it would be fantastic. If we have to jump to a higher percentage to fund government projects, so be it. We'll have to do it.'

'Is it right,' I asked, 'that the current indirect tax system is inequitable, given the estimated sixty-plus millionaires on the island?'

'I wouldn't use the word inequitable, but if you're looking for a tax system that does some social engineering, that taxes the rich more than the poor on a progressive basis, then it doesn't achieve that. If you're looking for a tax system that's easy to implement and simple to manage and easy to understand, then this system works—it's exactly what we've got now.'

Welcome to Norfolk Island, I thought. A place where simple is simply the best. The very lifestyle that attracted Janelle Patton and thousands of other TEPs. How long, I thought, can it keep the complexity of the outside world at bay? It had greater powers than any Australian state but was smaller than a local council. On paper it was ridiculous until you realised it had actually happened. Something radical, like direct taxation, has never happened because advocating taxes is akin to political harakiri and managing a complex system is beyond the island's capacity. Toon Buffett was the only minister who admitted to me the island's 'tax honeymoon' was over but until the community was prepared to contribute, people would continue to complain about the state of the roads and nothing would change.

After speaking with the finance minister I stopped off at the Sports and Workers Club, the location of Janelle Patton's fight with Susan Fieldes. The 'Sporties' is housed in one of the original Pitcairn family homes and still has a large front lawn. I sat in the sun and contributed to the economy by drinking several cans of VB. As the sun shifted to the west I thought about what made Norfolk so refreshing.

As a landscape, its difference from the rest of Australia was instantly appealing. As James Cook noted, Norfolk shares much similarity with the rolling landscape of New Zealand's north island. But Norfolk's improbable charm lies in more than just its geography or the fact that the community voted no in a referendum on mobile phones. To most visitors the charm comes from the people themselves. Hardly a week goes by when there isn't a letter of appreciation in the *Norfolk Islander* from another enamoured visitor who promises to 'return soon'.

What I liked about Norfolk Island was the business landscape. It didn't really have one.

Burnt Pine isn't the most attractive township for a good-looking island, especially when compared to the icy grandeur of convict Kingston. It's more a fudge job than anything else, and a sobering reminder of the demise of architecture since the emancipation of convict labour, but at least it looks *kind of different*, and within this hodgepodge collection of shop fronts lay, perversely, some of its beauty. On Norfolk, the business landscape isn't corporatised, franchised and sanitised. There are no fast food chains, multinational resorts or global petrol brands. Instead of BP there is Paw Paws Pump House. Instead of Avis there is Barry's Car Hire. It's all business owner-driven, just like the old days. Where else would the lingerie shop be called 'The Underworld'?

Norfolk's shops are independent of big business. They're quirky and amateurish and quaint. Not that the island has groovy shops—it's got daggy shops. Lots of them and all the tourist shops sell the same stuff: perfume, make-up, European casual clothes, sneakers and lots of Chinese cotton including T-shirts which say 'I drink on any day ending with Y'. I expected Norfolk to be a crafty place, its businesses exploiting a Polynesian soul or Pacific sensuousness, yet the cultural-retail mix struggled beyond Fletcher Christian, the *Bounty* and the cat-o'-nine-tails.

There are walls of teaspoons and tourism trinkets and endless collections of porcelain figurines. Norfolk must have more porcelain figurines per capita than any other place in the world. These figurines are priced at hundreds, if not thousands, of dollars and require endless dusting, which is what Janelle Patton spent a lot of time doing while she worked on the floor of World Traders. When I dared to ask, 'Who the hell buys all the porcelain?' then saw what was inside many island homes, I felt embarrassed. I saved these jokes for the understanding of outsiders.

I struggled to find anything to buy, although admittedly I was taken with the miniature glass bottles with a model of the *Bounty* inside. They rested on wooden cradles and were so kitsch they were almost cool. I experienced a sort of boyish captivation with them every time I saw one. I wondered if I could mentally coexist with it on my desk but feared I might smash it with my duty-free whisky the moment my writing threw a mutiny of its own.

There is no discernible Norfolk Brand, although efforts are underway to shift from the traditional and faithful market of 'nearly deads' to a younger, groovier, eco-oriented clientele. The new tourism brochure tagged Norfolk the 'Beguiling Isle' and flagged a move into adventure sports. It's no secret the island hopes these younger, more vigorous visitors will spend more cash than the oldies. It seems a growing number of business owners are tired of people with squeaky wallets. What the island has overlooked is that this new market will be infinitely more discerning. What the 'nearly deads' see as quaint, younger generations see as old and tired. This wasn't lost on Janelle. As she wrote to her family, 'Sometimes I can't believe how beautiful the island is, but they seem to market it only for the geriatrics.'

Railing against this move to a younger travel market, was, of all people, politician and lawyer John Brown, the de facto minister for privatisation and profit. He warned against any policy which would see the island disregard the market which has been the backbone of its tourism prosperity. He believed it was time for Norfolk to make a quantum leap in how it managed its affairs and how it paid its way but getting rid of its traditional tourist market wasn't what he had in mind.

If wealthier visitors were the new focus then island shops would have to change. Most remain a historical throwback to when Norfolk was a duty-free shopping destination, a claim it still uses to hoodwink tourists.

I finished my beer and drove to see Gary Robertson, head of the island Chamber of Commerce and a commercial printer. Gary is a tall, lean and keen squash player, originally from New Zealand. He immigrated to Norfolk in 1969. Twenty years ago he tackled Tom Lloyd's hold on the local media market by running a competing newspaper called, of all things, *Dem Tull*. In his back office he explains the dilemma of Norfolk Island's seventy-two retail businesses and the changing demographic of tourism.

'The shopkeepers moan like buggery about not having people in their shop, and I've told them, I don't know how many times, to turn around and have a look on their shelves. What have they got in the shop? There, I say, is your problem.

'This whole island used to spark on the builders of the nation, the pre-war age. Then came the baby boomers and now the later ones. These are the markets Australia and New Zealand are now aiming at, they're not the mums and dads who have saved up for years for a holiday, they're looking for more spontaneous things, better things, and we have to look at the goods they want. This is where the shopkeepers have to get their act together. Some are, some aren't. The ones that aren't are moaning.'

'Does this mean nobody's making a quid?'

'Yeah, that's a fair view of it.'

'What about all the figurines?'

'Originally shop owners made sure they had a product no one else had. Now, since the mid eighties, some of the new players walk down the road and say, "Shit, there's six people in that shop, what are they doing, what are they buying?" Then bang, they offer the same thing and the next minute six people become three. It's crazy. You can't stop it, it's free trade. You can do what you bloody well like.' Gary smiles and tucks his feet on the edge of the chair in a sort of yoga squat position. Perhaps he's stretching for a squash game.

'Are there too many shops?' I ask.

'Put it this way, every shop is for sale. Some sell readily, others don't. It's going to get harder before it gets better. Those that have kept their turnover and financial records have no problems. Business owners are realising if they want to sell they need to have some records, even till-takes. At the same time it's to their advantage because if they look closely at the business they might realise, Shit, I'm not making much here anyway.'

I felt for the retail owners because it was clear many were still living the old dream of 'lifestyle first, business second'. It's a reasonable aspiration on an island adrift in the Pacific—why else, I thought, would someone move to Norfolk and buy a business except to lig and loaf? This is why TEPs come to Norfolk, to escape the grind of mainland work hours and revel in an effortless island existence where social engagements are never more than five minutes away.

An important part of this culture is the shopping hours. Tradition- ally shops close at midday on Wednesdays. In wonderful defiance of its economy, even the tourist information centre shuts on Wednesdays. Shops also closed at midday on Saturday and all day Sunday. But cracks are appearing. New Australian and New Zealand business owners comfortable working seventy-hour weeks are ramping up the pressure by extending their hours. The concept of business and pleasure never clashing was clearly under threat. Still Norfolk was hanging in there, doing what it did best, resisting change it saw as unnecessary and un- Norfolk.

Before I left Gary, I asked him about his experience of running the newspaper. He smiles and, like bookends, pulls out a copy each of the first and last edition from a nearby cabinet, both printed in 1983. 'You can take those with you,' he says. On the front page of the last edition is the headline: 'TEPS Gain Ground in Quest to Get Vote'. Twenty years on, the issue was still alive—nothing had changed.

Gary Robertson employed two journalists from New Zealand to sort the myth from the truth on an island hostile to reality. It lasted a year. Not because locals went feral over its reporting. Gary says it was because the classified market was locked up by the *Norfolk Islander*.

'The intent was to do something journalistic and we got a written note from the Chief Minister of the day to say under no circumstances were any of the Assembly members to give stuff out to my reporters. It was easily fixed. There were three backbenchers who turned out to be most knowledgeable anyway, and they'd say what you wanted to know. It just made us more determined to get the stuff and make sure the correct news went through.'

Gary had been living on Norfolk Island for twelve years before he tackled a newspaper. I ask what would happen if someone came over and started something similar after just a few years. 'Would it be a problem?'

'It'd be a shitfight,' he says laughing. 'Quite frankly.'

———

On Norfolk there is no cultural reference point for media inquiries. When I asked John Brown, a tax exile, lawyer, businessman and island politician, a question about one of his employees losing both legs in an industrial accident while working for one of his companies, he called me a 'disgraceful journalist', aborted the interview and told me to leave. These were questions, it seemed, that must never be asked and by asking them I was breaking the universal rule that says outsiders shouldn't question the 'Norfolk Way' (the 'Norfuk Wieh' in the Norfolk language), an umbrella term which covers anything to do with the cultural mores of island life; how people live, govern, make decisions, all the important ingredients which create an ethos and tradition. 'It's not the Norfolk Way' is a common refrain and one used to justify many political and personal decisions. Reporting things to the police is not the 'Norfolk Way' nor is allowing mainlanders to voice opinions on how things could be done, say, differently, or better. These suggestions are seen as impertinent. The right to make them is to be earned, just like the right to vote. The passport to these rights is time; time living on the island and participating within the community.

Islanders enjoy respect. They like it, they want it, they seek it. Respect for who they are and what the island has achieved. By suggesting change after a couple of weeks or years, newcomers clash with the Norfolk Way: the fresh eye is blind to the cadence of island life and to the uninitiated there appears much to do, simple things like building footpaths or providing lighting for elderly tourists who plod the roadside with nothing more than a penlight to guide their way.

The Australian Federal Police are the consummate outsiders with an insiders' job. Three officers are seconded from Canberra on two year postings. For the past few years the police have been raising money for a footpath between the school at Middlegate and Burnt Pine so children don't have to walk on the road or the embankment to get to class. Local adults won't use the footpath much because they drive *everywhere*, even across the road, but tourists will find it a relief because it goes via a busy section of town. The construction money has been raised by charity golf days and other fundrasing activities organised by the police. Given the begrudging recognition of the need for law and order by the community, the police have got away with this rather crafty defiance of the Norfolk Way which is still to update itself on the need or otherwise for footpaths. If any other group of newcomers or temporary visitors had said, 'Let's build a footpath here,' they would have been told to butt out.

This very human reaction to resisting outside influences is due to decades of being told, particularly by Australian politicians, that the island should do things differently. This advice is not seen as helpful, it is seen as criticism, which is what it often is. If there's a sure way to get a rusted-on Islander to bristle in the wind, it's to suggest the 'Norfolk Way' might be the wrong way. People who do this are sometimes called 'seagulls'—those who fly in, shit on the community, then leave. The most common 'seagull' appeared in a suit and came from Canberra. Strangely, there are no actual seagulls on Norfolk. I was told Islanders shoot the birds as soon as they arrive.

CHAPTER 10

ROOTY HILL ROAD

I'VE GONE to see Detective Sergeant Bob Peters at the Norfolk Island police station. It's a windy day and the surrounding seas are rough. 'No workin' the ship today,' say Islanders. For nearly two weeks the *Norfolk Guardian* has been anchored off Headstone Point waiting to be unloaded. Headstone is adjacent to the old ocean tip and gets its name from two convict graves which forever face the ocean that imprisoned them.

The *Norfolk Guardian* has been waiting for the tail end of a cyclone to abate, leading to the longest delay in years. The hold-up has led to a crisis in supplies. The island has run out of frozen potato chips, along with building supplies and a number of other more serious things—but it's the lack of hot chips which is having the most obvious impact. Blackboard menus carry the chalk caveat 'No Hot Chips'. It appears there are no meat patties either, despite the island having two butchers and a rifle to pick off a roaming beast when one is required. 'They could bloody well make their own potato chips,' says Graham 'Struts' Struthers.

Struts and I downed a few whiskies the night before and it's thanks to Struts that I've been able to rent a house for a few weeks. Struts reminds me of Obelix from the Asterix cartoon. As a baby, Obelix fell into a cauldron of magic potion giving him super strength. 'Struts' looks like he fell into a cauldron of red cordial giving him hyperactive powers. The New Zealander lists Robert Muldoon as one of his political heroes. He works at least three jobs and despite having an artificial ticker implanted recently, he is still moving at a hundred miles an hour. 'We've been cutting up spuds all week,' he gasps, 'like in the old days, hand-made chips, but the others, they're bloody too lazy. They just wait for the ship and sit on their hands.'

Struts' favourite saying is, 'I can tell you some stories,' and he does. Plenty. About those 'bloody Pitcairners' and how he once told a local, 'You don't look like you came off the *Bounty*.' It was obviously a joke about skin colour and it didn't go down well. He laughs. 'That was the last time I drank there.' Struts has lots of stories about his years on Norfolk, I'm just never sure whether to believe them.

————

Bob Peters sees me approaching and mumbles hello. He has agreed to drive me around the island and detail Janelle Patton's movements on the Sunday she died. The detective shakes my hand, looks me up and down and says, 'How are the Islanders treating you?'

Bob Peters is wearing a white shirt, red tie, no jacket, black trousers and scuffed shoes. It's clear he's been doing some walking. He's just returned from the Old Military Barracks in Kingston where he addressed the nine members of the Norfolk Island Assembly. Today's subject was the forthcoming coronial inquest.

'Did they ask many questions?'

'Not as many as I thought they might. But one of them did ask why a coronial hearing was necessary.'

'Toon Buffett,' I say.

Bob nods.

Ivens 'Toon' Buffett had expressed similar thoughts to me a few days earlier on the veranda of the Golf Club. His view was consistent with the 'let it lie for the time being' theory. According to this notion, the crime could solve itself if only it was left to fester alone. It's a theory which is easily misconstrued because on the surface it doesn't make any sense. It isn't about denying justice, or letting the offender off the hook, it's about letting the nature of Norfolk Island take its course. It is an island approach to many things and grounded in a timeless attitude that truth is as porous as the island's sandstone and soil—eventually it will seep out. It was just a matter of time until the offender tripped, let slip, revealed or squealed, perhaps falling on their own sword during a night on the drink. Until this took place, Toon Buffett could only see the coronial inquest as a portal to further pain, disharmony, ill will and mystery: a prediction which proved accurate.

Detective Peters was having enough trouble getting Islanders to recall what they'd been doing the day Janelle disappeared. He figured to break the case he'd have to do the work. The notion that the truth might accidentally reveal itself sometime in the future was not one he was relying on. He describes this attitude as 'surprising' then rephrases it to 'disappointing'.

'I don't think it is a prevailing attitude,' says Bob as we walk to his car. 'It may be in some areas of the community but in general terms I don't think it is. I mean, a lot of people want the crime solved for a lot of various reasons. I know there is the other attitude that says "it's our business, go away, it's got nothing to do with outsiders". But Janelle *was* an outsider, so they can't say that. It's hard to say. I think you could live here for fifty years and still not understand what goes on and the movements of the place.'

Bob stops at a caramel-brown Mazda sedan. 'My usual car wasn't available and anyway . . .' he says, looking at me across the car roof as he jangles a set of keys, 'everyone knew the numberplates.'

Tracking where Bob Peters goes and who he talks to has been happening since day one. It's no longer as acute as it was in the months following the murder, when he had to issue a statement that people seen speaking to police didn't make them suspects.

The investigation team endured cars and tour buses passing their accommodation. There were times when locals strolled into their rooms to inquire on progress. One day fellow detective Tony Edmondson was in the shower and came out to find an Islander making himself coffee and offering sleuth-ful suggestions about cracking the case.

Bob unlocks the car, which shows he's a long way from going native because on Norfolk Island most people leave their keys in the ignition. He slides into the seat and reaches over his shoulder for the seatbelt. Norfolk is still debating mandatory traffic laws such as seatbelts, drink-driving legislation and kids riding on the back of trucks. There's a lot of noise about how such legislation could cripple the island lifestyle. The Norfolk Way is enshrined in laxity and the same debate was heard when motorcycle helmets were enforced. 'If people stuck to the speed limit then we wouldn't need to wear seatbelts', is the common sentiment in the local paper. Third party insurance demands minimum standards such as seatbelts. Yet again the real world was sprouting inside the glasshouse of Norfolk culture and people were finding it hard to accept.

I decide to belt-up but only because I'm in a car with a federal detective. It's the first time I've worn one for weeks and I feel instantly restricted, aware of the sash across my body. I've spent my whole life wearing seatbelts but in a short time the sensation of having no body restraint has become liberating.

We head off with Crosby, Stills, Nash and Young humming low on the radio. As Bob navigates the frail island roads he does what all locals do and what all visitors try to do: he waves to passing cars. I notice few are waving back. It's not surprising given Bob is wearing a seatbelt. And a tie. Could there be a greater sign of foreignness?

Everyone on Norfolk has a different version of the 'island wave'. It can depend on a driver's mood, speed, location or whether the other person is remotely recognisable—family, friend, lover or foe. As two cars approach it can be like a standoff, a countdown, a game of who waves first. The most common wave is not a wave at all, it's more a nervous twitch, a couple of fingers flicked off the steering wheel. Sometimes it's nothing at all, which makes the driver who did wave feel stupid. Some tourists wave like they're flagging the finish of a Grand Prix and I've been with rusted-on locals who have received similar, over-the-top flapping from people on the street. My favourite version is the double pistol wave: both hands off the steering wheel with raised thumbs and straight forefingers. No one gives Bob this wave. Not today.

Bob's take on the wave is to raise his palm above the steering wheel and offer a full frontal 'howdy' sign, like a native American Indian greeting a tribe. It's a bit unsteady, even clumsy, but it's passive and I give him full points for trying. It's a hell of an island to make friends on, especially if you're honest about why you're visiting.

As we turn up New Cascade Road towards Burnt Pine I try to coax Bob into a commentary on the case. Does he think it extraordinary? What strikes him as unusual? Isn't it weird somebody can just vanish at noon and no one sees anything at all?

I deliberately pepper my questions with an air of nonchalance but

Janelle shows off her island home. Taken by Ron Patton on Saturday 30 March 2002, one day before Janelle's murder.

Last sighting: the section of Rooty Hill Road where police believe Janelle disappeared.

The coronial inquest visits Cockpit: the witch's hat marks the placement of Janelle's body.

413 cm

364 cm

The major clue: the sheet of plastic found covering Janelle's body. A number of prints found on it are still unidentified.

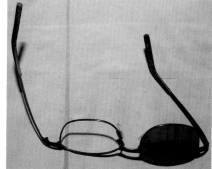

Sunglasses found on Rooty Hill Road. Believed to be Janelle's but forensics fail to prove beyond doubt.

The detective: Bob Peters at Cockpit, March 2004.

Laurie 'Bucket' Quintal awaits the coroner's findings inside the courthouse.

Carol and Ron Patton answer questions at the conclusion of the coronial inquest, June 2004.

The late Ivens 'Toon' Buffett (centre) offers his hands for justice in the Patton case.

Tom Lloyd: the editor of the Norfolk Islander *shows off his printing press.*

Bounty Day 2004: Islanders march from the jetty to the cemetery in honour of their Pitcairn ancestors.

David Buffett (aka the Colonel): Norfolk's statesman and longest serving politician. Every Bounty Day he re-enacts the role of Captain Denham, the man who welcomed the Pitcairners to Norfolk in 1856.

Political signs: protesting the island's relationship with mainland Australia.

Burnt Pine: the main street and home to Norfolk's only roundabout.

Quality Row: the main street of Kingston, and home to the island's government and bureaucracy.

Island paradise: Anson Bay and the steep cliffs of Norfolk.

it's an amateur effort. I can't get the detective to bite. My questions sink into silence. The only word he chews on is 'luck'.

'Yes. They were lucky,' he says.

I say, 'Audacious.'

He just stares through the windscreen.

In the mid 1980s, Bob Peters applied for a secondment with the Norfolk Island police but a Canberra homicide investigation held him over. He'd always wanted to visit the island for a holiday. It's something he now chuckles about. He no longer finds Norfolk as endearing as he did before he scratched its underbelly. He says he's 'not a travelling sort of man', and 'hates living out of a suitcase'. He also misses his wife. This is his twelfth homicide investigation in his career and perhaps his last. He won't admit it, but this is his most infuriating case.

After a period of silence he brightens up. 'I'd say, when you look at things, it's unusual for attacks of this nature to happen in daylight hours. Very unusual. Especially when you have the alternative of night-time here, which is, you know, you can't see your hand in front of your face. Similarly, disposing of a body in daylight hours is very unusual. I've got theories about that but no proof.'

'Is it unusual to disappear like Janelle did, to vanish from a public road? To not have an eyewitness?'

'Well, you've been on Rooty Hill Road. Sometimes you can sit there at midday and not see a soul for five or ten minutes. And other times it's just a steady stream of cars, not like peak hour, but steady. The same with Cockpit reserve. There can be no one or lots of people, with a tourist bus pulling out. So it's . . . I dunno, it may well be that no one else has ever seen or heard anything that is connected to the crime. That may well be the case and if that is the case . . .' Bob pauses and exhales, 'then I'm really battling.'

Time and time again Bob Peters says there is nothing to indicate Janelle Patton was in danger the day she died. Security camera footage from the supermarket shows Janelle moving along the aisles at 11.18 on Sunday morning, buying food for a Mexican dinner that night.

Bob shifts the car past the school at Middlegate where students' bikes lean against the side railings, or are scattered on the grass like an afterthought. We head along Queen Elizabeth Drive, nudging towards the island's southeastern corner.

'This is the route Janelle drove on her way back from Foodlands.' Bob doesn't look at me as he speaks, he keeps his eyes fixed ahead. 'She drove along here towards Collins Head Road and then turned into her street, Allendale Drive. She was in a rush to go for her walk.'

Bob pauses at the driveway of Ruth and Foxy McCoy's property where Janelle lived in the self-contained flat. From her front garden Janelle could catch glimpses of the ocean and hear waves rolling over the boulders of nearby Ball Bay.

Bob turns the car around. The street is misnamed: it isn't a road but a cul-de-sac. Bob Peters believes Janelle arrived home around 11.30. She dumped her purse and shopping on the kitchen table and switched her work uniform for a black singlet top with a red trim, a pair of faded drawstring shorts which police describe as 'multicoloured', and a pair of 'Asics Gel' runners. She gathered her hair into a ponytail, had a drink of water and left by the back door. Janelle liked gold jewellery and wore three chains around her neck, a gold ring on each hand, a gold bracelet on each wrist and a gold anklet on her left ankle.

Bob stops the car at the intersection of Allendale Drive and Collins Head Road. 'Ruth McCoy saw Janelle here, on the corner of these two streets, about 11.30 am. She was returning from shopping and church. She waved but Janelle didn't seem to notice. She said she was walking briskly. Janelle then walked up the left hand side and was again seen by several people.'

'Did she wave to them?'

'They can't recall if she waved or not.'

As Bob slowly drives I look to my left, staring at the thin, grassy verge of the pockmarked road. There is no gutter or kerb. Parallel to the road edge is a timber fence, behind that a low hedge. As with all roads on Norfolk there is no footpath. Sometimes there's a dirt track but here there is nowhere to walk except on the road. This is why people exercising stand out: a driver has to go out of their way not to run them down.

About a kilometre from Janelle's flat is the turn-off to Rooty Hill Road, which leads to Queen Elizabeth lookout and its windswept vista of Kingston and the islands of Phillip and Nepean. Bob is now driving Janelle's regular walking route. He explains that if Janelle was feeling especially energetic she'd extend her walk down the hill to Kingston, past the cemetery, across Bloody Bridge and up the steep hill of Driver

Christian Road, passing the burnt-out remains of the Cardno house. But on the day she died Janelle was pushed for time. Given she planned to meet her parents Bob Peters believes she only had time to 'walk to the lookout, then double back home'.

When Ron Patton returned to Norfolk eleven months after his daughter's murder, he told me he saw the island with 'new eyes'. As he traced Janelle's last known movements, trying to fathom how this unforeseen cruelty entered his world, he noticed the early bends of Rooty Hill Road are sunken from view. He mentioned how easy it would be to accost someone here and not be seen. This is true, particularly along the road's first two hundred metres where it cuts through a steep embankment almost two metres high. But Janelle didn't disappear here, instead she vanished several hundred metres further on while walking on a flat and visible section of road.

There are so few facts about what happened to Janelle Patton that what is known takes on precious significance. Bob Peters is confident he knows where Janelle vanished thanks to Jodie Williams. She is the last known person to see Janelle alive and the only confirmed eyewitness who can pinpoint Janelle's location on Rooty Hill Road. Jodie Williams is a cousin of Janelle's landlord Ruth McCoy and was driving around the island trying to put her twenty-month-old son to sleep. She turned a corner and saw Janelle walking alone, on the left hand side of the road. She told the coronial inquest: 'I just put my hand up to wave to her, looked in the rear-vision mirror and passed and kept going.'

Jodie Williams was heading downhill towards the lookout, which is where Bob Peters is driving now.

'What time did Jodie drive past?'

'We estimate about 11.40.'

'Did Janelle wave back?'

'She can't recall her waving back.'

'Then what happened?'

'Jodie Williams did a loop. She went down to the cemetery, over Bloody Bridge, up Driver Christian Road and back down Rooty Hill Road again. Based on a reconstruction of the drive we estimate it would have taken Jodie Williams between eight and ten minutes to complete the circuit.'

'And she didn't see Janelle the second time round?'

'No, not walking in either direction.'

'So Janelle disappeared in a ten-minute period?'

'That's the indication based on Jodie Williams.'

'So what happened?'

'I think Janelle got into a car, either willingly or by force,' he says.

———

Police gathered nine statements from people living or travelling along Rooty Hill Road at the time of Janelle's walk. No one saw anything suspicious but one did confirm Jodie Williams' sighting of Janelle, who at the time was walking past the entrance to John Huxstep's property. John Huxstep knew Janelle by sight but that day was toiling in his backyard. Police asked if he heard 'any sound which resembled a scream, argument or a car accident'. He said no.

Because there are no eyewitnesses to Janelle's disappearance, Bob Peters must rely on conjecture and dead reckoning to conclude she never made it to the lookout and disappeared in the time it took Jodie Williams to complete her loop. There is one additional clue which makes him confident he's right—a pair of damaged sunglasses, found by Sergeant Brendan Lindsay at seven o'clock the next morning during a line search of Rooty Hill Road. In her police statement, Jodie Williams confirms Janelle was wearing black sunglasses across her eyes.

The sunglasses were found not far from where Janelle was last seen walking. The glasses were splattered with mud and missing one lens. Forensic tests can't prove they're Janelle's but in a case where so little is known, near enough is probably good enough. A public plea, complete with photograph, failed to illicit any claim of ownership.

The missing lens has never been found.

On an island where lost and found items are advertised on the radio and find their way home successfully, let's assume the sunglasses are Janelle's. Was there such panic, or urgency, the sunglasses were knocked, dropped or somehow forgotten? Or were they dislodged in an argument? A roadside struggle? Sunglasses—an item separated from their owner only by accident or mishap. No one chooses to discard their sunglasses, not at midday on a bright summer day while out walking. These black, no-brand sunglasses provide the only clue to what took place, and they suggest Janelle didn't leave the road willingly.

Bob Peters stops the car so I can see where the sunglasses were found. The side of the road is like the edge of a fried egg; thin, bubbled and uneven. In the distance is a small rise before the road runs down towards the coast.

'The glasses may have been lying further up,' Bob says, 'but this is where they were found. The rain or wind could have pushed them down the hill.'

Bob Peters has always suspected Janelle disappeared from Rooty Hill Road in a vehicle. He simply can't imagine an alternative scenario. Rooty Hill Road is surrounded by properties which are, in turn, surrounded by fences. It's unlikely Janelle skipped off the road and into the meadows. The landscape angles everything towards the bitumen. It helps keep the cows on pasture.

Janelle had no past or present lovers living along Rooty Hill Road and she wasn't known to make social visits while she exercised. Friends say when she walked she didn't like to stop and talk to people. As Janelle also lived alone, a clandestine get-together on a public road during a midday walk doesn't seem likely but on an island of secret liaisons, it would be a mistake not to flag it as a remote possibility. If we assume nothing covert in Janelle's midday walk, that her motive was purely exercise, then logic points to her having disappeared in a vehicle. The immediate question is whether she got into the car willingly or by force.

Another theory, one more dramatic and chilling but not discounted by the forensic pathologist, is that Janelle was deliberately hit by a car. Mowed down and scooped up. As spectacular as it sounds, Janelle's injuries lend some weight to this theory: the broken pelvis, the fractured ribs, the grazing and bruising on her trunk, the massive abrasion on her right shoulder and lower back. Bob Peters calls them 'friction injuries', caused by contact with a 'rough surface in a sliding or dragging motion'.

The forensic pathologist in the Patton case, Dr Allan Cala, said he did 'wonder about the possibility' of Janelle being struck by a vehicle but pointed out that pedestrians hit by vehicles usually suffer 'many more fractures'. He said the fractured ribs could have been caused by kicking, and suggested there might have been a number of other reasons for the fractured pelvis, including 'possibly a stomp by somebody' as she lay on the ground.

Bob Peters isn't sure if Janelle was hit by a car. 'I don't know about you,' he says, 'but every pedestrian I've seen hit by a car seems to lose a shoe along the way and Janelle's shoes were both on.'

The detective does wonder if Janelle was lured into a vehicle with a ruse, a story demanding her immediate attention, perhaps a bogus emergency (involving her parents) or the promise of a reconciliation. If Janelle was baited with a lie then it was compelling enough for her to abandon walking.

If Janelle did leave the road voluntarily, then regardless of the reason given, the driver must have been somebody she knew, it must have been someone she trusted, or *wanted* to trust. But complicity with the driver doesn't explain the first mystery: the broken sunglasses. Is it too bold to suggest Janelle got in a car and was then immobilised, punched, assaulted and, slumped in the front seat, driven away? Or more dramatically, did Janelle climb in and, realising the vehicle's occupant/s were hostile, try to escape from the moving vehicle, losing her sunglasses on the way? Those who know Janelle say she wouldn't have thought twice about opening the door.

As any detective must, Bob Peters spends a great deal of time mulling over motive, including any motive Janelle might have had for getting into a car. He can't find an obvious one so he keeps this possibility up his sleeve, alongside a deliberate malicious attack or a sexual assault, as the most likely. It's not much to go on and it's this paucity of evidence, these rudderless clues and unconfirmed sightings, which make this investigation a nightmare for the dogged detective. Part of the problem is that Janelle walked this route so many times, he needs every sighting to be confirmed to ensure Islanders haven't mixed up their days. An example of this is Maria Forsyth, who lives closest to the lookout. She says she saw Janelle reach the lookout and speak with a couple of people in a car. Maria Forsyth can't remember the 'colour, make, or model of the vehicle' or the gender of those inside, so it doesn't leave Bob Peters much to go on. This reported sighting 'can't be discounted', he says, but nor can it be 'corroborated as having occurred on 31 March 2002'. Again police wonder if locals have got their days mixed up—after all, the rhythm of island life is innately repetitive.

Bob Peters shifts into gear and drives me over the incline, past a magical looking banyan tree and down the curving road to the lookout Janelle loved to walk to. The investigation team has tracked down fifty-six people using Rooty Hill Road or visiting Queen Elizabeth lookout between 11 am and 1.30 pm on Easter Sunday. Of note are two female tourists from Victoria who were reading books at the lookout between 11.30 and midday. They didn't see any females walking in the area and believe they would have noticed if someone had appeared on foot. One did remember a 'small white car' which pulled up with 'two people in it'. She said the driver was possibly a young male and 'both occupants looked agitated and the driver appeared to be peering around'. After a couple of minutes it sped off faster than one would expect. Her friend was reading and didn't notice any of this.

Around the same time there is another reported sighting of a man and a woman in a light-coloured sedan, this time at the bottom of Rooty Hill Road. The witness, Kathleen Wheeler, said the male driver had no facial hair, a round face and short, light-coloured hair. She said he 'did not seem to be sitting up straight', and the two people in the front passenger seats were 'sitting as far away from each other as possible'. Kathleen Wheeler did not know Janelle Patton but after seeing her photograph believed it was a close match to the woman she saw in the vehicle.

———

There's no one at the lookout as we pause to take in the view. For days now the island has been buffeted by a relentless southerly, the ocean a horizon of white caps. It's starving the island of supplies and surfers of a clean break. Today is no day for relaxed book reading at the lookout. Thirty metres below are the lowlands of Kingston, the rocky reefs where convicts mined the calcarenite sandstone to construct the Georgian buildings that are such a feature of the island today. Immediately beneath the lookout is the golf course. The club house and bar are inside the nineteenth-century magistrate's quarters. Working in the kitchen on the day of Janelle's death were two men who reported hearing screams around midday.

'What sort of screams?' I ask Bob as we sit inside the car at Her Majesty's lookout.

'Bloodcurdling screams,' says Bob.

'Did they really say that?' I ask. 'Did they really say bloodcurdling screams?'

Bob thinks for a moment as he pulls a three-point turn and heads back up the road on which Janelle vanished.

'Yeah, that's how one of them described it.'

Janelle Patton polarised people but all who knew her agree on one thing—she would have been defiant under attack. She may have been small and light but what she lacked in size she made up for in aggression and courage. Janelle Patton, like many women her age, was the embodiment of 'feisty'. Her family and all who knew her agree she would have matched violence and anger pound for pound. She fought with heart, muscle and sinew. We know she did, because of the extensive and varied nature of her wounds. All those who knew Janelle say she would have yelled her lungs out to let others know she was being savaged. A 'bloodcurdling scream' might be a clichéd description of a damsel in distress but in this case it's not outside the bounds of Janelle's character.

The man who described the scream as bloodcurdling is James Gardner. On Easter Sunday he was working with Arthur Keeping to prepare a lunchtime fish fry at the golf club. A 'fish fry' is the local Norfolk term for fish and chips. The two men say they heard a long scream sometime between 11 and 11.45. Arthur Keeping told police he heard what sounded like a 'high pitched scream' coming from 'some distance away', which seemed to go for 'about thirty seconds'. James Gardner says the scream was longer, 'about a minute', and sounded like a 'female or a child'. Both men walked out the kitchen door and looked around but couldn't see anyone. They went back to work and thought no more of it.

As the crow flies, the distance between where Janelle was last seen and the golf club is a good kilometre. The lookout is approximately halfway between them. The prevailing winds as Janelle walked along Rooty Hill Road were at her right shoulder, blowing from the north. It's feasible a 'bloodcurdling scream' could have carried to the golf course. What doesn't add up is why those much closer to the road where Janelle was walking heard nothing at all. James Gardner and Arthur Keeping reported what they heard in the days immediately following the murder. It wasn't until six weeks later that Bob Peters was informed of another possible scream. This scream was also heard on the golf course but the timing is different. Instead of being heard before midday, it was heard a couple of hours later.

Between 1.50 and ten past two, a local man called John Anderson was lining up a shot on the sixth tee when he heard a 'sound like an adult screaming'. He told police it was 'high pitched but faint' and 'lasted for three to four seconds'. The sixth tee is close to the Kingston escarpment but not one of John Anderson's golfing partners could verify this 'high pitched' sound. They didn't hear anything at all. John Anderson puts this down to his keen ear, an ear developed during a communications career in the navy and civil aviation. He told police he could register sounds others couldn't and is adamant what he heard on the sixth tee was 'a scream from someone in trouble'.

Bob Peters says these two separate screams, heard by different people at different times, 'can't be discounted but nor can they be confirmed by a third party', and that's the problem. Without independent corroboration he can't rely on them as fact—it's just one person's word and that is never enough for a court of law. These screams are another tantalising signpost in a trail which goes cold minutes before midday. Without more evidence, Bob Peters can't positively link these sounds with an attack on Janelle and nor can he dismiss them. All he can do is slip them into the large file of uncorroborated evidence and keep on walking—or, in our case, driving. The only thing he knows for certain is Janelle disappeared from Rooty Hill Road shortly before midday, that she probably didn't make it to the lookout, and she vanished in an eight to ten minute period.

Chapter 11

COCKPIT

Bob Peters is a cautious driver. As we leave Rooty Hill Road he lets a brown cow dawdle past the fender, then stops for a gangly calf with spindly legs trailing its mother on a narrow cattle track above the road. 'I don't trust those ones,' Bob says, his eyes following the strapping young beast which looks as flighty as a thistle. 'They're light-footed and liable to spring at all angles. At least the older ones are fairly docile.'

For a detective Bob Peters is unpretentious about his profession. 'There's no great genius to solving crimes,' he says in a deadpan voice as he directs the car east to Norfolk's more remote coastline. 'Either a person hands themselves in, a co-offender gives up a secret, a person is at the scene, like an eyewitness, or there is a glaring motive.'

The Patton case is missing every one of these factors. So the tactic is to think like the killer, which is what all detectives do when leads dry up. To me, thinking like 'the killer' is pretty open-ended—there are any number of scenarios, a myriad of gruesome outcomes. Bob agrees: 'For every scenario there is a counter-scenario. Even when I go home I can't say there've been too many waking hours without thinking about it.'

I ask about a profile—does he have one? Bob explains that profiling a killer relies on repeat behaviour, on having a pattern. 'It's of limited use when you have a one-off crime,' he says.

Without any of the standard methods for cracking the case Bob Peters has to focus on peeling back the past of the island and its people. It's what he has been doing for months, seeking signs of uncontrollable violence, rage, sexual frustration, perhaps sexual dysfunction. The process of digging into the mind and history of individuals capable of extreme violence. The murder of Janelle Patton is one of the worst homicides he's ever seen, and attempted sexual assault remains a strong motive.

Mulling over human responses to acute stress, anger and violence is what homicide detectives do and it's what Bob Peters is doing as we rattle through the downhill bends to Cockpit waterfall and reserve, the area locals simply call 'Cockpit' and where Janelle's body was left lying on the grass.

'Perhaps the killer or killers drove around for a while, maybe they took the body to Cascade jetty and it was busy, we just don't know.'

Since day one, Islanders have wondered why the body wasn't hidden in a ravine or dumped in the ocean. In all the intrigue surrounding the murder locals place great significance on the location of the body. They regard it as a sign that the killer was an outsider—a TEP, a visitor or a tourist—because Norfolk is a dramatic island of nooks and crannies, ridges and gullies, of high hollow cliffs and pounding seas—locals like to direct discussion to this rich landscape. They say only newcomers would be silly enough to leave a body in a public space.

The island has always used the site where Janelle's body was found as a defence against its own involvement. The implication is clear—if an Islander is going to conceal a brutal murder, there are better options than Cockpit reserve. I often heard people say, 'There are places on this island where you'd never find a body. All sorts of things go over the cliffs, never to be found.'

It's the brazen nature of Janelle Patton's murder which is so unsettling: a daylight disappearance and a daylight slaying. I've never heard a local suggest the cover of darkness would have been preferable; instead, all the talk is about concealing the crime.

Bob Peters suggests the killer probably 'didn't have time', or the inclination, to drive around the island with a body in their car. For a person who has just endured the evil of murdering another human being there are benefits in a location like Cockpit, namely, access and speed.

Bob Peters doesn't discount the significance of the body being disposed of in the open as a statement, a public display of the killer's deed, but he places no more weight on this than a lack of alternative options. He says people overlook the chill of 'sheer panic'.

Bob turns the car left off Cascade Road. We head north a couple of hundred metres and arrive in a small meadow dotted with cattle. This is Cockpit reserve. To our right is a grassy valley between two rolling hills. The sides are terraced from the tireless grazing of cattle. The reserve is part of an old flood plain so the land undulates and is mostly cleared of trees. In 1983 the area was being used as a temporary tip. There's a glimpse of ocean at the end of the valley but there's no beach; the rocky shoreline is reached by scaling down a four-metre rock face.

The entry to Cockpit is marked by a timber bridge and a dirt road. Blocking the turn-off is a bus, its motor running. This is awkward. It's a tourist bus on a half-day tour. The day before I'd asked Bob Peters if there was a good time for us to drive around together, retracing Janelle's last hours. He shook his head and said, 'I don't care, mate,' but it didn't mean he wanted to show me where Janelle's body was found in front of thirty tourists. We slowly approach the bus and ease to a stop. After a short moment it shifts into gear and blurts up Harpers Road, leaving behind a relieved detective and a whiff of diesel.

It's at Cockpit where Broken Bridge Creek and Cascade Creek merge and empty into the sea. Given the dry weather the creeks are matted with reeds and waterlilies. The waterfall is more like a funnel at the end of the valley, where the earth has cracked and tumbled to the ocean. Without heavy rain, the 'fall' is no more than a trickle. One day I followed the narrow cattle track, tracing the water flow to a wide rock ledge where it dribbled down a sheer wall until a wave rolled in and washed it away. It's clear from the stained rock ledge that a wide body of water once cascaded into the sea. This is what Phillip Gidley King saw in March 1788, when he was bobbing about in his longboat and trying to figure out how to set foot on an island he could smell but not touch. He noted in his journal a 'cascade' on Norfolk's eastern side, 'down which a very fine fall of water fell with great force and noise'.

With the tour bus gone Bob drives across the bridge. This is the main entry to Cockpit but it's not the only way in. There is another road down the northern ridge called Prince Phillip Drive. Police don't know which road the killer used and, given the wet weather, individual tyre tracks were lost in all the mud.

There are no eyewitnesses to what happened here. There is a large timber house with a direct line of vision over Cockpit but it wasn't completed in March 2002. No one saw a vehicle enter, a person act strangely or the body of a 29-year-old woman being discarded. If anyone did, they haven't reported it. For the Australian Federal Police it's another blind spot in its investigation.

We drive to the end of the dirt road and onto the grass. Bob parks next to several concrete slabs, the foundations of an old fishing co-op from the 1960s, another chapter in Norfolk's troubled economic history. He gets out, turns his back to the breeze to light a cigarette, then faces the ocean and inhales. For a moment he looks like Peter Falk in the TV series *Columbo*, but without the overcoat.

This area can loosely be called a picnic spot but there's little to entice people to linger. There are far prettier and warmer places to have a social gathering than Cockpit reserve. Like most of the eastern coast of Norfolk, it's sparser and less popular compared to the western side. Cockpit has an unkempt feel about it, an empty, weary spirit. There is no picnic table, just a low bench, roughly cut from a raw slab of untreated pine turned dark green in the weather. Nearby is an unused concrete barbecue and two steel drums for rubbish, one red, the other black. There's no toilet block, fresh water or shelter from the wind.

It's here, between the steel drums, the barbecue and the concrete foundations, that Janelle's body lay, her head, shoulder and feet poking out from beneath the plastic sheeting which was bunched and pillowed and flapped in the wind.

———

On the afternoon of Janelle Patton's murder, as the killer placed her body on the grass, the island was lashed with twelve millimetres of rain in forty minutes. When the rain eased, two separate parties made their way to Cockpit reserve, a family on holiday from Queensland, and four local lads armed with boogie boards and a video camera. The boogie boards were for grass surfing down a steep embankment, the video camera to record their stunts. Zach Sanders filmed his three mates in action, sliding from the edge of Prince Phillip Drive on the northern ridge of the valley into the reserve below where the body of Janelle lay. It was no more than thirty metres away but no one in the group noticed the clumped sheet of plastic or saw what was beneath it. Not even when they walked to the waterfall to wash off the mud, a route which took them much closer to where Janelle lay, did anyone notice the body.

The next day they took the video to the police. The footage is time stamped; the recording starts at 3.57. It shows the plastic faintly in the distance; it's not in every shot, and it's not apparent there is a corpse underneath it.

The person who did notice this morbid secret was fourteen-year-old Daniel Roates. The Roates family had driven into Cockpit just before four o'clock and parked next to the track leading to the waterfall. The family got out except for Daniel, who stayed behind in the rented van. As he sat gazing across the reserve he thought he saw some misplaced rubbish near the barbecue and the red and black garbage drums. When he looked again he realised it was a person, covered by some plastic. To give an idea of how close he was, he said the person 'appeared to be pale'. At the time, Daniel Roates didn't know he was looking at the body of a murdered woman; he thought he was looking at a homeless person using the plastic as a form of shelter. 'He'd seen homeless people before on the mainland so he didn't think anything of it,' says Bob. 'He made a comment to his sister but she didn't respond.'

When Bob Peters later revealed this evidence before the coronial inquest, one of the Christian clan in the public gallery shook his head, astonished at the double tragedy: that a visitor could imagine homeless people on Norfolk Island, and that Janelle's body could have been discovered three hours earlier, giving police a crucial head start.

Apart from the plastic sheet clumped over Janelle's body there was no effort to disguise the crime. Bob shuffles towards the creek and surrounding thicket to make his point. 'Janelle's body could have been placed further in here,' he points. As we look we disturb a black cow which groans and trots away.

For the killer to do as Bob is suggesting would have involved more time. The thicket is only ten metres from where Janelle was found, but to reach the safety of the bushes the body needed to be dragged over the bumpy ground. It seems there wasn't a second to spare to hide the crime.

Bob Peters goes through the motions with both hands. He explains how a driver could have circled in, pulled up to the foundations at our feet, heaved the body off the tray of a ute or a truck, or out of a car, hoping to hell nobody was approaching because once here, standing on the thick grass where Janelle Patton's body lay, there is no escape: we're cornered by ocean, cliff and creek. It's a dead end.

And from this position I can't see the main road, the turn-off or the timber bridge. I'm also blind to anyone approaching from the ridge above, until it's too late. As lonely and empty as Norfolk can be, it's impossible to be confident you're ever alone, or not being watched. There is no way the person who dumped Janelle's body at Cockpit could have been any more or less certain, unless somebody was watching out for them.

When Janelle's body was discovered on the grass at Cockpit there were pools of water lying on the plastic sheet and the grass underneath was dry. Bob Peters says the body was left 'either prior to or during' the afternoon rain storm, which started at 3.13 and ended forty minutes later, just before four o'clock. The best estimate of Janelle's time of death is between midday and three o'clock.

As far as homicides go, moving a body during the day is a risky business. It's so risky as to be stupid. It smacks of desperation, of the murder being unplanned rather than premeditated. Bob Peters doesn't think it was planned. He sees the daylight gamble as a sign of urgency. Bob wonders if another person was due home, the killer's partner or spouse, or even the owners of the property where the murder may have taken place. It appears the killer had no choice but to dump the body immediately—an act in which panic rode roughshod over logic. Time didn't afford the luxury of waiting for nightfall.

Before we leave Cockpit reserve I ask if I can take his photo. 'Jesus, mate, let me put my cigarette out first.' As I frame the shot he looks at me uncomfortably. I manage to get two snaps before he scrambles for the car door. On the way out we pull over for a car of elderly tourists. We wave.

———

At the coronial inquest Bob Peters named eleven separate motives, all permutations of a personal, random or sexually motivated attack, either premeditated or opportunistic. He doesn't know if the attack was to stop Janelle taking some form of unknown action, or to conceal a separate offence. There doesn't seem to be anything which isn't on the list. 'It may have been a personal attack on Janelle out of revenge, or out of lust, or by chance, Janelle was just the wrong person in the wrong place at the wrong time,' Peters admits to me as we drive back to the police station.

When I first interviewed Bob, eleven months into the case, he said, 'If a murder isn't solved within forty-eight hours, it'll take years.' Inside the Norfolk Island police station, now more than twenty-four months into the Patton investigation, I ask him if this police adage is proving to be a prophecy. Behind a desk piled high with loose papers, he sits on a low chair and nods in agreement.

'That's accurate and it goes for two categories: even if you haven't arrested anybody within forty-eight hours, you've got a fair idea who committed the murder—it's just a matter of finding the admissible evidence to prove it. But when you don't know who the offender is, and there are multiple choices—well, it's harder.'

And this is what Bob Peters is facing, a bizarre investigation where the killer is known but not identified. It is back to the list of every person on Norfolk Island on 31 March 2002—one of these people is the killer. It is the one absolute fact in this case, perhaps the only irrefutable fact Bob Peters has got.

'Yeah that's right,' he says, 'and that's very frustrating to know. I know people have been nominated and other people acted unusual, and everyone has their own suspicions, but we have to deal with facts, admissible facts. Suspicions and people saying something about somebody else isn't necessarily a fact but I guess that's the nature of the job.' He pauses and sighs. 'Perspiration, patience and . . .' he trails off. I try not to laugh. The detective has forgotten his motivation lines. 'There's another P,' he says, thinking for a second. 'Persistence.' He gives me a wry smile and starts again. 'Perspiration, patience and persistence.'

I mentally add a fourth P—Peters himself. It's clear he's in for the long haul.

'It's hot in here,' he says. 'Wanna go out the front for a smoke?'

CHAPTER 12

SINNERS TO SAINTS

SIX DAYS after Janelle Patton's murder a memorial service was held at All Saints Church in Kingston. People cascaded down the steps and across the surrounding lawn to say their goodbyes, except for Terence Fletcher Jope, a new friend of Janelle's and best friend of Brent Wilson, who Janelle was beginning a relationship with at the time of her death. Terry Jope was later named a Person of Interest and during Janelle's memorial service sat not in the pews, but in the cab of his green Chevvie pick-up truck at Queen Elizabeth lookout—the location Janelle was heading on the day of her disappearance.

Also at the lookout were two tourists enjoying a late lunch of fish and chips. They overheard Mr Jope say he was at Janelle's service on his walkie-talkie when clearly he wasn't. When questioned by police Terry Jope said he was at the lookout 'to observe other people driving around'. This, he thought, 'would be more useful than attending the actual service'.

Ken Rogers was the Uniting Church reverend at the time and conducted the service. From the altar he asked what to him seemed a pertinent question: was this crime not a 'wake-up call' for the island? All Saints is the beloved church of Norfolk Islanders because it is here, in the former Commissariat Store, where it's widely believed the new settlers came in from the rain to hold their first thanksgiving service after arriving from Pitcairn Island.

At Janelle's memorial service Reverend Rogers reached into the cupboard of Norfolk's living history and told those assembled that it was time to 'revisit' the faith of the island's forebears. 'You see they took God's laws seriously and island life developed around the fundamental of God-inspired human and community relationships. Perhaps it is now time to take a fresh look at those fundamentals. This means, I believe, taking God and his laws so seriously that the tragedy that has brought us here today can never happen again, and that the pain and scars of this day will heal in and through his grace and mercy.'

The service ended with one of Janelle's favourite hymns, 'Shine, Jesus, Shine'. 'Let us begin even now,' said Reverend Rogers, 'to believe that Janelle is in the nearer presence of God where evil, pain and death are now things of the past.'

———

Religion has been a foundation of island life since the early years on Pitcairn. It's now cracking as the wear and tear of modern life erodes and reshapes the social values of Norfolk, but the extraordinary story which gave light to the Islanders' historic faith remains legendary and compelling. The story has nothing to do with the convict era and is instead rooted in the first decade of life on Pitcairn Island. It took place long before the community of 194 outgrew their remote homeland and were relocated by the British government to Norfolk in 1856. The full story of what took place on Pitcairn Island in its first decade will never be known. It is a remarkable kaleidoscope of treachery, selfishness, switching alliances and desperate behaviour by men who knew they would never return to the world from which they had come.

The story's strength lies in its Christian imagery and centres on Able Seaman John Adams, who by considerable luck and savvy was the last man standing on Pitcairn Island following a cycle of sex and violence between 1790 and 1800. For the descendants of the *Bounty* mutineers, religion is what saved the community from itself. From the seed of murder and mayhem came redemption and salvation. For Islanders who can trace their bloodline back to the mutineers, religion is more than faith, it is also a lesson in the power of God's voice, an example of how He alone conquered the vice of the mutineer spirit and enabled the community to prosper. It is a terrific story, and was sold to the world as one of good triumphing over evil. It helps explain why many Norfolk

Islanders feel personally affronted by the murder of Janelle Patton. The crime is a slur on the community because the struggle to honour Christian values is supposed to be a problem confronting the outside world, not the world of Norfolk Island.

Four years after landing on Pitcairn, Fletcher Christian was murdered, along with four of his shipmates and all six of the Polynesian men: in total, eleven men killed at the hands of the small community. Most of the murders took place in the first four years of settlement, and stemmed from race divisions, and disagreements over possession of land, labour and, most of all, women. From day one there was sexual tension on account of the gender imbalance, but only the Polynesian men were forced to share their women. The boys from the *Bounty* made sure they didn't have to and this insistence was their undoing. There is general agreement the mutineers treated the Polynesian men like slaves.

After the Pitcairn community was discovered by the American sealer *Topaz* in 1808, John Adams was asked to explain the missing inhabitants. By now eight of his shipmates, six Polynesian men and several women had died. To every subsequent visiting captain he told a different story. These conflicting accounts have long irked historians, who question what role he may have played in the murders. Glynn Christian, a descendant of Fletcher and author of *Fragile Paradise*, a 1982 biography on the mutineer, calls John Adams a 'pious fraud' and suggests he may have been involved in plotting the murder of Christian and others.

After the death of his first wife it was John Adams who demanded the Polynesian men hand over one of their women, sparking the first wave of murder and payback. Glynn Christian, who travelled to Pitcairn in a failed bid to locate Fletcher Christian's grave, questions the failure of the religious community to mark the graves. It is this fact which convinces the author to declare that John Adams 'was not a benevolent old patriarch but a hypocritical manipulator of Polynesian women and young children . . . If Adams' flock was really so Christian, should they not have made some attempt to mark the graves of their forefathers?'

When I read about the violent wreck of Pitcairn's early years it underlined Thomas Hobbs' theory of individualism—that self-interest is the dominant motive in life. It seems that everyone in the Pitcairn community, women included, schemed and/or was involved in killing one another. There is a *Lord of the Flies* intensity to it, with an endless array of successful or foiled pacts to kill one another. The first five mutineers, including Christian, were murdered at the hands of the Polynesian men. Attempts to kill Quintal and McCoy failed and they ran into the bush to hide. There are many questions as to why John Adams and Edward Young managed to remain somewhat protected.

Caroline Alexander is another author who questions the motives of Adams. She writes in *The Bounty*:

> What importance is to be attached to the striking fact that Adams was one of only two men left standing in the wake of the massacres? Was it Adams's party that killed Christian? Could it even be—impossible as it would seem of the venerable patriarch!—that it was Adams who killed Christian?

There was no possible escape from this mayhem on Pitcairn and by 1794 many of the Polynesian women wanted to leave the island. Foes were neighbours or lovers and friends were murderers. The early history is a revolving door of fugitives hiding out, shadowed by imminent revenge as others were dispatched to try and coax them back to the community, either as a treacherous ploy to kill them or in an honest pact for peace.

If it weren't so violent it would be comical because the image of people hiding on an inescapable island one mile wide by one mile long is ludicrous. Just how Fletcher Christian met his death is still debated but most accounts suggest he was shot in the back while tilling his field. It's a terribly plain demise for such a legendary figure of the South Seas.

Of the remaining four mutineers William McCoy was the next to die, throwing himself off Pitcairn's steep cliffs, either in a drunken stupor or in suicide. (The Pitcairn Register records McCoy with a rock tied around his neck.) Not long after, Matthew Quintal's wife Sarah fell to her death, leaving him without a wife. When Quintal demanded Edward Young hand over his partner and threatened to kill him if he didn't, John Adams and Young decided there could only be peace without Mr Quintal on the loose, so they murdered him with a hatchet. This left just two mutineers and when Edward Young died an unprecedented natural death (from asthma), John Adams was literally the last man standing. He *was* the balance of power. The centre of Pitcairn Island has been called Adamstown ever since.

In all, Pitcairn's first decade is an extraordinarily brutal cradle for a community to emerge from. And it is in this context that religion arrived at the hopelessly remote and primitive island. The edification of John Adams began when he picked up the only two books on Pitcairn, the *Bounty*'s copies of the Bible and the Book of Common Prayer. These he turned to for spiritual guidance and community teachings. It's also claimed he had nothing else to read. It's a lovely image and in his 1929 essay 'Politics in Pitcairn' Keith Hancock wrote: 'It is possible Adams began his exercises in the Scriptures as a mere refuge from the unaccustomed tedium of peace. Yet in the end they mastered him and overruled him.'

After a decade of treachery and murder, Adams was now the supreme ruler of Pitcairn, the patriarch surrounded by a harem of surviving Tahitian women and the crawling offspring of his dead mates. For reasons unknown Pitcairn produced no full-blooded Polynesian children. So with Bible in hand, John Adams began daily prayers and the legendary Pitcairn Piety was born.

Sixty years later, this simple, classless community of 194 people stepped ashore on the convict pier at Kingston. From mutineers and murderers blossomed an honest folk with traditional English-Christian values which overrode the undeniable fact that all were born to Polynesian mothers. It was the equivalent of a modern-day spiritual makeover and the glue which made the piety stick was the teaching of the Bible. But the impact of Christianity came at a price. The contribution of the Polynesian women who made it possible for Pitcairn to survive and relocate was overlooked, and would be for more than a century.

Glynn Christian writes of the confusion caused by:

> ... having black blood in a community which began by hating black men ... The Christianity which can be credited with bringing some daily harmony to the island is also to blame for generations of hushed and hypocritical embarrassment, when it was forbidden to talk about the Tahitian women.

The best observation of the Pitcairn story, recast as the biblical tale that so captivated nineteenth-century Europe, is by Keith Hancock (quoted in Raymond Nobbs' *George Hunn Nobbs*):

> Evil men (the mutineers) and evil women (the Polynesians) ate the apple (unlicensed sex) and fell into discord and bestiality too horrendous to be more than hinted at. When all seemed lost, the word of God appeared through the media of the ship's Bible and Prayer Book, relayed by a regenerated John Adams (the island Moses), lone survivor of the evil men. This brought the little Pitcairn remnant to salvation . . . Here was living, flourishing proof of the efficacy of the Christian ethic and the salvation which lay in the Gospel and in religious attitudes and observances.

For the Norfolk Islanders of today, the now distant descendants of those violent years on Pitcairn, All Saints Church in Kingston is where the traditional Pitcairn service is held once a month. The day I walked up the steps was also the Foundation Day service—celebrating Philip Gidley King's first service on Norfolk 216 years earlier. Again the fusion of past and present was alive and squirming on this sunny autumn morning.

On the mainland, traditional services are as popular as a cold bath; on Norfolk it's the opposite. Once a month 39-year-old Reverend John Reed switches altars, leaving his ornate chapel up town for the salty air of Kingston.

In the last census seven hundred locals identified with the Church of England. Of that number Reverend Reed estimates ten per cent attend Sunday services throughout the day. It's a far cry from the numbers of a hundred years ago. On this Sunday morning there are about twenty-five people, mostly old-timers, and a handful of tourists and children. Everyone is friendly. In front of me is Reverend Reed's wife and their three children, the children all dotted with the freckles of their parents.

With his chiselled chin, cropped black beard and easy manner Reverend Reed is the modern face of religion—inclusive, laidback and on message. He paraphrases the Pitcairn tale as a 'remarkable story of redemption'. He uses the Foundation Day service to focus on the rules of society, the moral map by which we live. Reverend Reed speaks of the rules outlined by Philip Gidley King in March 1788. Like the Ten Commandments, these were the rules to follow, enforced by the threat of physical rather than moral punishment. He unravels a tourist copy of King's eleven orders and reads them aloud. He holds the fake parchment in both hands, adlibbing on some of the more antiquated orders, which gets a few giggles. He strikes just the right balance between past and present. On King's last order, Reverend Reed nails home his message, the one he has been warming to all service. It is a message of benevolence to one another, to be honest, obliging and hard working. 'The future welfare of every person on this island depends on their good behaviour.' From the pews comes strong singing and loud fine voices.

As I hand back my prayer books I tell Reverend Reed what I'm doing, bundling the words murder, politics and culture into one sentence. His face drops visibly, and he tells me to tread with care: 'You don't want to have the *60 Minutes* experience.'

'What happened to them?' I ask, knowing they had a tough time of it.

'They got locked out, nobody would talk to them.'

'That's okay, I've already done a story here.'

'Oh,' he says.

Sounding upbeat and refusing to be despondent, I ask if I can speak with him about the island. He's wary but I'm keen to know the relevance of the Pitcairn story today, two hundred years on, not only for locals but for him as the representative of the church. 'This must be a great place to work,' I offer.

'I'm not qualified to speak about the community,' he says, hands clasped over one another, his back straight and shoulders pushed back. 'I've only been here a couple of years.'

This is exactly why I'd like to speak with him. I shake his hand and promise to call.

Outside, the morning has blossomed into a wonderful autumn day. The best time of year, say locals: 'The humidity is low but the sun still warm.' At the foot of the steps I stop for a cup of tea and a double helping of biscuits. Nobody is sure where I fit in, and nor am I.

———

The Church of England rectory is located on Headstone Road, within earshot of the chapel. It is an address which raises a smile from its occupants, who travel from mainland Australia for three- to five-year stints. After the recent rain the grass is green and spider webs tattoo the shrubs. I park behind an old Volvo station wagon with weeds lapping its corroded rims. A timber swing hangs from a nearby oak tree—it's a picture book entry. The reverend opens the door and shakes my hand: 'Please call me John.'

'There're plenty of things I miss from home,' he yells from the kitchen as I sit down in a flowery chair in a flowery living room. 'I miss my mobile phone.'

'And you didn't even get to vote in the referendum on a mobile phone network?'

'No,' he says, handing me a coffee and raising the corner of his mouth, maybe in mirth.

Reverend Reed can lead his congregation in prayer and hymns, lead a traditional Pitcairn service broiled in legend, but is denied the vote. He has no say in the community. This is a privilege earned, not a right gained. Like a TEP or an Islander returning home from years offshore, he is banned from taking part in island politics and referenda. Only when he's done his time and has been accepted as a resident can he regain his political voice. He is spiritually employed, but politically disenfranchised. I saw a contradiction here. Few agreed with me—it was simply the Norfolk Way, complete with my favourite island disclaimer: 'If you don't like it you can bugger off.'

John doesn't see any point in engaging with the issue: he isn't here to reinvent the wheel, he's here to keep it turning.

John Reed is the child and grandchild of English missionaries, his parents still active in Tanzania. He left Sydney for Norfolk to enjoy island life, to act on the journeyman seed planted by his forebears. The attractions of Norfolk for his young family were the same as for others: the community life, safety, the physical beauty and rugged character of making do with what's available. These are the fruits of isolation. Norfolk is, he admits 'of limited appeal' to some: 'Lots of visitors come for one week or ten days and that's enough. There's so much that is available on the mainland that you can't get here. People talk about the things they miss. They range from McDonald's to the opera, and everything in between.' Reverend Reed muses on the time it takes to get a replacement fanbelt. That's what he's missing at the moment, an auto parts warehouse. His laugh is as laidback as his nature. He looks like he's from central casting, the young movie reverend, a modern day face of religion's push to stay relevant, here on an island mired in a tough past.

John agrees that Norfolk's compelling mix of religion and history is one of the thrills of the job, a sense of the 'history of the Church and its place in this community' that, he says, is not as prevalent on the mainland. But the grit of the Pitcairn story, its romance, treachery and moral salvation, isn't one he comprehended until he decided to take up the position which, for reasons he can't explain, the Church finds difficult to fill.

'It was only really when I looked at coming here that I took hold of it. It's a story which over time has not been lost but forgotten to some extent. During the 1800s it was a very well known story. From the time they were discovered on Pitcairn until the time they moved to Norfolk in 1856, there were a lot of people wanting to visit Pitcairn Island. The story captured the imagination; the higher spiritual society. The island Chaplain, George Hunn Nobbs visited England and was invited to speak and captured the imagination of the English world.'

'Is it a story taught by the Anglican Church now?' I ask.

'Not broadly, it's not widely known because of the distance now from those events. I guess in part because of this modern world we don't value the past. The modern world is so busy and all about the future, the stories of the past are neglected somewhat.'

But not on Norfolk, where the past is knitted so tightly with the present it is one and the same. It's this awareness of history and tradition which gives Islanders their sense of place. In the past decade many pillars of the community have made their final trip 'downtown', to the cemetery at Kingston. This includes some salty matriarchs who dished out guidance and discipline to those straying from the island customs of respect, love and community. Norfolk knows it's losing its colourful older characters, those who lived in an era which defined how Norfolk Islanders see themselves: as a generous, charismatic, hospitable people, deft at all manner of tasks and fond of a practical joke. The things which mattered most were mateship, family and Island. Everyone I spent time with spoke fondly of the generation of men and women born in the twenties, thirties and forties, and everyone seemed worried about the vacuum they will leave when they die.

When I seek Reverend Reed's personal observations of the Islanders and their ways, he says it's 'a little presumptuous to say'. To help me he recounts a line from his predecessor, Ian Hadfield. 'After his first year he thought he really understood the island, after the second year he began to realise that perhaps there were some things he hadn't understood so well, and after three years he began to think he really didn't understand the place at all.'

We both laugh.

I turn our conversation to the murder of Janelle Patton. John Reed's first visit to Norfolk was before Janelle's death. When he returned to take up his post everything had changed. 'I guess the community we first visited was happy, safe and secure, and then a few weeks later when we came back there was a community that was traumatised by that event. Women wouldn't walk down the street alone and, you know, when you did see a woman walking alone, people would comment on it. Whereas a few weeks earlier there was nothing to fear. So the island really was in a state of shock.

'They in a sense hadn't had to deal with that in the past, there have been deaths in the past, yes, and you hear mutterings, you've heard about Dem Tull, rumours will go around of other suspicious deaths, but it is the first demonstrably clear case of murder since the days of Pitcairn, since John Adams and the conversion. It's the first time since then that a member of the community has been clearly and obviously murdered by, one suspects, another member of the community.

'So there was a lot of talk and there has been since for the community to revisit the transformations of the past. Here we are with murder in out midst again. In a sense we need to undergo the same experience John Adams and his community did. We need change. People are talking now about how this community is not the idyllic innocent community that for a long time legend had it to be. Others will say, "Of course it never really was. It's a community of human beings and humans beings everywhere are far from perfect, bad things happen." But I think the murder really confronted people with the fact that there is evil in our midst, we can't avoid that. We can't pretend to ourselves we're immune. That was the big shock really, having to be confronted with that.

'At the time, in the initial months following the murder, a lot of damage was done with speculation. Who was guilty? What were the police doing? There was a lot of gossip and reputations and lives were harmed. Obviously Janelle's family and her life was literally destroyed and that is terrible. There was also a lot of damage for other members of the community as wild rumours swept around. I think people have learnt from that, we can't propagate rumour and innuendo, we just have to wait for some hard facts.'

'That must have been a whirlwind experience for you,' I say. 'The rumours are so vicious here, so defamatory and insidious.'

'I was surprised at the strength of some of it,' John responds. 'Australia's not as bad as America which is so litigious. But if in Australia people said some of the things that I heard said when I was first here, they would have been sued. There seems to be nothing to stop that here. I'm no expert on the laws of defamation as to whether they apply here. But it fed off itself. Good people that I would have trusted and respected found themselves caught up in that, repeating rumours that they had on good authority. They were immensely sorry when they found out they were a part of spreading untruths. But it caught on and got rolling and was very hard to stop.'

I mention to John the unsinkable rumour of the Pattons killing their own daughter. John says, turning in his chair, 'One of the things I realised very early on is people were, in a sense, desperate for it not to be one of their own. That would be too desperate to contemplate because everybody knows each other. Just about everyone is related to each other in some way. They didn't just go to school together, they work and play together, so the thought that it could be my work mate, my old school friend, my fishing buddy, my golfing buddy, it could be a relative, that's what really—apart from the horrific nature of the murder and the fact there was a murder—it was that sort of speculation. It was easier to think, "No, it couldn't possibly have been one of us, it had to be someone else. It had to have been a tourist or a short-term worker." I mean, the suggestion it was the parents, I think that is the most extreme example of shifting the blame from it not being one of us.'

'Are you surprised at how divided the community is over the island's future, over who they are?'

'Yes and no. Surprised I guess in the sense that I wasn't expecting that when I came. You pick up the image of this idyllic community living in peace and harmony. But in reality, and if you stop to think about it beforehand, it's obvious it is a community of human beings and human beings are fallible and sinful and so it's no big surprise in that sense. I guess the surprise was the reality didn't match the myth but on reflection the myth is a myth. No human society is perfect and some of the divisions are not unhealthy ones, like over politics and direction.'

'The issue of truth and myth is very hazy here, isn't it, where one begins and the other ends?'

'It is and so you need to be very careful because it can change. You know, you learn something as a truth and then you realise maybe it's just a myth and then later on, you realise there is some truth to it but it's hard to know. It's not just with the murder, but politics and the relation-ship between the island and Australia. Or whether Queen Victoria gave the island to the Islanders in the first place. There is so much—I call it myth—you hear things and it's so very hard to know what's true. One person will swear black and blue this is the case and somebody else will say that's the case. And even though books have been written and inves-tigations have been done, people will still say, "No, no, no that's not true". In a sense, sometimes what we want to believe will triumph over the facts as stated in an official document and if it doesn't suit, then we simply won't believe it.'

'Do you have to navigate a careful path through all of this?'

'I think you have to be careful. My job is to minister to the people. So their own self-understanding of who they are and what the truth about the nature of the community is and their history and so on, I have to take that at face value. It's not my position to dictate. It is my position to say what the truth of God and the Bible is, but it's not my position to say what the truth of island politics or history is.'

Like Gidley King's eleven orders, John Reed is sticking to his own to ensure personal peace and harmony.

CHAPTER 13

COOK'S PARADISE

PARADISE HAS always been more than a word; to many it is a lifestyle, a dream, a longing. Janelle Patton called Norfolk her 'paradise' and so do many who call it home. It's a word used to sell the islands of the world and spoken with great gusto on Norfolk as well. What's more it is said to have come from the ruby lips of Captain Cook when he discovered the island. According to Norfolk's official brochure, the tourism office, the airline magazine and online travel information, Captain Cook took one look at Norfolk and sighed, '*Paradise*'. 'Never one to exaggerate,' says a tourist fact sheet on what makes Norfolk unique, 'Cook did not use this word to describe any of his other discoveries.'

The theme of Cook and paradise infects Norfolk's tourism literature like a virus, contaminating everyone's copy. What's worse, 'paradise' is always written as a direct quote. But Captain James Cook said no such thing. He's not misquoted, he's entirely misrepresented; the quote is made up and whoever cooked it up, so to speak, has done a great job. There is no reference to 'paradise' in Cook's own log and the explorer was not known as a romantic but rather a 'great dispeller of illusion'. He was also a man whose veranda was the Pacific.

Cook was twenty-seven months into his second voyage of discovery in southern waters when he glimpsed Norfolk in October 1774. He was heading south after exploring the northeast coast of New Caledonia and was in a rush to return to Queen Charlotte Sound, New Zealand, where, in the serene waterways still popular with yachties, he planned to refresh, repair and restock the *Resolution* before sailing to Tierra del Fuego. He didn't bother to circumnavigate his new find, instead he tacked from the north in a zigzag fashion, rowing ashore in a small alcove now called Ducombe Bay. With the aplomb of a man who discovered more of the South Pacific than anyone else, Cook wrote: 'I took possession of this isle as I had done of all the others we had discovered and named it Norfolk Isle in honour of that noble family.'

Cook doesn't expand on the naming of Norfolk beyond his reference to 'that noble family'. But one of his fellow gentlemen on board the *Resolution* does. Naturalist Johan Forster says the island was named specifically 'in honour of the Duchess of Norfolk, who recommended it to Captain Cook to have one Isle name after her.'

Cook's landing spot on Norfolk's northeastern tip is now marked by a grey monument on a nearby headland. It's a simple, if ugly, triangular rock cairn, stuck together with off-white concrete. When it was unveiled in 1953 school kids got the day off to attend.

The first time I peered down the loose, rugged cliff at where historians believe Cook came ashore I was astounded. Like most visitors, I thought, how did he scale that? Anybody stranded at the bottom today would require rescue. Cook noted it was 'steep and rocky' but offered no other concessions. He wrote: 'We found no difficulty in landing behind some rocks which lined part of the coast and defended it from the Surf.' Near the Cook cairn is a much-needed diagram pinpointing how he may have done this. This spot is typical of Norfolk's coastline which is, on average, about 100 metres above sea level.

In the pub later that day, locals didn't offer any insight into Cook's landing spot; they shrugged their shoulders and talked footy tips. For many Islanders, the history of Norfolk starts in 1856, when their forebears arrived. Islanders are keen anglers, though, and this brings them into close contact with Norfolk's perpendicular edge. They're veterans of scaling the precarious cliffs with rods, dogs and buckets of bait hanging off their limbs. The island is peppered with ropes, ladders and steel rings fixed to the cliff face by long-gone fishing mates. They have plenty of tales of near-death experiences overhanging twenty- or thirty-metre drops. The coastline of Norfolk is a manly place and they assume Cook scrambled up the cliff without a bother.

James Cook *was* complimentary of Norfolk, though; he found it agreeable, just not as much as locals like to think. Cook believed the island had great potential: what he saw on Norfolk were many natural resources, particularly for naval use. He saw the vast pine trees and thought of soaring ships' masts. When he discovered the flax plant underfoot, he saw the manufacturing of canvas, sail and cloth. The importance of these resources is difficult to appreciate now. Robert Hughes frames it powerfully in *The Fatal Shore*: 'In eighteenth-century strategy, pine trees and flax had the naval importance oil and uranium hold today.'

The decision to settle Norfolk in 1788 was based entirely on Cook's upbeat assessment of the island's superior resources. Since its discovery no one had been back to do a stocktake. Despite having spent only a few hours on the island, what the mighty captain said was taken as gospel. He would never have imagined his fellow countrymen would turn it into a prison, or the island would one day harbour the descendants of a British Navy mutiny.

Throughout its history Norfolk has experienced a number of settlements. Archaeological research shows Polynesians were the first, living there around 500 years ago, although by the time Cook arrived the Polynesians were long gone and Norfolk was home to bush and birds and not much else. The clues of past human inhabitants came in the shape of bananas and rats—both could only have arrived with human help.

The first penal settlement established in 1788 was a mix of free settlers and convicts. It lasted twenty-six years until being abandoned in 1814. It's the second settlement, from 1825 to 1856, where Norfolk's notoriety as a place of extreme punishment was born. This was the penal colony for the worst convicts from mainland Australia—a hell-hole of destitution, despair and death. The legacy of this infamous reign by the British and its convict labour are the buildings and ruins which dot the foreshore of Kingston today, and which in decades to come are destined for world heritage listing.

When King George III dispatched the First Fleet from London there was no reconnaissance of Australia. It just sailed off the edge of the world. It's no surprise Governor Arthur Phillip did much the same with Norfolk Island. Within four weeks of the First Fleet's arrival at Botany Bay, the *Supply* slipped the heads of Port Jackson for the great unknown of Norfolk Island. The only guide in the hands of Philip Gidley King and his party of twenty-two settlers was the enthusiastic notes of Cook and his fellow journeymen. At the time of Norfolk's discovery Cook wrote in his log that 'on the whole there are many good refreshments to be got but we had no time to spare to benefit by them'. No doubt many tourists feel the same today.

To comprehend why the colony of Sydney felt the need to conquer Norfolk Island before it had even established Parramatta is to understand the strategic policy of 'pre-emptive annexation', a policy which still has a contemporary ring to it.

The instructions from King George III to Governor Arthur Phillip were to colonise Norfolk as 'soon as circumstances admit of it'. Phillip's commission describes Norfolk as 'a spot which may hereafter become useful' and one he should secure to 'prevent it being occupied by the subjects of any other European power'. French explorer Jean Francois de la Perouse—who is recorded as saying Norfolk was 'only a place fit for angels and eagles to reside in'—had just sailed from Norfolk Island but, due to the wild surf, couldn't land. As the story goes, La Perouse mentioned his recent visit to Phillip, which caused the Englishman a degree of mild panic and hastened the dispatch of the *Supply* to claim Norfolk for England and deny its historic rival an orgy of flax and pine. The aim to secure naval supplies on an uninhabited island while denying the Spanish and French—two nations interested in Pacific expansion—is widely regarded by historians as the strategy behind Norfolk's urgent settlement.

In early March 1788, Philip Gidley King spent five days trying to get ashore, no doubt cursing Cook, who had reported Norfolk as having 'good soundings'. In fact, Norfolk is like a castle in the moat of the Pacific. Today landing on Norfolk is still a headache and prone to delay. The only explanation for Cook's escalator-like access is good weather. In today's language we would call it dead calm.

The belief that Norfolk had good 'soundings and anchorage' was Cook's first mistake. Many others followed. The great hopes resting on Norfolk's flax and pine, wrote Robert Hughes, 'were proven a total delusion. The place would produce nothing for England; it would never pay for itself'. The Norfolk pine 'snapped like a carrot' and the quality of Norfolk's flax was no good for making rope or sail cloth. No ship, bar one, wrote Hughes 'ever had a suit of sails woven from Norfolk Island flax or sailed under the spars of Norfolk Island pine'.

By 1800, the expense and complication of maintaining Norfolk's mix of free settlers and convicts was beginning to tell. The island had failed to contribute much to the colony in Sydney and there were growing concerns about its lack of a harbour and distance from Sydney. A decade later Norfolk's population had dropped to 177 and the mood of the English authorities shifted to abandoning the island altogether.

In 1811 Governor Macquarie was ordered to withdraw the whole community. The secretary of state, Earl Liverpool, claimed, 'The impolicy of the original settlement of the island has been fully demonstrated.' Three years later the first settlement of Norfolk Island was abandoned, its huts and stone houses demolished, its animals slaughtered. In February 1814 the last people on Norfolk sailed away in a square-rigger called *Kangaroo*.

The legacy of Norfolk's first European settlement was an awareness by the English that Norfolk Island was a natural geographical prison. When the English returned in 1825, it was with the sole intention of turning it into a prison. There was nothing new in this idea; as early as February 1790, Governor Phillip had alerted Lord Sydney of the advantages of Norfolk Island for housing intractable convicts. In a dispatch to London, Phillip advised that if England didn't want convicts ever returning home, then Norfolk was the place to dump them: 'Convicts would very seldom be able to escape as there are only two or three places at which a boat can land, and from the badness of the ground, ships will seldom anchor.'

The Georgian buildings which form the backdrop of Kingston date from this second convict settlement, which closed before the Pitcairners arrived in 1856. These were the years when death was said to be a privilege compared to the punishment of life on Norfolk. The extreme harshness of this settlement put Norfolk Island in the school books and the buildings from which the colony was run stand today as the finest example of Georgian architecture in the world.

Philip Gidley King's landing spot of 6 March 1788 is at the base of Flagstaff Hill and immediately in front of the convict-built Kingston pier. It's marked by a sandstone tablet, engraved with the names of all twenty-three settlers who camped nearby.

Next to this list of names is a brick display panel showing nautical charts and drawings of the colony's first years. It took Philip Gidley King some time to identify the flax plant he was commissioned to cultivate because he didn't know what it looked like. To help tourists recognise the species which so bewitched King and co., the display panel points to three of the gangly green plants growing nearby. It's a cheeky irony mixing modern tourism with historic folly—because flax was Norfolk's first export failure.

This spot is where tourists now gather to watch the *Norfolk Guardian* unload its cargo. With no harbour or wharf, the method for getting goods ashore on Norfolk hasn't changed in one hundred and fifty years. Timber lighters are towed beyond the reef to meet the ship, and as they bob alongside the hull, a crane drops nets of cargo over the side. For larger items—like cars and buses—two or three lighters are tied side by side to balance the weight. This important function of the Norfolk economy is a spectacle in its own right. The ship comes every four to six weeks and when it's not being unloaded the foreshore is quiet and often empty. It is easy to stand there and imagine what it was like for King and his small party of settlers all those years ago, the water ripping at the ragged reef or slapping the black volcanic boulders of the shoreline. In the late afternoon the sun flares behind the muscular cliffs, dotted with the now strategically useless pine trees, and the salt spray is heavy like smoke.

It's possible to stand where King first did and take in a vista as natural and as challenging as that which appeared before his own eyes. The imprisoning nature of the ocean is as powerful now as it was for all those who came before. To the left of the first landing is Slaughter Bay and the infamous reef which scuttled the *Sirius*, the flagship of the First Fleet. It's now a popular surf break, with a quick right- and more manageable left-hander.

This is where the power of the Norfolk story lies, in its naked display of the past. The landscape is uncluttered by alteration or modern buildings. There's nothing standing that isn't at least one hundred and fifty years old. The 23-room Government House is still occupied by a figurehead from Canberra, a colonial anachronism of pride and privilege for a lucky man and his wife, all funded by the Australian taxpayer. On the commons roam cattle and geese amongst the spirits and ghosts and old stone waterways of Norfolk's convict past.

Kingston is no museum, it is a restored, functioning town within a heritage zone. Its main street, Quality Row, is regarded as 'the most extensive remaining pre-1850 penal settlement street in Australia'. It's along Quality Row where today's government and administration is based and at any single moment, it's possible to experience a glimpse of the then and now simultaneously. This is what makes Norfolk such a delight.

CHAPTER 14

POLITICAL QUICKSAND

EIGHTEEN MONTHS after the murder of Janelle Patton, an Australian parliamentary committee delivered the most damning report ever produced about life on Norfolk Island. It said the island's twenty-five years of self-government had been a disaster, its government had failed the community, and unless serious reforms were implemented Norfolk was going to be a basket-case economy knee deep in woe and muddle.

The committee rejected the notion that Norfolk Island was a 'shining beacon' in the Pacific, a model state in an otherwise troubled region. Instead it touched on the perils of speaking out and the fear of reprisal. It alleged acts of arson and physical assault were used to pressure people to leave. It said the abuse of political power was commonplace and telephones were monitored as well as email and postal mail.

I had heard these allegations before, although proving them was another matter. There is no question people are reluctant to speak critically over the phone and claims of postal interference are common. Some Islanders swear all manner of intimidation goes on, and those who feel it most are women.

It struck me as odd the Australian Federal Police couldn't tap phones but apparently everyone else on the island could. This idea is derived from the manual telephone exchange where, if someone wanted to, it was technically possible to listen to a call. It's illegal, of course, but it didn't mean things were being monitored by a Pitcairn descendants' version of the Stasi. 'Whether these acts are highly organised or not is immaterial,' said the report. 'The undercurrent of intimidation and the overt criticism of those who express a different view do not sit well with the image of a participatory consensual style of politics or cohesive community life.' It was clear members of the committee had never lived on a remote island.

The report cherry-picked 130 years of previous reports to deftly probe myth, history, rhetoric and reality. It also took evidence from Islanders in public and private hearings, written submissions and a litany of previous papers on the shortcomings of Norfolk Island. There is no lack of material. It threw lots of punches and isn't a bad read for those who enjoy a title fight on paper. Unsurprisingly this latest report from Canberra went down like a grenade; those critical of Norfolk's ability to manage itself liked what it blew apart. Others were repulsed and asked, 'Isn't anything sacred anymore?'

Despite Norfolk having no representation in the Australian parliament there is a parliamentary committee which oversees the island. This is another one of those strange Norfolk anomalies which, ironically, undermines the committee's own relevance. It's called the Joint Standing Committee on the National Capital and External Territories. It's known on-island by the acronym JSC. Ric Robinson and Colleen McCullough dubbed it the Joint Standover Committee. It's chaired by Western Australian Senator Ross Lightfoot, the man who claimed locals and police know who killed Janelle Patton. Colleen McCullough predicted the report would be given a 'fetchingly cute, witty title' and she was right. Lightfoot called it: 'Quis Custodiet Ipsos Custodes?' Translated from Latin it means: 'Who is to guard the guards themselves?' Islanders did their own translation and summarised the content of the report's one hundred and sixty pages into three words: 'Norfolk Island's fucked.'

The report was released in December 2003 and if the pomposity of the title didn't get locals offside then the contents did. It rejected what many on the island believe is a fundamental truth, that Norfolk deserves special status and recognition, saying: 'Norfolk Island is *not* an independent nation, but an Australian Territory and an integral part of Australia.' The notion that Norfolk Island was 'ceded' to the Pitcairn Islanders when they were relocated in 1856 was, it said, 'not supported by the legal or historical record'. The report said this historic claim was 'a myth perpetuated by a minority of Pitcairn descendants and other more recent, often wealthy, arrivals motivated by self-interest to resist the imposition of income tax'.

From this basis, the report proceeded to slam the management of the island and make thirty-two recommendations to introduce 'real and meaningful reform'. It was unequivocal about the need for greater Commonwealth scrutiny and said the power of Norfolk to run its own immigration regime should be removed. It recommended the island be stripped of self-government if the proposed reforms weren't implemented in a 'timely' fashion. The subtext was very much 'game over'.

Naturally, the Norfolk government was insulted. The notion that Norfolk was run by an elite minority who kept the island alive on a ration of myth while it exploited self-government for its own ends was an affront. The government and many Islanders regarded the report as an attack on its soul, not to mention its sovereignty. Others privately thought it was fairly accurate but didn't like the implication that the *entire* island was dodgy.

What's interesting about this thorny report is how opposing camps used it to successfully argue two divergent philosophies. Opponents to Commonwealth interference said it was evidence that Canberra was out to standardise, sanitise and once again colonise Norfolk. The report, they said, was not only biased, wrong, insulting and vitriolic, but ultimate proof that Australia wanted to destroy the island. Those who believe the island is a complete shambles and run like an amateur theatre production thought the report was 'spot-on'. It was held up as the last great hope, proof that only the Commonwealth could save the island from itself and its inability to push reform and make tough decisions.

All the hot evidence about the island and its secret ways was given in secret. The report was all about improving the accountability, transparency and governance of the island, yet the allegations of corruption, family fiefdoms, private bank accounts, the fiddling of documents, ripping off land, thuggery, arson, intimidation, changing wills—even the so-called identity of Janelle Patton's killer—were given in confidential, private hearings, in camera and on oath but unable to be seen by anyone but the committee which convened the hearings.

Some who gave evidence were too fearful to do it in public, which, given what they were alleging, was understandable. Thirteen people are listed as giving confidential submissions out of a total of forty-eight—that's twenty-seven per cent. The committee was amazed at what it heard; people appeared with documents and folders and carefully organised dossiers about other Islanders and what they might be up to.

When the committee took evidence on Norfolk Island, locals had the option of giving their submissions in private. But some refused because they still didn't feel safe. They claimed people were recording who was entering the committee room, their identity would hardly be a secret, it would be known within minutes.

The response of the Norfolk Island government to Canberra's blistering report was to argue a denial of natural justice. Norfolk Island Chief Minister Geoff Gardner said 'the taking of secret evidence raises issues about the quality of the allegations made, the credibility of the witnesses or their material and whether there has been any factual corroboration of the information'. There was no way, he said, the government or anyone else could test the 'truthfulness of that evidence . . . If the committee expects the Norfolk Island government to be transparent and accountable, it could start by applying those sorts of principles to its own actions.' It was a fair point, and when Norfolk Island asked for evidence so it could look into the allegations it was told it was privileged and it couldn't have it.

It was left to the federal government to decide which recommendations from the report would be implemented and for all the huff and puff about the changes advocated, John Howard's government hasn't yet responded to this or other recent reports slamming Norfolk Island's policies and practices—which goes to show that when it comes to the crunch, Norfolk Island is still off the map.

———

Three months after the release of 'Quis Custodiet Ipsos Custodes?' Norfolk Island hosted a meeting of Australia's Attorneys General. A large entourage arrived in their own jets, unloading lots of important men in suits who switched their mobile phones to satellite coverage to keep in touch with the big island to the west.

For the first time in Norfolk's political history it had scored 'observer status' at this annual get-together of federal, state and territory legal ministers. It was a political godsend at a time of tense relations with the Commonwealth, and a great moment for Chief Minister Geoff Gardner to showcase the little-big-man theme of Norfolk Island to the political elite. This is why the anti-Australia propaganda posters plastered all over the island were either an amusing or awkward act of rebellion, depending on one's point of view.

The posters were stuck to the back of road signs around Burnt Pine, the airport and other key spots. There were two alternating messages; one said CANBERRA BULLIES NOT WELCOME. The other said WE ARE NOT A PART OF AUSTRALIA. I first saw one of them as I was rattling through a tight bend on Ferny Lane on my way to town. After I flashed past it I screeched to a halt because underneath the large print was another word, in smaller type. I shooed away the cattle to take a closer look and there in tiny print beneath the bit about 'not a part of Australia' was the word 'Inasmuch'. I paused for a few seconds. 'Inasmuch' is on the Norfolk coat of arms and is also taken from the last verse of the Pitcairn Anthem. It is widely regarded as the unofficial signature of Ric Robinson and the Pitcairn Descendants Society.

The posters were simple A4 sheets in large bold type, printed off somebody's computer, but their message to the visiting dignitaries was clear. Even a half-blind tourist could see the dogma of one section of the community. Some of the posters had their edges torn, maybe by people who had tried to remove them, but overall the anonymous poster smearer had done a thorough job with the glue. Long after the men in suits departed the posters remained plastered to the road signs, as obstinate as the person who placed them there under the darkness of a Norfolk night.

Having political graffiti telling his political guests to bugger off was awkward for Geoff Gardner. In fact the posters were designed to vex Gardner as Chief Minister as much as to give Canberra the Norfolk finger. 'I was embarrassed at those, embarrassed,' Gardner says. He shakes his head in his Kingston office, repeating 'embarrassed' for a third time. 'It saddens me a bit because I think the only comments I've received about that, apart from general condemnation, are from visitors to the island who are now beginning to question, "As Australians, don't you want us here?"' The target may have been Canberra but he wonders if there mightn't be some collateral damage, given eighty per cent of Norfolk's visitors come from Australia. 'You don't have to go and do irreparable damage to our tourism industry with activities like that,' he says, looking a little weary. 'It's just unnecessary and uncalled for.'

Gardner came to Norfolk as a TEP in 1980. Like the convicts sent to Norfolk 150 years earlier, Gardner was doubly convicted: being a TEP was bad enough; to be a Kiwi, he says, 'was beneath being from Australia'.

'In my early days you had Norfolk Islanders, the residents, the Australians and then others, which included Kiwis.'

I ask if it is less demarcated now.

'Oh yeah, absolutely.'

From mere itinerant worker to Kingston's top dog, Geoff Gardner is an example of how politics on Norfolk is no longer an exclusive club reserved for those with Pitcairn blood. 'I used to scratch my head a little bit when I met some of the people who had made up the membership of the Assembly and say, well gee, if they're on there then there's an opportunity for anybody who wants to have a crack.'

So was born the political Geoff Gardner—a moderate. A disagreement with the 'inflections they used in those days' is how he diplomatically refers to the 1980s when the drive towards independence was greater.

'I didn't necessarily believe that was in the best interests for Norfolk Island that we take such a hard line. If the Commonwealth is prepared to grant you more powers and a greater degree of independence from the mainstream there's no need to kick them in the teeth about that, or to send them packing.'

As one of four island ministers he's paid $38 000 tax-free. There's nothing extra for the additional work as chief minister, the kudos comes free. And it's not easy being a politician on Norfolk Island. There's quicksand everywhere, and everyone is conflicted. There can be no escape for the four island ministers. Wherever they go people are in their faces about this or that. Out of the shadows float community members who like to tap them on the shoulder and suggest where they are going wrong and where they should tread carefully.

I switch to the theme of Norfolk's culture, which seems as complex and controversial as everything else that makes the island tick. How does he describe Norfolk culture? Surprisingly for such a proud little place it's a question many Norfolk Islanders don't dare answer, or don't feel qualified to answer. They may have lived on the island for twenty or thirty years but unless they have Pitcairn blood in their veins they choose to stay silent on matters of heritage and culture.

Gardner doesn't flinch and responds with the rich blend of Pacific and European history, the unique Norfolk language and cuisine. I start to doodle in my notebook until he says, 'Most importantly of all, the culture of Norfolk Island is not set in a period of history when the *Bounty* mutiny took place and I think for people who believe that is what the culture of Norfolk Island is about are misleading themselves. Because culture is right up until everything that happened thirty seconds ago.'

'So it shouldn't be all about the Pitcairners?' I ask.

'It's not!' he says. 'It never has been and should not continue to be just about the Pitcairners. They are certainly a major part of the development of Norfolk Island culture, but it's right down to people like Toffy, who is outside painting. He's a guitarist, he sings in Norfolk, but he doesn't necessarily sing about the Pitcairn era, he sings about the whaling era. They are the people who are developing Norfolk's culture. Toffy will be remembered as one of these cultural icons in years to come. But it won't be about what happened in Pitcairn but what happened in convict times, or whaling, or this day and age.'

CHAPTER 15

DOING TIME

ON ONE of my many afternoons strolling about the convict ruins of Kingston, where the spirit of suffering and sadism is never far from the senses, I realised 'doing time' on Norfolk wasn't abandoned to the past, it was still alive. It was now about learning a culture rather than dishing out a penalty—although for some it still involved a denial of rights: the right to democratic participation.

For the convicts exiled to the island penal colony in the nineteenth century 'doing time' on Norfolk was having the physical and mental strength to survive the terror of daily dehumanising punishment. Today 'doing time' is a requirement for the right to vote. Participation in island affairs is a reward for the initiated and hopefully like-minded, those who grasp the fragility of the environment and how they can fit into the subtle character of island life. In many ways it is similar to political pre-selection, learning a party's policies and the importance of not speaking out of turn. The reward was also similar—the right to participate in the decision making process. Or at least it was, until the federal government blew it apart in 2004 on the grounds it was unfair, unreasonable and a denial of rights for Australian citizens.

The right to vote on Norfolk was the best example of how the cultural philosophy underpinning the 'Norfolk Way' and 'doing time' made the leap into legislation. Its removal by Canberra after twenty-four years indicates a rocky road ahead for the island to remain 'distinct and separate' from the mainland. It also suggests Norfolk's defence of being 'different' may no longer be enough to protect its unique position within the Commonwealth of Australia. Norfolk regards this as a 'right' but in today's climate of centralised government and new federalism, it should probably see it as a privilege.

The voting eligibility rules were born with self-government in 1979 and they went like this: to get on the electoral roll and vote in an election or referendum, a person had to live on the island for 900 days within a four year period—in other words, for two and a half years. Nationality or citizenship was irrelevant. No matter who they were or where they were from, if the voter was away for 150 days in the 240 days prior to the closing of the electoral roll, then they could be disenfranchised. It was wacky. Even Islanders regarded it excessive. It disenfranchised born and bred Norfolkers for one reason only: being away from home for too long. If they went offshore for extended work or study they could lose the vote. The only way to get it back was to return to Norfolk and rejoin the queue. Surely, I thought, hadn't the natives proved to be the real deal? After all, these were not blow-ins, they were Islanders who called Norfolk their 'homeland'.

The length of time to reclaim the vote was held up as proof Norfolk didn't discriminate: it made everyone sit through the same waiting period. Not even having Fletcher Christian at the top of the family tree was enough to sneak in under the radar. But Norfolk discriminated on so many other things—on land holdings, on who could live on the island, who could get residency, on TEPs and how long they could stay . . . Was Norfolk's political environment so complex it took years to figure out who stood for what? Norfolk had perfected the art of moving slowly. Did Islanders returning home need two and a half years to catch up on gossip before they voted again, or had they forgotten John from Middlegate was always useless in school and shouldn't be trusted in government? And why wasn't due credence paid to the awesome power of Dem Tull in keeping Norfolk expats informed? Perhaps the system was really a brake on change. It certainly helped maintain the status quo and a familiar electoral roll.

Surprisingly, no one I spoke to in government or on the island defended the two year, five month waiting period to get the vote. They all agreed it was a little excessive. But collectively they refused to change it. For many years they fought hard to retain the system and refused to heed the call from Canberra to reduce the legislation to six months. A majority of Islanders are paranoid about giving its temporary work force the vote. 'If people don't know the past and present,' locals said, 'they might suggest something rash for the future.' Hence the suggestion of a six month wait was viewed with great fear. There were suggestions of 'being swamped' by ignorant Australians and amid all the noise it was easy to believe Norfolk was facing radical and dangerous change until a look in the history books showed the six month clause wasn't new.

Norfolk Islanders like to give visiting mainland politicians a history lesson on their unique polity. This time the roles were reversed. In a cheeky paragraph the Parliamentary Committee advocating electoral reform said 'traditionalists on Norfolk Island may take comfort [that six months] was the qualifying period for enrolment on the electoral roll for over a hundred years from the earliest days of Pitcairner settlement'.

As with all contentious issues between Norfolk and Canberra, the debate over the right to vote was really about the right of Norfolk Island to determine its own laws. It argued the terms and conditions under which a person should remain on Norfolk Island was up to it to decide, not the Commonwealth of Australia. It resented this interference from 'offshore' calling it provocative and confrontational. It played to the fierce localism of the island and was rewarded with support for keeping Australia 'at bay'.

When Norfolk won self-government in 1979 and rejected the 1975 Nimmo Royal Commission proposal to integrate Norfolk into Australia, the 'probationary period' before residents became eligible to vote was set at 900 days, just under two and a half years, or thirty times longer than the one month period of residency required in most Australian states. The federal government of the day wasn't bothered with this. Nor was it fussed six years later when, in 1985, all references to Australian citizenship were repealed in the Norfolk Island Act. This came about from some spring-cleaning of Commonwealth legislation which removed the arcane term 'British Subject' on the grounds it was discriminatory. The Norfolk Assembly of the day agreed it too would delete 'British Subjects' and at the same time get rid of all citizenship requirements in the Electoral Act. This was in line with what local governments in Australia were doing and, in 1985, the Commonwealth regarded Norfolk as not much more. Of course Norfolk Island regarded itself as far grander than a local council; it was on the road to full self-government, it was in the business of accumulating extraordinary powers never before handed to a state or territory. It was happy to un-burden itself of Australian citizenship requirements. It gave the island an independent feel, which satisfied those who regarded Australia as an oppressor. Even though every child born on Norfolk is automatic-ally an Australian citizen.

This is how Norfolk Island ended up with an electoral system which years later caused Canberra great distress and embarrassment. Slowly, it seemed, the bureaucrats got around to reading the rules governing Norfolk Island and thought, hang on, this is kind of weird. And the closer one looks the stranger it becomes. Canberra then started to try and scale back the differences but by then Norfolk Island was happy with its bag of anomalies—it was its badge, it was part of being 'distinct and separate', and it was what it had been promised in 1979.

By 1990, the alarm bells were ringing for Canberra. In the five years since 1985 the federal government had devolved considerable powers to Norfolk, including many federal and state functions such as social security, immigration, customs, health, industrial relations, and telecommunications. The justification for not requiring Australian citizenship on the grounds that this was the rule for local councils was, said the minister, no longer appropriate. Technically the Norfolk government could be run by people who had never declared their alle-giance to the Commonwealth of Australia. The system on Norfolk was not only missing a cornerstone of representative democracy, giving Australian citizens the vote in a timely manner, but to coin a phrase from the Howard years, it was literally 'un-Australian'.

In 1991 a committee recommended the citizenship provisions be extended to Norfolk. The Island said no. And in a display of how successful Norfolk is at resisting change, it managed to delay this for thirteen years. But Norfolk was on a loser to begin with. Despite all the talk about protecting its lifestyle, it couldn't really explain what the lifestyle was, or what needed protection. If Norfolk had played its politics smart it would have realised its position was untenable. It's tough to argue why a particular group should be denied the vote in the twenty-first century, especially when they're fellow citizens. Someone should have twigged that Canberra's new-found obligation to provide all Australians with reasonable access to the vote was unstoppable. One look in the rear-vision mirror of the previous thirteen years showed the island had done well to get as far as it had. Instead it got a bill forced down its throat and Norfolk's cherished autonomy was compromised. After waiting so long for change, the federal government wasn't interested in anything but parity with its preferred policy—a six month wait for the vote and citizenship. It disregarded the Norfolk Island legislation and banged in its own.

The sorry part for Norfolk Island was that it reinforced the perception held by many federal politicians that Norfolk was obstinate, difficult and its government so divided it couldn't make decisions. More worryingly for the island, it set a precedent for federal parliament to veto island legislation. This in turn heightened the willingness of some federal politicians to iron out the many other differences inherent on Norfolk.

With no majority support for these changes the island was outraged. It forgot all its own divisions and focused its anger on Canberra. 'Norfuk for Norfuk' was under unilateral attack. In the unfolding anger it became clear the despair wasn't over the changes, it was over the Commonwealth's right to make them. It was a matter of principle. It reinforced what many Islanders already suspected—the Australian government had ditched its policy of uniqueness and adopted a policy of sameness. 'If the feds are going to do this,' I heard people say, 'where might it stop?' And this is what frightens the Islanders: if Australia wants to flatten Norfolk's anomalies then there will be nothing left because Norfolk *is* an anomaly.

The following Saturday an 'Open Letter' addressed to the Parliament of Australia appeared in the *Norfolk Islander*, headlined: A BLACK ARMBAND DAY FOR NORFOLK ISLAND, FOR DEMOCRACY AND FOR HUMAN RIGHTS. What followed was a dense four-page manifesto printed in a mix of bold type, capital letters, question marks and quotes. It centred on the principles of democracy, freedom and the right to choose. It argued these tenets of Norfolk life were endangered. It was rare for Islanders to go to such lengths to air their political outrage. Usually there were a few paragraphs in the letters section of the paper signed by the usual suspects. This was different. This cut deep. The Open Letter was signed by Robin-Eleanor Adams, an 'Australian National' who had lived on the island since 1966. She turned out to be none other than the clerk of the parliament. The covenant for people in such positions is to be silent and apolitical. Her four pages, at $85 a pop, were anything but.

At the Assembly offices Robin Adams strolls across the lawn waving a rolled-up piece of paper at me like a police baton.

'I know who you are,' she says on approach. 'I saw you in the Assembly chamber.' She stops and sizes me up. 'My God, you remind me of Mitchell.'

'Who's Mitchell?'

'He's my son.'

I shake her hand and explain I'm writing a book.

'Yes, yes.' Looking at me like I'm stupid. 'I've heard that. Come in.'

Yet again, I'd forgotten Dem Tull negates the need for introductions.

'I don't read the newspapers or listen to the radio,' says Robin as we enter her office. It seemed an odd declaration. She has been clerk of the parliament since 1984 and deputy clerk before that. She says she thought long and hard about voicing her opinion of the electoral changes, then realised she was so angry she couldn't remain silent.

'Fear. There is so much fear,' she says, falling into a chair a little out of breath. 'What has Australia got to fear? We're just a little place of a thousand or so electors.'

'How many people will be affected by these changes?'

'Oh, I don't know. I'm just interested in the principle of the thing.'

I sit down and take out my notebook.

She shoots me an inquiring look and projects a stern parliamentary voice: 'I won't talk to you here in the office,' she says, 'it's not appropriate. I wrote that letter as a citizen, an Australian citizen, not the clerk of the Norfolk Assembly. I even wrote it at home.' Her full stop is her smile. She is very excited with the response to her declaration of democratic despair. There've been whispers of support in the short corridors of Norfolk's convict buildings.

Robin agrees to meet at the Golden Orb the following day.

The next morning I wake to a misty drizzle. It clouds the landscape, hiding the summit of Mt Pitt and making the main street of

Burnt Pine look drearier than usual. The cloud billows on the ridges, then drifts reluctantly out to sea. The tops of the pines emerge like arrow tips before vanishing in another whisk of whiteness; a Pacific dew, heavy and laden.

The Golden Orb Bookshop and Café is surrounded by a remnant slice of old rainforest and tucked back from the main street. It's the sort of place I thought Norfolk would be full of but isn't. There's the timber interior, high roof, bookshelves and couches. On the deck outside feral chooks walk beneath the tables pecking for loose salad droppings. In twenty years the island will probably have many places with a new age, Byron Bay feel about them.

As we order—a coffee for me and a red herbal tea for Robin—she pulls out a photo of her son to prove our likeness. I think she sees this as a sign. 'It's all the crystals,' joked one local when I said I was going to see her.

Robin slides a folder across the table, a copy of a letter she sent to John Howard. It ends with the question: 'Prime Minister, has there been some misunderstanding that could lead to international misinterpretation?' I like the use of the word *international*. She's sure hot under the collar about being steamrolled by the Commonwealth parliament and its disregard for the voice of the Norfolk people, who, she reminds me, were happy with the electoral system the way it was: 'I do not believe the national interest can be used on this occasion to override a community which has had its democratic say. These are basic, basic, principles of humanity that we're trying, as a human race, to work towards. What is the rhyme or reason for that? I can't quite crystallise this into words, but I know it's nonsense.'

When frustrated, Robin squints her eyes or shakes her head. To hammer out a point she chops at the table with the edge of her hand. I ask if the Australian government has trodden on the island's much loved referenda.

Robin is chopping at the table now. 'Trodden on and denigrated. Denigrated! To the point where in their parliamentary debate—' She stops mid sentence and changes tack. 'Have you seen the musical, oh what is it called?' She starts singing. 'Tell the rabble to be quiet we anticipate a riot. Da-da da da da . . . what's that called? Oh, come on, Tim, it's so well known.'

I don't know what she is talking about.

'*Les Miserables!*' she blurts out. 'You know we often quote that . . .' and she starts singing the chorus line again. For someone with such a dour job her personality is effervescent.

'I object to being called a rabble. In order to speak out in my democratic way I will be seen as a rabble. How can they denigrate a referendum process which is direct democracy? It is the ultimate in direct democracy.'

'You used the term Black Armband Day?'

'Yes, that just came to me! It was such a horrible day. A day of mourning for democracy and human rights because they were stamped on. Remember I'm not speaking out against Australia or Australians because I'm one, but an Australian who has lived here for six months can now vote and I'm sorry, you cannot know Norfolk Island in six months and what's going on.'

'Why not?' I ask. 'Are you saying it's too complex?'

'You don't know the people for starters.' She looks around the café and lowers her voice. 'How can you even get to know the people who are standing as candidates?'

'But in any other election you don't know the candidates.'

'Yes I know. That's an argument, I suppose . . .'

'But is that important here? To know the candidates?'

'Yes! Yes. It is important because there are some people that you know here who stand for office and you would never vote for—they may poll four or eight votes. Now a whole community can't be wrong. Can they? There must be something the community knows that says they shouldn't be there.' At this we both laugh.

'And you don't want newcomers hoodwinked?'

'I don't know. That's going beyond where I come from. I come from principle.'

I ask Robin about island traditions. The Norfolk Way, what does she reckon it is?

'I don't think I'm the best one to talk to about that.'

'But over the thirty-eight years of living here, you must have some ideas?'

'The Norfolk Way.' She murmurs it to herself with a nervous giggle. 'You can't codify it. I can't codify it. It's not a tangible. And because of that fact, it's what creates the dilemma for others from outside, because there's nothing codified.'

I listen to the rain bounce off the dead palm fronds below the open window. Robin is explaining how there is 'absolutely no evidence of Australia, none at all', in the history of Pitcairn and Norfolk. Outside it was still drizzling, Mt Pitt still shrouded.

A couple of hours later, in the epicentre of island society—the supermarket—I ran into a former island politician, one of a handful of locals who were happy for me to bounce ideas off, provided they remained anonymous. 'I saw you with the clerk of the parliament this morning,' he scoffed. 'It's outrageous she's talking to you. I would have sacked her years ago if I'd had the chance.' With that he picked up a couple of cartons of long-life milk and walked away, leaving me to the ponder the sparse vegetable selection. Apart from green beans, nothing else seemed to be in season.

———

I needed to talk to David Buffett, the statesman of Norfolk Island, the only person who has managed to be re-elected to office at every election since 1979. David Buffett is political velcro, although his electoral support is now waning. On every Bounty Day anniversary he dresses up as Captain Denham, the man who stood in the rain and welcomed the Pitcairners to Norfolk in June 1856. When Mike King was chief minister he almost pulled the ultimate political coup by getting David Buffett to be the island's first home-grown administrator, a position he would die for. Alas, the 23-bedroom colonial house in Kingston is still occupied by 'Canberra's man'.

David Buffett's preferred position is speaker of the Assembly, a role he has nearly always held. Sometimes he is also a minister, which forces him to shuffle from the speaker's chair to the Assembly floor to answer questions. He is short and thin with a grey goatee and walks as upright as a colonel might. He is fit, verbose and speaks his hundreds of words with a crisp English accent whose origin no one knows. Unlike many of his colleagues, he doesn't have a beer belly. In the days after Janelle's murder he offered the Pattons free tickets to the island's museums. Ron and Carol didn't know what to think.

Islanders call David Buffett the colonel because he was once a reservist in the Australian army. As the story goes, someone took one look at him and said, 'You look like a colonel.' When I asked if the name bothered him he said, 'I've been called worse.'

Shortly after self-government David Buffett drove around with a Norfolk flag on his car and the numberplates A1. He says at the time Norfolk needed to fly the flag and he was happy to do so. Others mocked him for acting like a president and cut him down to size. The A1 numberplates were removed and placed on the island hearse, where they remain today.

David Buffett says the pillar of his electoral success is his understanding of 'the 1856 families'. It is these seven families that distinguish Norfolk from everywhere else: 'Without those values and without that group of people, Norfolk Island is a suburb of another place,' he said.

'And how would you sum up those values?'

'Oh, now that's a very tricky question, a very tricky question. The tricky bit is the expression of it. One can turn to a number of things. You can talk about food, or song and music, one can talk about some elements of writing, crafts, and language, that doesn't take account of a whole range of other things that you would never see. And I'm now talking about appearances; people, the shape of your head, how tall you are. Not always the colour of your skin—although that could be a mix. I'm talking about your voice and the timbre of your voice, I'm talking about your accent in some set of circumstances and people who are of *the group* know those things. One of the difficulties is people have a conception, they've had it for a long time, that unless you can verbalise something it doesn't exist and that's a load of rubbish.'

'But unless you can verbalise a culture, isn't it difficult to argue what it is, or what needs protecting?'

'That's very true, but it doesn't mean it doesn't exist and that's part of Norfolk Island's difficulty—some still say that's none of your bloody business and I don't give a bugger whether you recognise that or not. That doesn't change us or mean we don't have it. Another difficulty is that regrettably, many of the things I've referred to are being diluted and in some instances some have almost disappeared. Maybe thirty or forty years ago the culture didn't need protection because it was so dominant. If you were in a conversation it would be Norfolk that would be spoken, that would dominate. And if you wanted to exist in the community then you needed to make your mark, you would have to meet the Norfolk Island culture, you couldn't exist in an enclave on your own. It dominated the scene. Now it is the reverse. That is only thirty years ago. Now the reverse is the situation, in terms of language and a whole range of other things.'

'What dominates now?' I say. 'If it's the reverse, do mainlanders dominate?'

David Buffett looks at me sternly and says, 'It's an amalgamation from elsewhere.'

On my way back to Burnt Pine I dropped in on Tom Lloyd, the man who was instrumental in getting Norfolk into the Commonwealth Games. Having run the local paper for forty years I figured he'd have his finger on the island's cultural pulse. He paused at my question. 'The culture's not easily defined,' he said. I tried not to roll my eyes and begged him to expand.

'It's the amateur sports, the dancing, you realise what we have lost on Norfolk Island. The culture is something we sometimes imagine in our mind. The cooking, the language, the hymns, the singing, most of these things can be found in any small Christian community.'

I was astonished at what Tom was saying. Norfolk used its culture as a platform for special recognition from Canberra, its unique powers over immigration, deportation and government were all based on the island needing cultural protection. Here was an elder of the community, a member of the Pitcairn Descendants Society telling me that Norfolk was not much different from any other small Christian settlement.

'The Tahitian dancing is something which is trying to be revived,' Tom continued, 'but that part of the culture is bred out of Pitcairn. For the life of me, I can't find anything else to recommend. I'll get roasted for that, but that's my view.' He sat silent for a moment then said, 'I mean there is a great move afoot to teach young people Tahitian dancing and I suppose when you take it back to its original roots that's probably the main source of the culture. If we are to consider ourselves Pitcairn Islanders with a Tahitian background I would say "fair enough", but I think the Norfolk Island culture today, or as we believe we know it today, only started on Pitcairn. From all I've read and seen on Pitcairn when I went there, there was no concentration on that Tahitian link because it was never engendered. Even the Tahitian mums of the *Bounty* era decided to have their children speak English. I don't know—maybe it was John Adams—but the concentration was on the English heritage.'

Everyone was aware of the outside pressure on Norfolk's culture. What Tom had just revealed were some of the internal pressures, especially when it came to the current revision of its Polynesian history. It reminded me of a comment by an Australian man married into a Norfolk family. He didn't want to be named but he showed considerable insight when he said: 'Love of the island, its culture and lifestyle is one of the few unifying threads. Yet at the same time, it is also a cause of social division as no one can agree on how the Island and its lifestyle should be protected. This is the island's Catch 22.'

CHAPTER 16

BRUTAL ATTACK

JUST LIKE the murder of Janelle Patton, the coronial inquest into her death was equally audacious. It was raw, harsh and impersonal. It was also intimate. Norfolk Island has a natural intimacy about it when confronted by pain and anguish. The community blossoms in times of need—it is the ultimate unifier.

The inquest bruised many reputations. Janelle's friends, lovers and enemies were all tested, if not soiled, but it was nothing compared to what Janelle Patton weathered. It is she who suffered the greatest indignation. It was her character, her fears, her soul which were probed, blunted and in some cases debased by an inquest operating on multiple levels, and at the core of it all was the story of a woman who wanted to be loved and needed to be wanted.

When Janelle's body was dumped at Cockpit reserve it hit the ground in an unnatural position. She was on her chest, face down, the ponytail limp across her forehead. Her head was turned ever so slightly, one eye staring into the dirt, the other across the grass. The right arm was splayed at an angle away from the body, the left arm also pointed in the same direction but much higher, the shoulder wrenched in tight. It was as if the left arm caught the grass first and was dragged beneath the torso in the moment before the body landed on top.

It is only from one angle that her left buttock is visible. The shorts are almost completely pulled from the waist; scrunched, bloody and resting mid thigh. So too are the black underpants. These have been cut at the right hip and hang loose. The knife has left a jagged zigzag tear in the cotton. There is no associated injury to the skin beneath. It is smooth and uncut. Bob Peters believes the killer gathered Janelle's black underpants in one hand and slipped the blade of the knife beneath the cloth, slicing upwards and severing them from her hip. It's unknown if this occurred during the struggle or after death, but given the fight Janelle put up it is telling that the skin on her right hip is unblemished.

The front of Janelle's singlet was cut in a V-shape between the breasts. It was also pushed up from the bottom, leaving the belly button and stomach exposed. The cuts to the clothing are a mystery. In the autopsy report Dr Allan Cala wrote: 'There was evidence of possible sexual assault as her clothing was disturbed and her buttocks were exposed.' The forensic pathologist later told the inquest: 'I don't want to be drawn into suggesting a motive to this.' The cuts, he said, may have had a 'sexual motivation' but this theory wasn't 'absolutely water-tight'. 'It may have been the clothing was inadvertently or accidentally cut by somebody slashing at Miss Patton with a knife,' he told the court.

As always, Bob Peters is of an open mind: the cuts to the clothing may have been staged, he says, to make it look like a sexual attack. The third possibility is the cuts were made in the process of a sexual assault.

Other than the cuts to Janelle's underpants, singlet top and shorts, Dr Cala found no evidence of sexual assault: 'There was no sign of bruising around the genital regions,' he said, nor was there any 'sign of disturbance' to a tampon that was found in the 'correct position' in the vagina. Allan Cala said he was 'quite firm' on his finding of 'no assault to the genital region at all'. This included no evidence of interference in the anal region.

In total Dr Cala lists sixty-four separate injuries in his autopsy report. The injuries are broken down for each section of the body and include stab wounds, bruises, superficial wounds, cuts, gashes, grazes, abrasions, dislocations and fractures. It is a grisly, ordered detailing of what Janelle suffered in a prolonged attack. Based on Dr Cala's observations, Janelle had been 'punched about the face'; her fractured ribs may have been caused by a 'heavy fall' (he doubted a punch could deliver such force); her many head injuries may have been caused by a blunt, flat object, like a 'heavy piece of wood or a brick', and the fractured pelvis may have been caused by 'a stomp', although he didn't discount

Janelle having been hit by a car. When asked how long the violence may have lasted Dr Cala shocked the court by saying 'perhaps ten or fifteen minutes'. He estimated a large part of that time Janelle was 'fully conscious and able to mount or try to mount anyway, some defence'.

Keeping this in mind makes the listing of Janelle's injuries even more terrifying. Was Janelle fully conscious when she was stabbed in the left eyebrow? Like so many this wound is deep, extending into the skull bone leading to a fracture directly surrounding the left eye.

It's clear Janelle did her best to thwart her attacker; the gruesome injury sustained to the webbing between her right thumb and index finger is testament to her terrible, desperate struggle for life. The thumb is not quite severed but it is close. During the attack it seems Janelle has grabbed the blade of the knife with her right hand and tried vainly to keep it at bay. As the knife came at Janelle she most certainly looked the killer in the eye. In an act of pure instinct, Janelle sacrificed one part of her body to protect the whole. It is impossible to imagine the sensation of grabbing naked steel as it moves through the air, the blade gorging into the grip of her right hand. The depth of the injury between Janelle's thumb and first finger is not from one neat blow. Clearly she has wrestled with the knife time and time again. This section of Janelle's palm carries the brunt of the attack but thin nick marks, almost as innocent as paper cuts, line the tips of several fingers.

Janelle's courage was both tremendous and frightening. It is not only the right hand which is butchered by her fight for life—her lower right leg is also dreadfully wounded. Across Janelle's shin are two parallel injuries a few centimetres apart. They are inflicted by a knife but appear so ghastly it's easy to imagine they were produced by a cleaver or a hatchet. They are not so much cuts as raw hacks, deep into the shin bone about ten centimetres above the right ankle. They are most likely defensive wounds inflicted while Janelle was prone. Bob Peters offers one scenario: Janelle lying on her back and kicking at the attacker, her shin being repeatedly gashed by the knife as the person tried to keep her at bay.

These two injuries would have bled freely and are possibly connected to the dislocated left ankle. Dr Cala has an 'open mind' on the cause of the dislocated left ankle: he said it could also have been caused by a 'heavy fall or by running and tripping', or it may have been twisted by the attacker. He told the court, 'someone may have held her foot and she was very forcibly struggling, trying to get away, pulling her leg away from the attacker'. Bob Peters believes the left ankle dislocation and the two wounds on the right shin occurred at the same time. He offers another scenario, of Janelle kicking, squirming and fighting to defend her body as her attacker drags or holds the left ankle, in the process forcing a dislocation. Once Janelle sustained this injury, Allan Cala said her 'ability to then flee that situation would have been quite considerably impaired'.

The post mortem lists Janelle Patton's cause of death as multiple injuries, 'with the provision some were clearly more serious than others'. Of all the terrible wounds Janelle suffered the fatal blow appears the most harmless. It is a neat but irregular V-shaped wound one centimetre to the left of the chest midline. The wound is deep, measuring fifteen centimetres long, which suggests the blade was also that length.

After entry, the knife travelled at an angle, moving further left as it penetrated the upper part of the left lung and into the inner chest cavity. This injury caused severe blood loss in the 'left pleural cavity', which in turn led to the immediate collapse of the left lung. Dr Allan Cala explained to the inquest how the introduction of 'atmospheric air' into the pleural cavity would quickly remove the negative pressure required by the lungs to inflate and deflate with breathing: 'Once that happens the combination of those two things would be catastrophic for the person and they would be very short of breath, they would be suffering the consequences of acute and very rapid blood loss and I think that death would have followed fairly shortly . . . within several minutes perhaps.'

Before being pulled out of her chest the knife which punctured Janelle's left lung was twisted and, on exit, produced the V-shaped wound. The twist of the blade may have been deliberate—a spiteful roll of the wrist by the killer—or it was a result of Janelle's thrusting but futile defence. Because there is no bruising on the skin surrounding the wound, Dr Allan Cala concluded the knife didn't have a hilt. On this evidence alone, the popular idea that Janelle was killed by a fishing knife doesn't hold up. It appears more likely to have been a long, thin blade, such as a filleting knife, the sort used to de-bone fish.

It appears it is this same long thin knife which has slashed the right side of Janelle Patton's face. The wound starts below the middle of her mouth then fans across the right cheek to the end of the jawline, then continues onto her neck. It has been caused by one continuous movement and at first glance looks like someone has tried to decapitate Janelle. This is not the case, but it is horrifying to see such a gruesome gash across the fine skin of a pretty woman's face: a face which I have seen smiling and laughing in so many photographs.

At first this wound cuts deep. This is where the most force has been applied and where the knife first engaged the flesh. The depth tapers off as the blade moved across the cheek and then onto the neck. The knife travelled 180 degrees, one long swoop from mid chin to the mid neck vertebrae. Allan Cala said the injuries 'could have all been caused by the same weapon but it's also possible a number of weapons were used'.

Norfolk Island's Crown Counsel Graham Rhead asked if Janelle's facial injuries suggested 'deliberate disfigurement'. Allan Cala replied: 'I don't know about deliberate disfigurement but clearly the weapon and the attacker have been very close . . .'

Graham Rhead then posed one of the most important questions of the coronial inquest: 'Are you in a position to say how many people [were] involved in the assault?'

'I'm not,' said Allan Cala, 'but I favour one person and I say that because if there were more than one person I would have expected there may have been less injuries, perhaps one person may have been able to restrain her while another person produced injuries which would have killed her in a more rapid time than I think happened. So whilst I favour one person, I can't absolutely exclude the possibility that more than one person was involved.'

––––––––

Three days before the inquest I visited Graham Rhead. Only a handful of people had an insight into what was about to be unleashed and he was one. As counsel assisting the coroner he'd seen the brief. He knew it probed the dark crevices of Norfolk's after-hours drinking activities.

Graham worked on the top level of the island's tallest building, the third floor of the New Military Barracks. The tourist guide to Kingston's historic area describes the building as an 'excellent and rare example of a pre-1850 fortified military compound'. Just the spot for the island's top lawyer to operate from. The building was finished in 1837 and in its day housed 164 soldiers, which must have been a real squish. It has a wonderful circular stairwell and now houses the island's administration staff and court registry. Every time I walked into the stone foyer a hefty black labrador dozed in the open doorway; it rarely bothered to stir, seeming to have embraced life through the tunnel of eternal slumber—a criticism I regularly heard about the administration workers themselves.

I found Graham in a small corridor upstairs and he indicated the way to his corner office. His desk was covered with piles of papers and on the bookshelves were volumes of legal statutes, fat chunks of Australia's state and federal jurisdictions. Where Norfolk fitted in was anyone's guess. Through the salt-streaked office window I had an elevated view of Kingston pier. The federal government had just committed three million dollars to the historic cargo jetty to stop it sliding into the ocean. This bucket of fresh cash from unaware Australian taxpayers was going down like a cold beer. It helped appease locals hot under the collar about the report 'Quis Custodiet Ipos Custodes?'

'People like to come in and just drop piles of paper on my desk,' Graham says as he walks in. 'It's amazing how busy it is here. Since we're dealing with three tiers of government, there are lots of piles.'

Graham Rhead is a former Brisbane policeman and one-time 'document expert' who analysed people's handwriting. He then switched to law, becoming a Queensland police prosecutor. He worked in Hong Kong for six years and then headed back to Brisbane and entry to the Bar.

Needing a change of lifestyle and pace he washed up on Norfolk Island in July 2002 as Crown Counsel, three months after Janelle Patton's murder. Robyn Murdoch, the CEO of the public service, had just been sacked and paid out after trying to push through reforms. There was an almighty crisis in the hospital flaring between local nurses and three doctors employed from the mainland. This tension festered like a infectious wound with allegations of bullying, unprofessional behaviour (alleged plastic surgery on the side) and corruption. It culminated in a case of fraud against Dr Damien Foong but it never went to trial and the allegations were never investigated.

2002 wasn't a vintage year for Norfolk Island but it was a cracker introduction for Graham Rhead, who shrugs and flicks his hand as if to say 'let's not talk about that'.

Graham is tall and thin. Easily over six feet. When he stretches back in his chair there's a lot of torso. He clasps his hands behind his neck and talks about his role. It is, he admits, a legal 'jack of all trades'.

We talk about the Patton inquest and the media coverage. I ask about names. He hints at what is to come. 'It's not going to be a pleasant place to be here next week, there's going to be a lot of pain and anger.' He drops forward in his chair and says, 'Plus there'll be some embarrassment, the community won't be too happy.'

In the week leading up to the inquest the *Norfolk Islander* ran a front page notice signed by Coroner Ron Cahill. It was part community notice, part legal advice. The first paragraph was orderly: the date and time of the inquest. The second asked if anyone needed legal representation and if so, told them to contact Graham, as Crown Counsel.

The need for legal representation went over most Islanders' heads. Only a few did their homework and realised names would be revealed and, of those, a couple escaped the island for the duration. Most locals went about their daily business in the belief they wouldn't be involved. They might have known Janelle, shared a few beers with her, maybe they even fancied her, but they had nothing to do with her *murder*. The Coroner's notice was just another item in the Saturday paper. Readers had no inkling the dead hand of Janelle Patton was looming. Or that a hand so long gone could deliver such dirty, damaging secrets. The reaction of those named was shock and disbelief. A few days later it mutated into anger and telephone calls to lawyers. No one fathomed the intensity of the media interest, or how suffocating it would be for those named.

Tom Lloyd hinted at what was coming when he wrote 'a media contingent of 20' was expected to cover the case. Unfortunately this was sandwiched between a long and boring federal treasury article about Norfolk adopting the Australian taxation system, an unsavoury idea for sure and one most certainly skipped by readers. If locals *had* known what was brewing Graham Rhead would have been swamped by wide-eyed people. As it was, the Crown Counsel received no formal inquiry about legal representation. 'I remember a couple of people querying the note,' he said, 'but not for their benefit.' When I asked how people were supposed to know if they needed legal representation, Graham said, 'That depends on what questions police asked them or if they were guilty.'

The coroner's notice was more than legal magnanimity, it was also a tactic. The police were interested in who might seek legal representation and why.

Two days before the inquest commenced David Buffett, Minister for Tourism and Police, put out a statement. He said the government welcomed the inquest and hoped justice would be done. Beyond this he was mum. It was in the 'hands of the coroner', there would be 'no further comment'.

As the community creaked under the strain of what eventually took place, the government remained silent. There was no political leadership. As misunderstanding, fear, anger and confusion ricocheted around the island, its leaders were nowhere to be heard. 'Business as usual,' joked some.

Sensing a readership thirsty for more information Tom Lloyd wrote a short article called 'What can we expect from the Coronial Inquest?' But the article didn't tackle the major concern within Dem Tull—would people be named? It was dawning on the community that people might be named as *suspects*.

––––––

The 1834 courtroom is on the bottom floor of the Old Military Barracks and directly beneath the Assembly chamber. It has large latticework windows open to the sea breeze. The walls of the room are peach-coloured, the carpet an apricot-orange. It is a warm room—the colour scheme of a day care centre. It was a tone which didn't match the evidence to come.

Inside the tiny courtroom everyone was tripping over each other. As is the practice these days, Coroner Ron Cahill invited the media in to film and photograph the court. He sat in his high chair while the media crews scrambled about, shooting footage of the case folders and Patton family and anything else which didn't move. This shameless tactic in the pursuit of justice is not new but it is very un-Norfolk. The island had never experienced anything like it and the inquest hadn't even commenced.

'Notice how I'm covering up my notes,' joked Coroner Cahill as one TV camera nudged closer. There was nothing subtle about how Ron Cahill ran his inquest. His modus operandi was maximum publicity, a frank admission he made several times. The aim was to fish, flush and quash—fish for leads, flush out facts and quash the rumours. For two years the investigators had been tight lipped, revealing so little Dem Tull had floundered to the point of impotency. Now it was time to lift the curtain and hear from Bob Peters' explosive dossier.

The coroner got things underway by laying down a few home truths. In his opening address he said, 'In the words of Norfolk Island "Dem Tull" is no substitute for evidence. In this case there are probably hundreds if not thousands of people that have suspicions and theories . . . [but] suspicion and innuendo is not a substitute for evidence.' Then, in a line he must have drafted on the flight over, he said, 'This is not like Jessica Fletcher in *Murder, She Wrote*. Angela Lansbury is not going to walk in that door and say he or she did it. Equally, Quincy is not going to have a forensic solution, although we are still looking and examining very carefully the forensic evidence in this case, particularly the DNA.'

Ron Cahill then quashed any expectation of immediate justice by saying the court was not about to point out an individual for immediate arrest: 'If it does it will be a miracle . . . We still need help. I am confident without pre-judging the matters . . . that someone must know something particularly on this Island that will help solve this mystery.'

This line irritates Islanders but Ron Cahill is qualified to say it— he's been coming to Norfolk in a legal capacity since the mid seventies. In 1985 he was appointed chief magistrate of the Australian Capital Territory and Norfolk Island. He is a solid man with a square jawline and an inquiring furrow between his eyebrows. He was dubbed the Tardy Coroner because he always waddled in late and looked more than comfortable with the notion of island time.

Ron Cahill tries to get to Norfolk every six months and because his appointment is between the island government and the Canberra court, he doesn't feel the chilly welcome reserved for other visitors from the national capital. At night the coroner likes to drive to the end of Kingston pier, turn off the headlights and soak up the sea, sky and spirits. He loves the locals. He told me, 'they're the soul of the island'. I got the feeling the sixteen on the list weren't in his social network.

With Ron Cahill's assurance of no quick justice dispensed on a now sober gallery, a red Bible was produced and Bob Peters sworn into the witness box. Chin down and stony faced, Detective Sergeant Peters began reading his statement. It was a mammoth task. One hundred and sixty statements and documents to be tabled.

On an island where personal accountability is at best fickle, a 227-page document exposing the seething underbelly of life in paradise was to be read aloud, line by line, in a court of law. The story of Janelle's murder was always a story about island life; she wasn't a TEP who lived on the edge, she steamrolled into the middle and was invited into the lives and beds of established Islanders. Now Detective Sergeant Bob Peters was to reveal all in a speedy, monotone voice, punctuated by gulps of water. The delivery did nothing to hide the fireworks contained within, but did make me nod off a little.

As one sparky woman said to me, 'It's like reading a book where you know all the characters.' She was a newcomer, a Norfolk resident of only six years. She would jot down notes when certain names were mentioned and tap her pen when the going got slow.

'You're writing that book, aren't you?' she said.

'Yes,' I whispered.

'Fascinating,' she said, 'who is being named.'

And it was fascinating. It was a sizable cast of people who knew, had known or wanted to know Janelle Patton. Two and a half years of her life fleshed out in four days, a lot of it ugly, all of it uncomfortable.

The first people named were those right in front of me: Ron and Carol Patton.

When Carol Patton walked into the courtroom her voice was already on the way out. By the end of the day she couldn't speak at all. From her hand swung a plastic bag containing two frosty bottles of 'No Frills' water. The weeks leading up to this moment had been stressful and the pressure showed in her face. It was a portrait of resigned fortitude.

'All Carol has ever wanted is to be a schoolteacher and a mother,' said Ron Patton over the phone when he explained why he wouldn't meet me for a pre-inquest coffee. A fortnight earlier Bob Peters had spent five hours with the Patton family in Sydney going through his statement.

Knowing what was ahead didn't ease Carol's nerves. She knew they would be the first people named. She looked beyond pale—there seemed to be no blood pumping above her shoulders. Ron looked more composed while Janelle's brother, Mark, seemed aloof but ready. He was chatting to Laurie 'Bucket' Quintal and Bob Peters. Only on Norfolk (or Pitcairn Island) could the brother of the deceased speak with a Person of Interest in the presence of the homicide detective investigating the case.

Ron had wished for a solid media turnout and was satisfied with what he saw. Carol was taken aback by the scene. She turned to Ron and said, 'Janelle would have loved all this attention.' The irony struck the Pattons but they could hardly afford a smile. I'd heard the same comment on the court lawn from Bucket who, when he saw the camera crews, turned to me and said, 'Nel always loved to be the centre of attention.'

Janelle's parents sat with their son Mark at the bar table. Like students at a university lecture, each carried a notepad and pen. For long periods, father and son sat like clones, their posture a mirror of one another's hands clasped on the table, their eyes dead ahead, interrogating the peach wall in front of them for answers.

Fifteen minutes into proceedings on day one, Ron Patton's watch alarm went off. 'For God's sake,' said Carol, giving him a glare of dismay. Not knowing how to turn it off, Ron smothered the watch with his right hand and feigned ignorance. When this failed to quell the beeping he unstrapped the watch and buried it in his trouser pocket. Mark looked at his dad, shook his head and returned his gaze to a corner of the wall behind the coroner's right ear.

Ron and Carol Patton read to themselves from a copy of Bob Peters' statement as the detective read it out. When certain names or events were mentioned they would form a huddle with Mark Patton and point, nod or whisper. At other times Ron or Carol would let out audible moans when excerpts from Janelle's dairy were read out.

At the lunchtime adjournment on the second day Ron and Carol Patton broke down. They hadn't moved from their chairs since hearing Graham Rhead read from the autopsy report detailing many of the sixty-four separate injuries on Janelle's body. Court Registrar Allen 'Ikey' Bataille sensed the need for privacy and emptied the court, closing the door behind him. Until this moment, the Pattons' façade of composure had been so measured it had made some wonder if they felt anything at all. Now they needed a moment of privacy to come to terms with the evil they had just heard outlined in a clinical fashion.

When Ron and Carol were revealed as the first Persons of Interest they focused on not looking anywhere but immediately ahead. It's common practice for police to start from the inside out, and this means investigating the family of the deceased first. 'Unfortunately,' said Peters, 'in some instances this speculation has extended to malicious gossip and unfounded innuendo.'

The Pattons were named Persons of Interest because some locals claim they killed their daughter. This claim was derived from the assumption that 'Nutty Nel' was 'mad', and therefore so were her parents. Some who made this claim to me were later revealed as Persons of Interest themselves. The fact that Janelle's parents arrived on Norfolk Island twenty-six hours before their daughter's death was, in their eyes, enough to suggest guilt. It was part and parcel of blaming the entire Patton family for the whole affair.

Outside the court on day two Ron said he 'wasn't surprised' about being named, given the statistics on family homicides: 'Right from the word go we expected we would be under investigation in some way.' But he was putting on a brave face. For weeks after the inquest he stewed at his treatment by the police as he mowed Sydney lawns for his landscape business. In his eyes, being labelled a Person of Interest made him no better or worse than others named. Except he'd lost his daughter, they hadn't. He was furious and he cut the grass faster and faster as his mind worked double time. Mark and Carol also had to work double time to stop him lodging a formal complaint with the Australian Federal Police. They reminded him that the police were one of the family's few allies in the search for the truth. Ron Patton's anger was understandable—it was central to his long-term fear that justice for Janelle was slipping away.

For her part, Carol said being named by the court was distressing: 'We did arrive on the island twenty-four hours before she was killed, so obviously amongst some people there would be a question in their minds: "Was this a coincidence or not?" But it's upsetting though—you don't like to see yourself portrayed as a person of interest in your daughter's murder.'

Bob Peters told the court the Pattons had been 'fully frank' in discussing Janelle's private life and 'all aspects of her personality and character traits'. They both provided fingerprints and ensured the investigation maintained 'momentum'. There was no 'factual or forensic evidence' to indicate their involvement in Janelle's death. This last line became the 'not guilty disclaimer' and was attached to each of the Persons of Interest. In effect, what this disclaimer said was 'we can't arrest you because we don't have enough evidence, and you can't sue us because we've cleared you of any connection to the crime—for the time being'.

With every name on Bob Peters' list, the detective followed the same pattern. He would outline the case, warts and all. He would detail what Dem Tull said, what the facts said and what the evidence suggested. Having established these tenets, which sometimes contradicted one another, Bob Peters would then proceed to dismantle it all by stating there to be no 'factual or forensic evidence' to connect them to the murder of Janelle Patton or the disposal of her body at Cockpit reserve. If anything, his statement was rhythmic.

CHAPTER 17

FORENSICS

KATRINA GATES is a crime scene investigator. She attended the autopsy and was involved in searches of vehicles and properties. At twenty-seven, she is the eager face of forensic science. Halfway through her evidence Coroner Ron Cahill made her blush when he asked, 'You're what's popularly known as CSI, aren't you? It has become very famous in recent TV times . . .'

'That's correct,' she said, smiling awkwardly.

Katrina Gates had flown to Norfolk to outline the forensic clues in the case, providing a tally of progress inside the walls of the Australian Federal Police forensic laboratory. What was revealed was, again, how little Bob Peters has to work with. It reinforced the fragility of the police case and how fortunate or smart the offender was.

For anyone familiar with crime scene TV shows, 'trace elements' refer to the tiny, fiddly little bits and pieces collected by people in the field like Katrina Gates. These exhibits are sent to the lab with the hope that new clues will be unearthed for the weary detectives working the case. The 'trace elements' collected from Janelle Patton's hair, body, clothing and the sheet of black plastic are as follows:

- green plant material, including seeds, leaves and grass clippings
- fragments of broken glass, yellow in colour
- flakes of rusted metal
- five human hairs foreign to Janelle Patton

- particles of green paint found in her hair and clothes and underneath one fingernail
- a 'three centimetre long' facial hair, lifted from the pair of sunglasses found on Rooty Hill Road the day after Janelle's murder.

Bob Peters told the court that these bits and pieces, which he called 'particles', were 'considered to be of potential significance' in that these tiny clues could help identify three unanswered questions: where Janelle was killed, the vehicle used to shift her body and where the black plastic came from. Along with the unidentified fingerprints on the black plastic, these 'trace elements' are the only forensic leads police have revealed publicly.

It is important to note the list of 'trace elements' includes no DNA evidence. There is a misconception that Norfolk residents were all DNA swabbed. This isn't the case. Mass fingerprinting took place on Norfolk Island but not DNA testing. This is because the body of Janelle Patton failed to produce the lead every detective wishes for—some foreign DNA. As Katrina Gates told the inquest: 'no DNA profiles from unknown sources were obtained. This includes the fingernail scrapings and clippings as well as the oral and anal and vaginal swabs . . . A number of further samples from vehicles, knives, clothing and residences on Norfolk Island have been analysed since the 31st of March . . . On those that were successful none of the DNA profiles obtained could have come from Janelle Patton.'

In the early days of the investigation police did gather DNA samples. Many of the sixteen Persons of Interest readily agreed to mouth swabs but this occurred before forensics delivered the bad news: the only DNA identified on Janelle's body was her own. There are two main reasons for this: either the killer left no DNA, or the killer did shed DNA but it has been destroyed, degraded or 'swamped' by Janelle's own blood loss. A third possibility, and the one police are clinging to, is that the offender did leave a smidgin of DNA but it can't yet be detected and won't be detected until forensic science advances. The forensic equation is not helped by the movement of Janelle's body, which may have destroyed other trace elements. Then there was also the torrid rain storm which did to Janelle's body what nature does best: helped erode the sins of the past. There is no way the killer could have foreseen this, or known the quantity of DNA they shed.

It's worth remembering that the location of Janelle's murder remains a mystery. The island is only five by eight kilometres but police have no idea where Janelle met her death. This crime scene is the honey pot police failed to find—and without a confession, probably never will find. On this fact alone, the investigation team has failed because it would have been a forensic goldmine, especially in regard to pieces of flesh, tissue and blood spray patterns. It would have been a real lead to the identity of the offender. If the murder occurred in a domestic environment it would have been a grisly job to clean up. If it was outside, then once again the heavens were a godsend for the killer.

Two years on, Coroner Ron Cahill told the inquest it was unlikely any new DNA samples would be found; instead, hope rested with the minute but non-reportable samples already gathered and now stored in Canberra. Only through new and more powerful forensic techniques can these microscopic samples be analysed for identifiable DNA clues. Throughout the inquest regular reference was made to the 'advance of technology' and what future forensic methods might hold. The message was also to comfort the Patton family, in essence telling them, 'If we don't have the killer yet we still might later'.

The forensic snapshot was equally bleak when it came to six mysterious human hairs detected by Dr James Robertson, the national manager of Forensic and Technical Services with the Australian Federal Police. Five of these hairs were found on the black plastic covering the body and one 'three centimetre long facial hair' was taken from the broken sunglasses found on Rooty Hill Road. Janelle had long dark hair and, not surprisingly, there were plenty of broken hairs found on her body. Testing proved these loose hairs were Janelle's, as were the hairs collected from the plastic sheet—all except 'three scalp hairs'.

Katrina Gates told the inquest that these three hairs were 'not suitable for nuclear DNA testing, however may be suitable for mitochondrial DNA testing'. As she explained it, mitochondrial DNA testing refers to actually examining the shaft of the hair as opposed to the root. Most of the human genome is located in the nucleus of each cell—this is where DNA is found. If the nucleus is not present, as with a broken strand of hair, then clues are revealed in the mitochondria, which are located in the cytoplasm of the cell. Mitochondrial DNA testing is valuable because it can be lifted from severely degraded biological material. But it comes at a price. Any testing destroys the sample.

'A once-only effort?' asked the coroner.

'That's correct,' said Katrina Gates. 'Therefore you would no longer have the hair for any comparison at a later stage should a hair comparison be required. There is also no database of mitochondrial DNA for which you can compare the sample to, as there is with nuclear DNA.'

Katrina Gates then told the court that mitochondrial DNA testing was unavailable in Australia but in fact, while testing is limited, it has occurred in New South Wales and is available in Victoria and the Northern Territory. There are also numerous Australian cases where this technique has been utilised, although the Australian Federal Police have never used it.

Also found on the black plastic were two additional hairs foreign to Janelle. They consisted of 'a body hair and a facial hair'. Like the scalp hairs, these were only suitable for mitochondrial DNA testing. 'No conclusion can be made about these hairs in the absence of known sources,' said Katrina Gates. Which meant 'we've got no clue who they belong to'.

The precise details and limitations of these hair samples are explained in a report by Dr Robertson, but as with every exhibit tendered in the public hearing, bar two, I was denied access to this report.

The last of the hair exhibits is the longest, a three centimetre facial hair lifted from the broken sunglasses. Katrina Gates described this particular hair as a 'very light brown facial hair'. She said it was highly unlikely to have come from a female. It seemed obvious it could only be from a man's beard. Like the other hairs, this had no root and would only be suitable for mitochondrial DNA testing.

The coroner called this hair 'fairly significant' and declared its identification a 'distant hope'. The problem with the sunglasses found on Rooty Hill Road was the failure by forensics to positively identify them as Janelle's. No trace DNA or hair samples from Janelle were ever found on the frame or remaining lens. Even if the three centimetre facial hair is linked to an individual, any further connection to Janelle and her death will be difficult to prove without conclusive evidence that the sunglasses were hers.

As a final rider to the fickle limitations of this facet of forensic science, Katrina Gates revealed that mitochondrial DNA is inherited 'along the maternal side of the family, so it's not individual'. This means the mitochondrial DNA sequence is identical for siblings and all maternal relatives. In other words, members of the same family 'could have the same mitochondrial DNA'.

'It might be difficult,' said the Coroner. From what I'd just heard, it was something of an understatement. Not to mention very expensive. When I later asked the AFP what it costs to undertake a mitochondrial DNA test on a single hair I was quoted the overseas price of £8000.

———

When the body of Janelle Patton was rolled over on the autopsy table a piece of glass was found lying on the steel bench. It had been dislodged from Janelle's back. It was a curved, yellow glass fragment, measuring ten by twenty millimetres. On its edge 'was a section of a white label'. Two more pieces, slightly smaller, were found lodged in her skin. Janelle's hair also contained a large amount of smashed glass. Katrina Gates said the glass was 'similar to wine bottle glass and different to that of headlight glass or window glass'.

Police have since collected bottle glass from various sites on Norfolk Island but failed to match the glass found embedded in Janelle Patton's body and hair. It appears that in her struggle against her attacker, a bottle of some kind has been smashed over her head, possibly from behind. A wide, deep gash at the bridge of Janelle's nose may also have been caused by the slicing movement of cut glass.

Removed from the back of Janelle's clothing were 'small circular brown seeds'. Botanical evidence has become important in forensics because of its ability to pinpoint time and place through seasons and specific locations. Many cases have been cracked when flowers, seeds or species of grass or plant have led to a property or an offender. The problem with Norfolk Island is always its small size—nearly all its flora is endemic. The seeds on Janelle's back were identified as *Soliva Sessilis*, known as grab-a-leg. It grows all over the island, including Cockpit reserve where Janelle's body was found. These seeds provided no insight into where Janelle might have been killed. The only material inconsistent with the vegetation of Cockpit reserve were 'grass clippings' and 'leaves and pods from the guava plant'. Again this was of little help as the guava plant is common to the backyards of Norfolk, and it also grows wild in the national park where walkers can help themselves to the small red berries. In this case, the botanical evidence was not informative.

Perhaps the most gripping piece of trace evidence lifted from the body of Janelle Patton are flecks of green paint. This paint is distinctive and was recovered from 'Janelle's hair, shorts and underneath one fingernail'. After extensive testing and analysis by 48-year-old forensic chemist David Royds, it was established that the top layer of the paint was different from the bottom layer. The key point of difference was that the top contained chromium while the bottom didn't. Bob Peters told the inquest the paint particles were 'relatively smooth' on top with 'multidirectional scratches'. The bottom layer was 'a rough, dimpled under-surface [which] may indicate the paint had been applied to a concrete, brick or similar surface and possibly exposed to a high wearing environment such as flooring'.

David Royds concluded the paint particles recovered from Janelle all came from the same, unknown location. The immediate assumption is the paint came from where Janelle was killed but Bob Peters says the particles could also have originated from the black plastic or the vehicle which transported Janelle's body. However, his own evidence suggests a strong likelihood these flecks of paint came from a domestic residence, like a concrete floor or patio. If this is the case then this is most likely where Janelle was murdered. Chromium paint is regularly used on hard wearing, outside surfaces to help protect against corrosion and rust. Locating where these green paint particles came from has been a priority for Bob Peters and his team. It's also become a priority for Islander Ray Yager, because he wants to clear his name.

Eleven days after Janelle Patton's murder Ray Yager's white Toyota Landcruiser was searched by two federal agents including crime scene investigator Katrina Gates. During this search they discovered a single paint particle matching the paint found on Janelle. Of all the forensic evidence submitted, it is this paint fleck that excited Coroner Ron Cahill the most. He told the court, 'It could become very, very significant. I say could because there's still a number of issues about it. It's one of the few pieces of evidence that establishes a possible connection with a motor vehicle.'

Raymond Yager is a forty-year-old carpenter who often works in Cambodia. His nickname is 'Tugger' and the day Janelle died he spent at least three hours water-blasting, vacuuming and polishing his truck. Katrina Gates told the court that when she searched his truck it 'was in a very clean and neat condition'. Yager said he was in the habit of cleaning the ute every Sunday to keep away the rust.

Two days after Janelle's murder Ray Yager opened the doors of Burnt Pine Travel to ask about flights to Perth. At the time there was only one talking point on the island—the suspicious and unconfirmed reports of Janelle's murder. While in the office he was asked by the manager, Angela Judd: 'You nowa killar gal, did you?' (You never killed that girl?)

Yager replied: 'Yeh yeh, whatsar word, premeditated?' (Yes yes, what's the word, premeditated?)

Angela Judd told police this was said in a jocular manner and Ray 'Tugger' Yager appeared to be his normal self. She didn't notice any injuries to his body, arms or face.

The next day Raymond Yager departed Norfolk Island on a four o'clock flight to Sydney. He then flew from Sydney to Perth to visit his ex-partner and young son. After landing in Perth he discovered police were interested in his movements and relationship with Janelle. From Perth he contacted the Norfolk Island police station and said he wanted to clear his name. He consented to a police search, provided finger-prints and a DNA sample. He also agreed to be medically examined if police thought he carried any 'suspect injuries'.

Ray Yager's vehicle was extensively searched by police. DNA swabs were taken along with 'hand pickings', which are small objects collected with sterile tweezers. Reference samples of rust and paint were also removed. The interior of the driver's cab was searched and samples taken. The entire tray of the ute was then subjected to a tape lift, which is a common technique to gain evidence from a crime scene or an exhibit. It involves laying clear adhesive tape over a surface then lifting the tape to remove microscopic particles. The tape is then placed on a clear sheet of acetate and searched under a stereomicroscope for particles like hairs, fibres or glass. It is on one section of tape lifted from Raymond Yager's truck that the matching fleck of green paint was found.

It took twelve months for forensic chemist David Royds to reach his conclusion that the paint fleck from Yager's truck 'supports the proposition the vehicle and the deceased, Janelle Patton, are associated'. In the extensive search of Raymond Yager's truck, his flat and separate land holdings, this is the only particle of green paint found. Unlike the particles located on Janelle, which consist of two separate layers, the one lifted from Ray Yager's ute is only one layer: the bottom layer. And it is very small—in fact it is invisible to the naked eye. This is what worries Bob Peters. He describes the paint fleck as '0.25 of a millimetre at its greatest length'. He told the court, 'I can't exclude that the paint particle could have been blown in on the air, carried in the water system or a variety of other methods of getting into that vehicle.'

What the media wanted to know was if other paint particles were washed away during Ray Yager's car cleaning session on Easter Sunday. Coroner Ron Cahill was thinking the same thoughts when he asked Katrina Gates: 'The finding of one particle, it could have been more?'

Gates replied, 'Impossible to answer. We don't know how the paint chip came to be in the back of that utility so it's impossible to answer whether it's a part of more, or one of its own.'

Raymond Yager could only offer one suggestion about the source of the green paint found on the tray of his ute. He told police it could have come from a green-coloured trailer he owned. A sample was taken and tested but it didn't match the paint found on Janelle's body, nor did it match the fleck of paint in Ray Yager's truck.

Bob Peters asked Ray Yager if he had ever transported green concrete. He replied, 'I have no recollection of any green painted-concrete being in contact with my vehicle.'

The police have since combed the island collecting samples of green painted concrete, all to no avail. The police have found plenty of green paint but not the green paint they're after.

———

Raymond 'Tugger' Yager first met Janelle Patton in December 2001 during the South Pacific Games. Norfolk Island was hosting the sporting event and Janelle was doing some casual work for his sister.

Yager told police he regarded Janelle as an attractive and intense person who 'could make mountains out of molehills'. Like most Norfolk men who spent time with Janelle, he was more than happy to pursue her. One drunken night he invited her back to his flat. According to Bob Peters' statement, Yager told Janelle 'she had nothing to worry about and that he was not going to try and "jump her or anything" and Janelle accepted his invitation'. After another beer at his flat at the back of his mother's property, the pair crashed on the bed, Ray Yager in his underwear and Janelle fully clothed. Yager told police that they didn't have sexual intercourse or kiss and cuddle, they just went to sleep.

Janelle's diary entry supports this. For Wednesday, 12 December 2001 she wrote: '1/2 day. Didn't clean Frans. Watched midday movie and foot soaked. Worked at night. Went to Brewery. Govs. Sporties. Crashed at Ray's (no sex).' When Bob Peters read this diary entry out to the courtroom Ron Patton groaned and Carol yelped, crying out, 'Oh, Janelle.' If this was the end result of one's most private scribbles then keeping a diary was a dangerous and embarrassing activity.

When Janelle made the above entry she was still seeing Laurie 'Bucket' Quintal. Bucket himself was named one of the sixteen Persons of Interest and asked on television, 'Did you kill Janelle Patton?' His response was: 'If I did, would I be talking to you?' It was an appearance which deemed him guilty in the eyes of many viewers. When he went to Queensland to visit his daughter, people in shops asked him the same question. He was horrified at the power and reach of television to cast aspersions. He told me he went to Tasmania to claw back a solitude that on Norfolk Island now eludes him.

According to Ray Yager, Janelle asked him not to say anything to 'Bucket' about her staying overnight in his bed. He told her he wouldn't. A few weeks later, in the final days of 2001, Ray Yager and Janelle Patton crossed paths again at the Brewery. The drinking and conversation continued later that night at the Compound—the late night BYO venue among the ruins of the nineteenth century convict prison at Kingston. When Janelle left with a friend she declined Yager's offer to stay on. After her departure and some time later that same night, Raymond Yager decided to pay Janelle a visit. Bob Peters told the inquest: 'He sensed a mutual attraction between Janelle and himself and decided to go to Janelle's home to see her. He stated that when he arrived and walked on to the veranda he heard Janelle call out, "Go away". He stated he realised at that moment he was not welcome and that it was not the right thing to do so he left immediately. He stated that following this incident he made no attempt to contact or see Janelle.'

Laurie 'Bucket' Quintal disputes this evidence. He says when Yager approached Janelle Patton's flat that night he knocked on the door and pretended to be him, Laurie Quintal, 'as a means of trying to get into the flat'. He confronted Yager with this allegation in the RSL Club on Thursday 28 March, three days before Janelle's murder. There was a verbal argument and Raymond Yager denied the accusation. Janelle was also in the club that night and Laurie Quintal says he challenged Yager to go and speak directly with Janelle about the matter of the late night, undesired visit, but he declined.

This incident is an example of the claims and counterclaims which riddle Bob Peters' investigation, because Raymond Yager denies that any conversation of the sort took place with Quintal. He agrees Quintal was at the RSL that night, but that's all. Yager says Quintal walked past him and said something unpleasant, to the effect of 'older guys being better than younger guys or something like that'. There is only one thing both men agree on in regard to this frosty evening at the RSL. It was the last time either saw Janelle Patton alive.

Bob Peters says 'initial concern was raised about Raymond Yager due to his alleged uninvited attendance at Janelle's flat, the thorough cleaning of his motor vehicle on 31 March 2002 and his departure from Norfolk Island within three days after Janelle's death. These concerns were increased by the finding of the particle of green paint in the tray of his utility.'

But Yager's story and his loose comments at the travel agency are perhaps more promising than the insubstantial circumstantial evidence against him. By itself, the fleck of green paint found in Raymond Yager's truck is at the same time confusing, compelling and weak. As the coroner said, it is the only piece of evidence linking the body of Janelle Patton to a vehicle. But how it got there is a mystery and at this stage cannot be proved one way or the other.

Bob Peters told the coroner the paint 'standing by its own' was not a link to any involvement in the crime. The coroner then asked if Yager's truck could have been used by somebody else. Bob Peters said that wasn't possible based on Ray Yager's account of his movements on the day of Janelle's murder. However, Yager's account is riddled with holes. Yager told police that Mark 'Oot' McCoy and his girlfriend paid him a visit mid morning on Easter Sunday. Yager said he then went and helped Oot do some rubbing and sanding on the hull of a boat. In separate police interviews ten days later, neither Mark McCoy nor his girlfriend mentioned visiting Raymond Yager's house or his presence at the boatshed. Bob Peters came to two conclusions about this fairly dramatic inconsistency. Either poor memory was to blame, with one day being confused for another day (a common occurrence on Norfolk Island) or there had been an attempt at a false alibi. 'If that is the case,' said Bob Peters, 'it has been a generally loose and clumsy effort to do so.'

What can be confirmed independently is that Raymond Yager drove to Paw Paw's Pump Shed and purchased car cleaning products with his credit card at 12.39 pm. This is near the time of Janelle's disappearance. There are no reports of Yager being seen on Rooty Hill Road and police have confirmed he made inquiries about travelling to Perth in the week before Janelle's murder. Bob Peters agrees there *may* have been many more green paint particles in his truck before it was water-blasted and that at some stage Yager may have placed an unknown object on the tray which was the source of the mysterious green paint. Alternatively, the particle may have been the only one which ever existed. Bob Peters doesn't know; nor, says Yager, does he.

Despite the mysterious paint fleck and the 'ambiguities regarding his movements and associations' on the day of Janelle's murder, Bob Peters concluded Raymond Yager couldn't be linked to the crime. He said Ray Yager had continually cooperated with the police investigation, 'in some cases at his own initiative'. When I rang Ray's mother, Anne Watson, she accused the cops of 'hanging my son out to dry' but she also said he 'needs to learn from this'. This last reference was to his comments in the travel agency which Anne Watson thought somewhat foolish.

Other than the green paint fleck, the other major clue revealed by police and the one they go back to time and time again is the four by three metre sheet of black plastic. Bob Peters feels guilty that he keeps sending the fingerprint specialists back to the lab to study these muddied, overlapping partial palm prints, eight of the ten prints unidentified.

Despite a time-consuming finger and palm printing exercise which recorded the prints of 1311 locals, only one match has been made, to local man Stevie Cochrane. After extensive follow-up investigations and search warrants, police said there was nothing to indicate Steve Cochrane was connected to the murder of Janelle Patton. Neither the police nor Cochrane could determine when, or under what circumstances, his prints were placed on the plastic. In my first interview with Bob Peters he said 'our interest in him has lessened'.

Obviously the killer of Janelle Patton had fast and easy access to the sheet of plastic. Determining where it came from could lead police to where Janelle was murdered. Identifying more of the prints on the plastic could lead them to the killer or an accomplice. Through a series of interviews the investigation team arrived at one explanation. It involves the company Roadstone Constructions, its then employee Terence Jope and one of its work vehicles.

Bob Peters spent considerable time outlining a convoluted theory to the court. He explained how a large sheet of plastic once seen in the back of a Toyota ute driven by Terry Jope may have been the one used to move Janelle Patton. But the evidence was circumstantial and speculative. The best the police could do was trace this particular sheet of plastic to the last weekend of January 2002—two months before Janelle's death. After that it was anyone's guess where it may have gone and who could have used it.

As a self-employed builder, Terry Jope handles pieces of 'black polythene' all the time and he can't imagine how anyone can readily recognise one from another. His property and truck were extensively searched, swabbed and tested, with negative results. Police could make no link between Terry Jope and the crime. Nor are his fingerprints on the piece of plastic found around Janelle's body. But Terry Jope's daily access to builders' plastic is not the only reason he was named a person of interest.

———

Janelle Patton met Terry Jope through her friend Steve Borg. It was February 2002—one month before her death—and Steve Borg was having a 'roof raising party' at his new, partially built house. Steve Borg has often claimed the black plastic came from his building site but he has no evidence to support this and police can't find any either. The small party consisted of a bunch of people drinking beer and eating chips under the new roof. The builder was Terry Jope and he was knocking back a few beers like the rest of the crowd.

A couple of weeks later Janelle ran into Terry Jope again, this time at Mariah's restaurant and bar. It is here, readers may recall, that Janelle was introduced to Jope's mate Brent Wilson, the man who in the final weeks of her life became 'the lover in waiting'. Terry Jope was dining with his wife Angela and Brent Wilson. When Janelle entered the restaurant with a friend Terry Jope said to Brent, 'Here's a nice girl worth getting to know,' and he called her over and introduced the pair.

During the inquest, Bob Peters told the court Janelle had some 'undetermined concerns' about Terry Jope shortly before her death. This is based on a third-hand account and one Jope dismisses. He denies ever being 'at loggerheads with Janelle', or that 'she was afraid of me'. Terry regarded Janelle as a 'new friend', a person he had invited into his house; they had played cards and drunk beer together, and she had once cooked Angela Jope a birthday dinner.

Terry Jope is built like a builder. He is well over six feet tall and of strong part-Polynesian build. His mother is a Norfolk Islander (a Christian) and his father a New Zealander, which is where he was born. The forty-four year old has lived on Norfolk Island for twenty-four years.

In October 2004 he was a candidate for one of nine positions on the local Assembly. Bob Peters wondered what it might mean for his next briefing to the Norfolk Legislative Assembly if, as a Person of Interest, he was elected to office. 'It could be awkward,' he said to me in his typically droll manner.

Stephen Gibbs, a journalist with the *Sydney Morning Herald*, rang Terry Jope for a comment about his dual status as Person of Interest and potential politician. Jope replied, 'This Person of Interest thing is totally finished. I'd rather not have anything to do with it, frankly. I've tried to put it behind me and I know the people of Norfolk have. They realise what absolute crap it was.'

The island's 1252 voters didn't agree. Of the fourteen people who ran for office, Terry Jope achieved the lowest number of votes in the proportional system (112) and just 2.2 per cent of the overall vote. He came a distant second last and was not elected. With this, Bob Peters breathed a sigh of relief.

When I spoke with Terry Jope he was pissed off with how the *Sydney Morning Herald* quote had come across. He confirmed its accuracy but claimed the context was wrong. The reference to 'absolute crap' was not about the inquiry or the pursuit of justice, but, he said, about the court process of naming people who had no chance to defend themselves. He called the procedure 'totally inappropriate', and was horrified that he had been named.

'I am sick of it,' he told me over the phone. 'It has changed the way I think of the law. Now I have my name plastered all over the papers and people keep calling—like yourself—and I can't answer any of this in a court. It can smash my life to smithereens and there is nothing I can do about it so I just go *stumm*.'

'Did the inquest damage your run for office?' I asked Terry.

'Yeah, it probably did,' he replied, 'but I have to move on and try and put it behind me.'

After declaring his political intentions in a long letter to the *Norfolk Islander* Terry Jope was criticised by one anonymous local for being unable to speak Norfolk and not being a 'real islander'. But it was one piece of unfavourable evidence documented during the coronial inquest that damaged his character and made his candidacy for office audacious given half the electorate were female. It involves Terry Jope's reputation as a 'consummate womaniser'. At this he laughs and says, 'All my women friends have said yeah, Terry, we wish.'

After Bob Peters outlined Terry Jope's tenuous link with the mysterious piece of black plastic, he went off on a long tangent, which at the time of the inquest had me wondering what he was up to. It was another familiar island story about strange happenings after dark, and alcohol consumption. It involved Terry Jope and a schoolteacher called Leonie Newton. Bob Peters explained that sometime in April 2003 Leonie Newton woke up between '2 and 3 o'clock in the morning' and found Terry Jope standing next to her bed, 'within touching distance'. The two were not strangers—they had known each other for seven years. For some time Terry Jope had been trying to sell her a house but negotiations had fallen through. During that time he had turned up several times in what she called a 'flirtatious' manner after drinking. On one occasion she explained his size and presence late at night made her feel uncomfortable. He assured her he would never hurt her.

Bob Peters says Leonie Newton's first reaction on seeing Terry Jope standing in her bedroom in the early hours of the morning was 'panic', because she didn't know who it was. When she realised it was Terry Jope she tried to remain calm. Bob Peters read to the now attentive courtroom the following:

> She remained in the bed and Terence Jope sat on her bed. She stated she could not judge if he was sober as she was not particularly sober herself. She stated she tried not to demand from him what he was doing because she was trying to keep the situation calm. She stated he was talking about his relationship with his wife and his beliefs that there was an Australian Government conspiracy to take over Norfolk Island . . . She stated that Terence Jope never actually said why he was in her house and in her bedroom uninvited. She stated she did not want to ask because she was trying to keep the situation calm and in control. She stated that Terence Jope was in her bedroom for a minimum of one hour and a maximum of two hours . . . She stated she did not tell him to leave but for some reason he just decided to go . . . she had not given Terence Jope permission to enter her house or enter her bedroom that night. However she was adamant she did not want any Police action taken about this incident and was making the statement on the understanding that it would not be used in any way to take action against him for entering her house that night.

Bob Peters told the court this was an example of how 'over an extended period of time [Terry Jope] displayed a propensity for behaviour towards women which causes serious concern'.

Of course Terry Jope is not the only man guilty of sliding open Norfolk Island doors in the moonlight. He just got caught out. I heard half a dozen stories of similar behaviour over the years, including one where a woman heard a guitar being played and walked into her living room to find a man strumming on the lounge, clearly drunk and most definitely uninvited. Nor is being a 'consummate womaniser' a tag unique to one man—many women on the island apply it to local men and it's a reversible tag. Sex and alcohol are two of Norfolk's many social traditions, as is never locking the front door.

Terry Jope's movements during the day Janelle died are supported by his second wife, Angela Keogh-Jope, who says they spent the day together between 11 am and 6 pm, except for a period between one and two o'clock when she went shopping.

Terry Jope says he's offended by any suggestion that his wife might be providing an alibi for him. He told me he went to the lookout during Janelle's memorial service in an honest attempt to play detective. 'I was hoping to see somebody who may be acting strangely, a look of guilt or something like that. A new friend of ours had been murdered, a person we had welcomed into our home and sometimes people do revisit the scene, you know, they may have a look of guilt on their face and that shows up. I just thought I'd have a better chance of recognising somebody looking strange than the police who don't know the island as well. I'm not trying to big-note myself, I just thought I could help.'

Bob Peters concluded his rather detailed evidence about Terry Jope in the same way he did for every person of interest. He said there was 'no factual or forensic evidence' to connect Terry Jope to the death of Janelle Patton.

He then paused, downed some water, cleared his throat and started on the next person on his list.

CHAPTER 18

NAMING NAMES

BEING NORFOLK Island, the inquest coexisted in close proximity with
the travel industry. Tourist buses would swing past the courtroom every
few hours and elderly travellers would wave to the media camped on the
lawn. God knows what the drivers were telling their passengers. A few
tourists even managed to break free of their busy schedules and nab a
seat in what was the only free show in town. During one adjournment
two grey-haired spinsters driving a rental car stopped me on Quality
Row and asked if they could listen in.

In the absence of any local news coverage it was a reasonable
question. A staff memo at the community-run but government-
controlled radio station instructed presenters not to mention the inquest.
The morning news bulletins, which are little more than community
notices, carried not the slightest whisper of what was on everyone's lips.
Once the inquest was underway the radio 'news' didn't even mention it
was on. Instead, the hourly 'news and information' was the same repetitive mix of sports notices, shipping updates, museum hours, the lost
and found segment and the weather. It was clear community notices
didn't extend to murder inquests, even if half the population was being
mentioned in court.

Showing considerable initiative, the two elderly women who had
approached me on Quality Row sat in wonderment in the far corner of
the courtroom. They nestled their handbags under their chins and
clasped the leather handles as tightly as a roller-coaster bar. At the first

opportunity they took early retirement, declaring it to be both sordid and confusing. 'So many names,' one said, looking sideways. The picture emerging from beneath Detective Peters' magnifying glass jarred with the tourist tales they'd been sold. They decided the community was better viewed from afar rather than from within. Together they trotted off towards the maritime museum to see the historic bits and bobs salvaged from the wreck of the *Sirus*.

By day two locals were asking why they had to turn to the Australian press to get coverage of what was happening on their own island. In desperation, a call was made to Tom Lloyd to ask if he could publish a special midweek edition of the *Norfolk Islander*. He said he couldn't because, like many other Islanders, he was in the courtroom trying to understand the complex web emerging from Bob Peters' evidence.

By mid morning on day three Bruce Walker, manager of the Norfolk Island Tourism board, had reappeared resplendent in a Hawaiian shirt, complete with name badge. He was not there to offer sympathy but to drum up tourism stories. He had been cock-a-hoop at the concentration of media on the island since meeting reporters at the airport where he handed out his business card. Now he was trying to persuade TV reporters to do travel stories before they went home. The timing of his appearance was shortly before the gruesome details of Janelle's injuries were read out.

Bruce Walker was on the fringes of the courtroom, lingering around the front steps and back corridor. He gave me a nod and said, 'You gotta turn a positive.' It was more than a lack of tact. It was shameless. The tourism board is government run and his presence suggested only one thing—the unsolved murder of Janelle Patton was a great opportunity for Norfolk tourism to profit. This sat uneasily with the government's own position of remaining at arm's length from the 'judicial process'. As so often happens, one arm of the Norfolk Island government was oblivious to the other.

Inside the court, Bob Peters continued giving his evidence and it was becoming increasingly apparent some of the sixteen people named were actually of little interest. They were on the list because the community nominated them as individuals who *should* be Persons of Interest. Rightly or wrongly, Bob Peters was now reporting back to the island about what he knew, about what was true, what was spurious and what didn't make any sense at all—which was considerable.

Some people were named for more innocuous reasons than others and it was clear the criteria for getting on the list correlated with suspected motives, those being a personal attack, a sexual attack or a random attack. Because police had failed to narrow down the motive, they couldn't narrow down the number of people on the list. Anyone who'd spent time with Janelle was a potential starter. So was anyone with a history of friction with her, hence the three members of the Menghetti family and, by association, Robyn Murdoch—the woman who replaced Janelle in Jap Menghetti's life and eventually married him on a white sand beach of Rarotonga.

Given the animosity between Janelle and Jap's eldest daughter, Dana Menghetti, people weren't surprised when she was named. Dana told police they generally tried to avoid each other and agreed the two never got on. But they did live together for many months. In a letter to her parents Janelle wrote: 'For some strange reason, last night, Dana asked me to help with her English essay. Thank God it was Romeo & Juliet based on obsessive love! Because at least I had some idea!'

This last line is a reference to Janelle's love for Dana's father, which was also cause of great tension. During the investigation police heard varying accounts of Dana and Janelle pushing each other at the Brewery. One anonymous source claimed Dana Menghetti was 'prone to violence when arguing with people'. Again police couldn't verify this report or the motive of the person who made the claim. In Dana's defence Bob Peters said, 'Janelle felt more resentment for Dana Menghetti than Dana felt for her.'

At the end of the inquest I asked Dana Menghetti if she wanted to make any comment. She looked astounded at the idea and quickly returned to her office in Burnt Pine. Unfortunately for Dana, she features prominently as a model in Norfolk's 'Beguiling Isle' travel brochure. It was launched a few weeks before the inquest and it is from one of these shots that the media lifted her photograph.

Dana's uncle Charles Menghetti made the list because he was the brother of Jap and a friend of Sue Fieldes, who Janelle alleged was having an affair with Charles. After Janelle's failed tenancy in Charles Menghetti's house the two rarely saw each other. A number of different people dobbed in Charles Menghetti on the basis of a fire in his backyard on the afternoon of Janelle's murder. Bob Peters said, 'The possible inference that the fire may have been used to destroy evidence has not been substantiated.' A search of Charles Menghetti's house and property revealed nothing suspicious.

Less than two weeks after the murder, another 'community source' rang police to say Janelle had been in the Leagues Club in early 2002 and Charles Menghetti had 'allegedly approached [Janelle], pulled her hair and said words to the effect: "Stop this shit or I'll sort you out."'

Beyond this unsubstantiated allegation, which was only given on the condition that the informer would remain anonymous, Bob Peters said there was no indication of 'ongoing animosity between him and Janelle'. Bob Peters told the court that, like many people on the island that day, Charles Menghetti 'has no one who can account for his where-abouts and movements approximately between 11.30 am and mid afternoon on Sunday 31 March 2002'.

When I spoke to Charles 'Spindles' Menghetti he was brief. He said he found out he'd been named a Person of Interest in his kitchen while watching the Australian TV news. 'I nearly fell off my feet. My son rang me and asked what the hell was going on. Why wasn't I told? I should have been told.' Like the others named he was furious about not being informed. He said he was disappointed 'with everyone's behaviour'—the police, first and foremost, but also the actions 'of my kin,' he said. As for the police, he didn't waste too many words: 'I grew up to respect the police but not anymore, they can get fucked.' This fitted with his overall tone on the telephone. 'Just make sure you get it right,' he said at the end of the call. The conversation lasted less than two minutes, so there wasn't much to get wrong.

From day one there had been a lot of Dem Tull slander about the Menghetti family and I encountered several men who seemed to bristle at the mention of Jap Menghetti. I've even had it suggested I should look at Francis Menghetti, the father of Jap and Charles who died of old age in 2003. In fact the entire time I was on Norfolk Island I was constantly astounded at who had what to say about certain people. It is of course circular, and Robyn Murdoch and Jap Menghetti can give as good as they get.

Everyone knew Janelle hassled Jap and everyone knew the saga of their break-up. Everyone also knew Jap was now with Robyn Murdoch. It was enough of a love triangle for some locals to make all manner of wild allegations. Bob Peters emphasised there was no evidence to support the gossip. It's clear Robyn Murdoch is not well liked in some corners of island society. I realised just how much when people rolled their lips around her name in spite. One island politician said to me, 'And what do you think of Ms Murder-ock?'

To understand why is to understand Robyn Murdoch's sacking from her position as CEO of the island administration. The Norfolk Island public service is a work force of about two hundred people. If it votes as one bloc, it can deliver considerable political muscle. When Ivens 'Toon' Buffett left the position of CEO to enter government, he was replaced by Robyn Murdoch. She was employed from Queensland and her task under the then Ninth Assembly was to bring about reform. She set about implementing a change agenda with gusto in 2001. As an outsider it took her a while to realise the quicksand she was in.

Robyn Murdoch says she found savings of up to one million dollars but when she advocated cuts the political reaction was chilly. As she continued to push, so did others—to get her out of the job. According to Robyn, when she approached one member of parliament about how much money could be saved, she was told, 'And what do you want me to do about that?' In the end, her growing opponents within the administration and government won out. Her three-year contract was paid out after eighteen months in the job. It was another case of the island simply being unable to work with anyone from the outside world. She would have left Norfolk except her relationship with Jap Menghetti was underway. And despite all the friction at Kingston she was starting to enjoy a slice of Norfolk Island from the tranquillity of Jap Menghetti's 100-acre farm, just like Janelle Patton before her.

Then there is the naming of Susan Fieldes, the former friend turned enemy who still feels great resentment and bitterness towards Janelle. The subsequent assault charge and AVO following the skirmish at the Sports and Workers Club meant she was always going to be named by Bob Peters, although the detective found no evidence of any 'direct personal contact between the two women' in the eighteen months leading up to Janelle's murder.

The possibility of having a sexual motive was another criterion for being named a Person of Interest. Any lover, former lover or aspiring lover was as good as on the list, provided they were on the island on the day of the crime. Hence twelve of the sixteen named are men, like Rodney 'Moose' Menzies, who worked at the airport and was also a contract 'grass slasher' who emptied septic tanks on the weekends. According to secondhand information denied by Menzies, he once placed his hand on Janelle's knee. Hardly an offence, but enough to bring him to the attention of an investigation struggling for clues. Janelle once told a friend that Moose sometimes gave her the 'willies' but said she wasn't afraid of him.

Bob Peters found a number of contradictions in Moose's account of his social relationship with Janelle. According to evidence from Brent Wilson, Moose had 'invited her home for a cup of coffee' and approached her several times 'while sunbaking at Kingston'. Bob Peters told the court 'anecdotal information' given to the investigation team suggested Moose was a man 'known to stalk women. However it is stressed that no direct source for these allegations and no factual evidence to support these allegations has been uncovered.' Again the community was nominating to the investigation team individuals who they considered *should* be of interest to the police.

Another man named, largely on information from members of the community, was Michael Prentice, who goes by the nickname 'Boo'. Michael 'Boo' Prentice is the father of modern tourism on Norfolk Island. He owns Pine Tree Tours and any visitor to the island will see his white buses plying the roads of Norfolk night and day. He offers all manner of tours and events, convict light and sound shows, poems by Archie Bigg under the moonlight . . . He is a powerful and successful figure in the tourism game and his reputation is crucial to his continued profit and success. Not surprisingly, he was furious after being included on the list of Persons of Interest. He even made inquiries about suing Bob Peters and the Australian Federal Police for defamation. But a close reading of the evidence against him suggests very little except for some damaging and anonymous information by fellow locals, including the claim 'he does not know the meaning of the word no'. This information came from an employee of the Castaway Hotel, where Janelle worked until her death. Prentice had made calls to the hotel looking for Janelle, and the anonymous employee warned Janelle against forming 'any close relationship' with the 52-year-old business-man for this very reason.

In January 2002, Janelle's diary contains references to Boo Prentice (who Janelle called 'Bu'). She notes phone calls to her flat, including a 1 am call, watching TV, meeting for a drink and one dinner date. In her entry for Tuesday 29 January, for example, she wrote: 'Went to Francis's [Menghetti] for a coffee & to drop off some plun [the Norfolk word for bananas]. Saw Bucket @ Foodies—invited me out to tea (chicken & salad). Basically only wanted a root so I left. Went down to Bu's for a coffee after he rang. Home by 1ish.'

According to Michael 'Boo' Prentice's police statement, Janelle downloaded her relationship problems onto him in January 2002. She spoke about Jap Menghetti and Laurie 'Bucket' Quintal. It is during this time she alleged Laurie Quintal had 'attempted to choke her' after 'refusing to have sex with him'. (Quintal denies this allegation.) Michael Prentice said that Janelle didn't appear to be threatened by Quintal and 'appeared to have him under control'.

The investigation team was informed much later on of a so-called relationship between Janelle and Michael Prentice. Again, this proved untrue. Police found nothing beyond the social contact of early 2002. Michael Prentice told police he had invited Janelle back to his room at Governors Lodge but there had been no sexual contact. Police have found no evidence to suggest the pair were ever intimate, and nor does Janelle's diary support the proposition. On the day of Janelle's murder Michael Prentice says he was watching rugby on TV at his mother's house and at no time did he leave the house. The first he heard of Janelle's death was the next day, on April the first.

Of the sixteen Persons of Interest Stevie Cochrane is the only one with a forensic link to Janelle's body. The carpenter's palm prints match two of the prints found on the black plastic. But Cochrane is also the only person Bob Peters has ever admitted to no longer actively pursuing.

Stevie Cochrane and Janelle Patton didn't know each other and no other forensic evidence has been found that links him to the crime. It's not known how his prints got on the plastic but it appears police had concluded the prints were placed there innocently, as part of his trade. Cochrane's work mates were also fingerprinted in the hope the building site where this plastic may have been used could be identified all to no avail.

Others on the list were named because the community regarded them as unsavoury, and therefore suspect. One was Andrew Ian Rowe, a 32-year-old TEP from New Zealand who was working as a carpenter. Like the locals, he too had a nickname—Buzz. He came to the attention of police thanks to the pervasive power of Dem Tull. It was said he had a reputation as a 'voyeur' and 'potential pervert'. There was no documented evidence of sexually aberrant behaviour but Bob Peters did tell the coronial inquest he once observed Buzz in action; Andrew 'Buzz' Rowe, he said, 'was prone to sit and stare at attractive young women to the point where he made them feel uncomfortable and on 22 August, 2002, I had occasion to speak to him about this practice'.

Andrew Rowe was nominated as 'acting strangely' at the tennis courts on the day of Janelle's murder and despite being interviewed by police only nine days later, struggled to recall his movements on that Sunday. He didn't know Janelle Patton and there was no evidence he had ever tried to approach her. Bob Peters described him as an 'insular person who made no apparent close friends of either gender while living on Norfolk Island'. His 'solitary lifestyle' and 'generally vague nature' made it difficult 'to establish exactly where he was or what he was doing at any given time on 31 March 2002'. Police executed a search of his house and car and found nothing. When Buzz departed Norfolk Island for the last time in October 2003, he was caught at the airport carrying a knife. It was sent to forensics in Canberra but it did not match Janelle's injuries.

Fisherman Kim 'Frenzy' Friend was nominated 'as a person who may be of interest to police' by his former mate, David Fraser. Of all sixteen Persons of Interest, Kim Friend gets the least number of pages in Bob Peters' report—barely three. But his background story says much about how the investigation into Janelle Patton's death is also an investigation into the lives of many others.

David Fraser sticks by his story and says he believes what he saw on Easter Sunday 2002. He told police he passed Kim Friend driving his Toyota Landcrusier on Taylors Road around 11.45 in the morning. In the cab of the truck was a woman he believed to be Janelle Patton, along with another male.

Kim Friend denied this and said it was a case of mistaken identity. The people sitting next to him were two visiting friends from Queensland. This was confirmed by police when they questioned the visitors, who also corroborated Kim Friend's account of his movements that day.

Bob Peters dismissed the sighting and told the inquest he had 'no reason to doubt David Fraser's motive for reporting the sighting of Janelle Patton in the company of Kim Friend [but] I have found no factual evidence to support that claim'. He then cleared Kim Friend of any involvement in Janelle Patton's murder but before he went further the coroner interjected and asked if there was any animosity between the two men. Bob Peters replied. 'Only anecdotally, Your Worship. I understand there is some ill-feeling and bad blood going back a number of years between the two.'

This ill-feeling wasn't spelt out at the inquest but Islanders knew about it because the ill-feeling had been spelt out ten years earlier, in the very same courtroom and it was more than anecdotal—it was on the public record. In 1993 Kim 'Frenzy' Friend was charged with rape. It is one of the few rape cases to be tried on Norfolk Island. The woman Kim Friend was charged with raping was the then girlfriend of David Fraser—Olivia Christian-Bailey.

Like so many rape cases, this one came down to a question of consent. There were no witnesses; it was one person's word against the other. The court transcript is a blunt account of what allegedly took place and makes for uneasy reading. On a fine Sunday evening in March 1993, Kim Friend drove Olivia Christian-Bailey home after dinner at David Fraser's house. At the Supreme Court trial, Olivia Christian-Bailey said that during the drive he told her:

> 'You can either suck me off or fuck me down at the guide hall,' and then I said to him, 'It's the wrong time of the month,' because I didn't want anything to do with, you know, anything sexual to happen between me and him and he then said to me, 'I've worked in a meat factory with blood up to my eyeballs' . . . and then he said 'How would you like a big fat cork sticking right up in your cunt so, fill you right up and make you scream and cry,' and he said, 'What do you reckon about that?' And I said, 'No, I don't want to.'

According to Olivia Christian-Bailey's evidence, Kim Friend drove past her house and towards Kingston. He then stopped the car, turned off the headlights, lifted up her top and started sucking her breasts. As she ran from the car he chased her and pulled her down a bank where he wrestled her to the ground, and this is where she alleged the rape took place. She told the court: 'His penis entered my vagina and he couldn't get it in so he asked me "help me put it in," and I said "no, no" and then he grabbed, I think it was my right hand, and he made me touch it.'

Olivia Christian-Bailey testified that after Friend ejaculated 'he sort of pulled me gently up the hill and I hopped in his car'. Kim Friend then dropped her off at home and said, 'Don't tell Frase'.

Kim Friend's defence was that the sex was consensual. He told the court Olivia made the first move, that she placed her hand on his, an action which prompted him to ask: 'What about a quickie for the road?' According to Friend's evidence, she replied, 'It'll have to be a quickie cause I've got to get home.' Under-cross examination Kim Friend admitted to the 'meatworks' comment and said it was voiced in a jesting tone.

On 23 November 1993, the jury of twelve Islanders decided to believe Kim Friend's account of the night he had sex with his good mate's girlfriend, and acquitted him of rape. Olivia Christian-Bailey has since left Norfolk Island. Kim Friend and David Fraser no longer speak to each other.

Back at the coronial inquest where none of this was outlined, Coroner Ron Cahill said to Bob Peters somewhat cryptically: 'But there could be some motivation for the David Fraser approach due to some animosity.' Bob Peters, who knew about the case, replied, 'That's possible,' but he repeated his view that there was nothing malicious in David Fraser's sighting.

When I spoke to David Fraser he was mighty pissed off. I wanted to confirm he stood behind what he had told the police, which he did, but in the process he delivered more than a sermon. He said, 'You listen to me. I don't want anything to fucking do with it. The cops didn't believe me and if you mention my name in any fucking article, or paper, or anything like that, I'm going to sue your fucking arse off.' When I said it was all on the public record and I just wanted his point of view, he repeated his earlier threat and said, 'I don't give two fucks—they didn't believe me and I don't care what you want.' He then hung up.

The last person on the list of sixteen was Greg Magri—Janelle's confidant and one of her closest friends. Greg Magri made the list on the basis of two reported sightings—one of them by a relative—of his black Honda Civic on or near Rooty Hill Road between 11.30 am and 12.30 pm. He denies this and told police it may have been one of the other two black Honda Civics on the island, including one owned by Andrew 'Buzz' Rowe. The owners of these vehicles also denied being on the road at those times of the day, which left Bob Peters back where he started—with another reported sighting which couldn't be verified.

What can be confirmed is that Greg Magri was at a family function at the restaurant Branka House from 12.30 pm till shortly before three. If he killed Janelle Patton then he had only thirty minutes to grab her off Rooty Hill Road, commit the crime, get cleaned up and make the family lunch. It didn't make sense but then no one ever said this investigation made any sense. Bob Peters was just reporting back to the community what it had told him.

Greg Magri was shocked and saddened that he was named. Like the others, he was also furious that he was given no notification before the inquest. He told me, 'All that's come out of this are sixteen innocent people have been named who can't defend themselves.'

Greg Magri is one of the few people I spoke to who showed concern for the damage the inquest inflicted on Janelle Patton's character. He called the hearing a 'betrayal of Janelle's good side'. He said, 'We didn't hear about Janelle's bubbly spirit, her fun side.' He then bemoaned the nature of the media coverage in reference to Janelle's relationship with Dana Menghetti: 'How many times have you called someone a cow? And to see it highlighted like that, like that's the only thing you ever said.'

Greg Magri says he was friends with Janelle right up until the last day and reports of a verbal argument between the pair three days before her death were probably correct but overblown. 'I was often telling her to bugger off, but I loved her for who she was. Sure, she annoyed people, but not to the extent of that kind of violence. When I heard the news of her death I asked myself, what has she done? What has she done to herself?'

The idea Janelle Patton was killed because she knew something has always been included in the list of possible motives. It was offered by members of the community from day one as a plausible explanation for her death. This theory usually relates to illicit drugs and involves Janelle Patton being a possible whistleblower who had to be silenced. The drugs involved are marijuana or amphetamines and this theory dovetails into another Dem Tull story without substance—that Janelle was tortured. This suggestion came shortly after details of Janelle's injuries leaked from hospital where the autopsy was performed. Bruises around Janelle's wrists, the terrible wounds to her right shin . . . according to Dem Tull these injuries indicated 'restraint marks' and signs of applied and controlled violence, something the autopsy report rejects.

When Brent Wilson gave evidence relating to his phone conversation with Janelle twelve hours before her death, he was asked specifically about Janelle's position on illicit drugs. Wilson told the court he regarded Janelle as 'anti-drugs' and not involved in any drug scene. This is corroborated by all who knew Janelle. She was a drinker and smoker, but didn't dabble in other substances. Graham Rhead asked Brent Wilson if Janelle ever mentioned she was going to blow the cover on people who 'were growing marijuana or something like that'. Brent said, 'Not that I can remember, no.'

A couple of minutes later, Coroner Ron Cahill tackled the issue again but came up blank. The coroner described Janelle as a 'fairly determined and almost obsessive personality'. Brent agreed and said, 'If there was something that annoyed her she was inclined to confront the problem . . . or definitely confront the issues.'

'So in looking for a motive for her murder we have to explore these sorts of things. Do you feel if she had information that someone was doing something that she regarded as totally inappropriate, for example, dealing in drugs on the island, she would be the sort of person that would go and do something about it?'

'Definitely, if it affected her or her friends. I can imagine they [sic] going and taking stuff into their own hands.'

'She never mentioned any mission that she had in that respect to drugs?'

'No,' said Brent, 'not that I can recall.'

Throughout the hearing the Pattons remained stoic, running on pride and raw courage. The family always planned to read a Victim Impact Statement at its conclusion. Carol, Ron and Mark all drafted individual versions and together they melded the best paragraphs into a four page statement. It was a final act for Janelle. She could no longer defend herself; it was now up to the family to guard her spirit, which it did, unflinchingly in the face of a barrage of negatives about Janelle's life.

Carol Patton spoke for everyone when she read to the court from the Victim Impact Statement:

> What sort of person would inflict these horrendous injuries on another human being? We cannot begin to imagine. To date there has been no indication of any remorse for this despicable act from the perpetrator. This was a brutal, savage and vicious crime. If a person shows no remorse for a crime, in all probability this person believes that their action was justifiable. In all probability they have some sick sense of pride that they have avoided detection to date.

Carol Patton's reading of the impact statement was exquisite and it nearly brought the court to tears. It's not often a courtroom is captivated. It's a pretty tough environment. Lawyers have heard it all before, the worst of the worst of humanity is fleshed out, the business of the court rarely stops toiling for an outcome, in the face of terrifying evidence papers are ruffled, lawyers whisper, people shuffle, the gallery coughs and splutters—life goes on, but Carol Patton steadied herself and she nailed her audience from the first sentence.

For the next ten minutes she delivered a legal eulogy for her only daughter, a parent fighting to salvage her child from the court of public opinion, doing what any parent would do, defending their kid in life and death. It captivated all, it stopped the court in its tracks. Carol delivered the statement in her best, clearest, schoolteacher voice. She tripped up only twice. Coroner Ron Cahill rested his chin on his hands and watched from the bench. Graham Rhead, sitting next to Carol at the bar table, stared straight ahead at a large satellite map of the island on the wall. Bob Peters sat to the side on a black chair, head hanging down, his hands clasped between his legs. The media took notes then stopped and simply listened. It was a moment of enormous power, a small victory over the person who killed Janelle. The statement over-powered the grisly details of her death and became the story of the day. It was powerful and compelling, an argument for cameras in court and an argument for Victim Impact Statements as a necessary adjunct to the character assassination and pain the court procedure inevitably inflicts.

———

In his closing remarks the coroner declared he was 'frustrated'. This was one of the most violent homicides he had seen in his thirty years in the law and the 'investigation team and myself need a break'—meaning a new lead, new information, anything to keep the wheels turning. Ron Cahill then focused on motive, which remains one of the great riddles in this case. What he had to say was significant, although it was lost in the avalanche of gossip that followed. The coroner said not one of the sixteen people named by Bob Peters 'stands out as having a driving motive of hatred to inflict such a frenetic attack in an uncontrolled fashion . . . Is it because someone felt so passionately angry with her?' he asked. 'Is it because she was about to expose something and the attack took place for the purposes of protection of someone doing something wrong?'

'The inquest at this stage is closed,' announced the coroner. 'It would make me a happy man, not only just to come back to beautiful Norfolk Island which the media have no doubt shared, but also to bring a resolution to this tragic affair. It's closed but still open.'

That afternoon Bob Peters' 227-page statement went on sale. It was sold to the media on a pre-ordered basis for fifty dollars a copy. Overnight it was discounted and sold to Islanders for five dollars. I remember standing on the landing of the Commonwealth admini-strator's office when the man himself, Grant Tambling, walked up the stairs. In his hands were a couple of court registry receipts which he was folding into the breast pocket of his shirt. He greeted me with a large grin.

'Just picked up a few copies of Bob's statement,' he said. 'Five dollars a pop.'

'You're joking.'

He flashed the receipts at me. He looked like a man who'd scored an unbelievable bargain. 'Just went down and ordered them. They're going like hotcakes. There's a bit of a waiting list.'

Whether this charitable act of discounting was always planned I don't know. But I went down and got a few more copies anyway. The first pages of my fifty dollar edition had been photocopied at an angle and were missing the first words of every sentence. Quality service is not always Norfolk Island's forte. The registry kindly deducted the costs from my initial payment.

The story was that David Buffett, the police minister, decided to sell the AFP statement for the price of hot chips in the name of justice. It was a government-sponsored literature drive creating a demand the registry photocopier struggled to cope with. There was a constant flow of cheery people picking up copies, or ringing to place orders. Stacks of statements sat on the front desk, each with personal receipts clipped to the front page. This went on for days and made Bob Peters the island's top-selling author. The demand was understandable: the inside account of the Patton investigation is a gripping read and there was no better teaser than the coverage of the inquest itself. The stories published and broadcast in the mainland media over the week made locals thirsty for the complete yarn. They wanted to read more about their mates or, if they were unlucky enough, about themselves. It made Bob Peters more widely read than Colleen McCullough, although her whodunit wasn't yet published.

CHAPTER 19

OFF THE ROCK

THE FALLOUT from the coronial inquest was anger and confusion.

Before the inquest the details of Janelle Patton's murder made little sense. Four days of evidence and tens of thousands of words later the equation hadn't changed. The community was now privy to Janelle's private life and the violence which engulfed her last minutes, but little else. Who could have done this and why remained unanswered.

That it was a brazen crime was beyond question: Why did the killer, or killers, strike at midday? It's unimaginable someone would logically commit to such a plan of attack. Was it impulse or malice which drove this desperate act?

How can a woman as well known as Janelle disappear within ten minutes? Is it possible her disappearance went *unnoticed* rather than unseen? Or did somebody glimpse something, only to turn a blind eye?

Perhaps the crime was random, a simple, reckless act, a fleeting and awful twist of circumstance which plunged into murder. Perhaps the killer was a stranger? Are there strangers on Norfolk Island? Maybe there is no link, no dwelling motive, no connection between Janelle and the person who took her life. Is it this which blinds the police? The hardest homicides to solve are those where the victim doesn't know the offender.

The only way to be invisible on Norfolk Island is to be anonymous. And the only way to be anonymous is to be an outsider, someone new to the community and its many eyes: a person living within but outside the community. If no one knows who you are then it's harder to be seen. The island has always wondered how the guilty party could stay mute, how the truth could be hidden from the pressure cooker of Norfolk's inquisitive community.

The thinking killer would leave the island, escape the scene of the crime. If the Island's internal consciousness is correct, if this murder is at the hands of an outsider, then the police have been looking too close to home. Maybe the answer lies with the many who have been and gone— the temporary and itinerant workers who man the island's economy.

One of the most insightful things I've read regarding Janelle's murder is a letter in the *Norfolk Islander* from April 2002, three weeks after the crime. It was written by Jenny Gilbert, a woman who had grown up on Norfolk Island in the 1960s. She wrote: 'It probably started out as a harmless approach by someone who was fascinated by Janelle and when she resisted the approach, rejection was something they just couldn't handle and lost control.'

The $300 000 reward remains on offer for information that leads to the arrest of the person responsible. Every edition of the *Norfolk Islander* carries a small notice calling for information, but only after the Pattons asked for it to be included in the weekly police news. They were worried the community might forget the need for justice.

The reward money is provided by the Australian and Norfolk governments, although the Norfolk Assembly hasn't yet passed an appropriation bill for its share. If the reward is called on, the island will have to dig around its empty savings box for $100 000. For critics who claim Norfolk has never wanted this crime solved it's worth knowing the initial $50 000 reward, announced in March 2003, was donated by an anonymous Islander. It was a touch of judicial philanthropy sold as a government initiative. The $50 000 donation remains in the reward pool. The reward also includes a conditional offer of indemnity from prosecution for any accomplice, provided they didn't take part in the actual slaying.

Under Norfolk Island law, any arrest for Janelle's murder must occur on the island. If that person is living offshore, they must be extradited to Norfolk to be charged. Extraditions can be slow affairs and subject to appeals. Once on Norfolk, any person charged will have to remain on-island, awaiting trial. The prospect of bail seems improbable, if not dangerous. These local laws make the course of justice a mine-field. So too is any prospective trial, which must be before an island court and an island jury, making jury selection a fascinating prospect. Is there, I wonder, an Islander who hasn't followed this case? Is there an Islander who doesn't know or isn't related to at least some of the sixteen people named in Bob Peters' dossier? If a local is charged, can we expect a home jury to be impartial? If an outsider is charged, will they be hung and quartered?

Financially the trial brings its own challenges. Justice and sentencing must be paid for by the Norfolk Island treasury. While the majority of the investigation's costs have been funded by the Australian taxpayer (the Australian Federal Police won't disclose what it has cost) the delivery of justice should be carried by the island. After all, it is a central tenet of its political autonomy. Australia shouldn't carry the tab. This prospect worries the Norfolk government because it is a bill it cannot readily afford.

———

With the inquest over and the media gone I lingered on Norfolk to soak up the aftermath. Around the corner was Bounty Day, 8 June, the most important day on Norfolk's calendar. It took place the following week and the community used it as a rallying point. Bob Peters decided it was best to stay away and took the opportunity to catch up on paperwork in the police station.

Bounty Day is when the blood of Norfolk's original families assembles on Kingston pier in 1850s period dress. The day is a national holiday, unfolding in a series of events celebrating the past. It begins with a re-enactment of the Pitcairners' arrival on Norfolk, which is why everyone gathers on the same pier that greeted their descendants 150 years earlier. Visitors and non-Islanders are held back behind a rope. The descendants greet each other with a commentary on outfits and slaps on the back. It's a laidback affair and a mock landing is staged, depending on the swell.

Then the crowd, which is nearly the entire island, strolls from the pier to the cemetery, pausing to sing 'God Save the Queen' at the cenotaph. They walk past the sandstone walls of Kingston's rich past and follow Quality Row to the historic graveyard where the dead have been going since 1788. Many still walk barefoot, as their ancestors did. After the pain and confusion of the preceding week it was a sunny day with bright smiles and a good turnout.

At the cemetery, wreaths are laid and there's more communal singing. Locals talk fondly of their final resting ground, where they will be buried next to their parents, siblings, cousins and friends. It's a long rectangle of a field, fenced in with timber slats. Hardly a week goes by without a fresh plot being dug and a more peaceful lodging would be hard to find. Its sandstone headstones carry stories of executed convicts and drowning, of mutiny and foreign whalers, of *Bounty* descendants and Pitcairn legends. These crosses lie on a gentle incline leaning towards the southern reef of Cemetery Bay. In one corner is a country lane, in the other the golf course. Around the fringe the ocean swell heaves onto coral banks, peppering the greens with a salty spray that chews at the grass, exposing little sand bunkers to thwart the wayward golfer. On any given day the sexton hears balls whistling midflight through the air, a downwind chorus of chatter mixed with the swoosh of clubs. Most of us have no idea on which plot of earth we'll spend our afterlife; on Norfolk Island locals drive past theirs every day.

After a pause for remembrance, Norfolk's thoroughbred families are honoured at an exclusive gathering at Government House. 'No entry without a blood test,' joked those on the other side of the white picket fence. It's a day of exclusivity but togetherness. In a time-honoured tradition, children roll down the grass embankment while their parents drink from the well-stocked Commonwealth liquor cabinet.

Bounty Day afternoon is consumed with eating. A communal feast is held within the 'compound' or convict prison walls. Each family has a specific corner where they gather and picnic. The Quintals in one alcove, the Christians in another. It's a lovely occasion, although staunch Pitcairn descendants shun the event, disappointed with how compromised their culture is by prying tourists.

You have to be invited to feast within the compound walls—it's one way to keep the outsiders at bay. I was delighted when several people from different families asked me to join them. I felt more accepted than ever before.

At dusk, Bounty Day is formally celebrated at the Bounty Ball, held in the local community hall.

The following day, as the descendants slept in, I returned to Norfolk's remote east coast. A place of fat pines and rotting needles and little else. It resounds in magical silence and is mostly national park. The air is so pure the lichen known as 'old man's beard' hangs from the branches like faded Christmas tinsel.

I walked to Bird Rock, one of a series of rock outcrops dotting the coast. It was here I met two retirees rejoicing in their seventh trip to Norfolk in seven years. Margaret and Trevor were upright and thin, with droopy hats and thick spectacles. They came from Terrigal on the New South Wales central coast, a seaside town that's suffering the blight of traffic, development and a popularity that's asphyxiated the very atmosphere people went there in search of. It is the usual plight of coastal over-adulation which will never afflict Norfolk. Trevor called Terrigal a 'rat race' and to really stick the knife in said, 'it's no different from Sydney'.

I'd just emerged from one of the bush tracks and was moving from the tree canopy to the burning light of mid morning. Before me lay a vast, dormant Pacific, barely breathing. From the cliff height of 100 metres the ocean seemed to rise up to greet me. The horizon wasn't flat, like it is from a beach or a boat, rather it was curved, its edges tilted, flexing in the sunlight. The ocean looked horrific in size. In the distance a lone boat headed out from Cascade jetty, its wake the only ripple in a windless sea. I watched it fade like a vapour trail in the sky.

The water below was translucent, an emerald smooth liquid. When the swell pushed beneath it the colour drifted from aqua-green to blue then back again. In the air were fairy terns, hundreds of them darting around, snow white against the sky blue, the white of a dove, the pure white of a bird never known to touch the earth's surface. It's said the fairy tern only lands on the branches of the Norfolk pine. There it lays its egg, precariously and miraculously balanced on the fork of a branch.

What Trevor and Margaret enjoyed most about Norfolk was the *quiet*. And what brought them back every year for a fortnight was a chance to meander along this coastline even though they had done the same walks countless times. They each wore skimpy, anaemic backpacks from which they removed a water bottle and a local orange, a hard blotchy fruit the size of a boule and covered in a thin, tough skin. It was rare for visitors in their seventies to tackle the bush tracks of the national park, what with its steep climbs and loose dirt paths.

As we stood whiffing the ocean breeze and sharp avian scent I listened to the couple's admiration for Norfolk. Their effusive love of the isle lay in it being just the way it was. The locals might be resistant to change but these visitors were even more hardline. Trevor offered the sound if unoriginal insight that Norfolk was twenty years behind Tasmania: 'And we all know Tasmania is twenty years behind the mainland,' he said.

A quick calculation suggested Norfolk was entering 1964 and I wondered, given that I hadn't been born then, if Norfolk really exuded this old world charm or if it was a line visitors hooked themselves on to quell anxiety about their own mortality. I wanted to ask but didn't wish to sound rude, so I deferred to their visible wisdom and asked anyway, in a nice way.

'But that's what we like about it,' they laughed. 'We meet people our age and everything is simple and easy—that's what we love most.'

'And the people are nice,' Margaret added. 'There's no rush here, no get up and be gone by yesterday. The world never used to be frantic. Here it still isn't.'

Together we stood in a line facing seaward, watching another boat being slung-shot into the never-never of the Pacific.

'But it's changing,' said Margaret, twirling a yellow daisy in her hand. 'We loved it when they had cattle on the main street, oh gosh, moaning and mooing at shop doors. The shopkeepers hated it. They were always shooing them off, but we thought it was really fun.'

She was right. Up until 1990 cattle grazed the length of Burnt Pine, nudging the windows of the duty free shops and, when they could, stealing food. Cattle grilles at either end of the street now keep the common stock out, much to the chagrin of long-time visitors who reminisce about the quaintness of dodging cowshit to get to the duty free cosmetics.

Margaret has faded blue eyes and a face etched like Lake Eyre. She clutches Trevor's hand and smiles at me. 'Why are you here?'

'I'm doing some writing.'

Her eyebrows arc. 'Well, what a perfect place.' After a pause she continues: 'The young dear who served us tea this morning said it is fine as long as you can get off for a while.' Trevor chuckles, keeping his eyes fixed on the horizon, like he's looking for the vapour of a spouting whale. 'Every six months, they say, if you can get off the Rock every six months it's not too bad. I don't think I could live here, but we don't holiday anywhere else now. I didn't see your car in the car park—which way did you walk in?'

I explain I parked at the first gate and walked the couple of hundred metres. He remembers the car. 'We drove that bit,' he admits, a shade embarrassed.

I watch Trevor and Margaret walk to the cliff edge, where a brown timber fence with the trajectory of a roller-coaster stops people falling off the side. In unison they gently squat, one hand on the railing, the other on their lower spine. They let gravity do the rest. Once planted, Trevor rustles in his bag and retrieves a pair of binoculars to study the birds. Margaret leans towards him, nestling her head on his shoulder. All around is ocean, birds and silence.

Aided by the dramatic height of the cliff I sense the power of Norfolk's elevation in offering these spectacular views. It's these visceral inputs which whisper 'paradise'. To me it meant more than just a pretty place, it said this is a *soulful* place. A place devoid of humanity. For me, the joy was found in the replacement of people, politics and murder with ocean, bird, wind and rustle. Solitude. Nothing less. I saw no paradise in the community and its squabbles, I saw it here, in the emptiness of the east coast.

At the park gate on my way out, I paused at Trevor's hire car. I was intrigued to see if it was locked. The driver's side was but the other three doors weren't.

It reminded me of the note in the house I was renting, which said: 'It is not necessary to lock doors on Norfolk Island. If this door and the glass sliding door are locked, re-entry will prove difficult.'

I had wanted to ask Trevor and Margaret if they wore their seatbelts on Norfolk, or drank more than they should and revelled in the idea of driving home, lucid and unstrapped, as free as in their breezy, innocent youth.

I wondered if coming to Norfolk made them feel young again because for me, it was the opposite, it made me feel weary, confused and often alone. I was relieved to be going home. I hungered for the city. I was tired of being the outsider. I wanted to be no one at all.

As I packed my bags I thought about the myriad pressures facing Norfolk. The island's isolation was always its challenge and its protection. Tourism, television, travel and wealth, they'd all combined to whittle away its natural defence—the ocean. The moat of the Pacific was now breached and many were deeply worried about what the incoming tide would bring.

Today Norfolk's remoteness is a lure, not a hindrance. Life is no longer the struggle it was for the old families, instead it's comfortable. Ingenuity is no longer a requirement for survival. The hard old days have been eclipsed with imports on demand. There is fresh milk and butter from New Zealand. The island doesn't even have a dairy. With this prosperity comes greater and greater demands and these pressures are mounting. Government has become big business, one far more complex than the model born in 1979 when Norfolk won back its self-determination. No longer could simple solutions solve the challenge of going it alone. Norfolk had much on its plate and rattling its foundation was one question the contentious 'Quis Custodiet Ipsos Custodes?' report failed to ask: was Norfolk Island fit to be a territory?

—————

The island airport is the next best meeting place after the supermarket and as I parked my hire car, leaving my key under the driver's seat, I saw Bob Peters and his team rocking on their heels in anticipation of departure. Inside the terminal was Adrienne Coles, Norfolk's only social welfare counsellor. I had spent an evening with her at the country music festival and she'd made me spit out my drink in laughter when she joked about opening a sex shop in Burnt Pine. She managed a community coup in 2004 by getting the island's first condom vending machine into the public toilets at the shopping mall. Before this, teenagers had to buy condoms from the supermarket. Mothers at the cash register would tell their friends, 'Guess what your son bought today?' It meant only the brave or the foolish purchased protection.

Adrienne Coles was constantly twisting her mouth around a reality the local Assembly didn't want to know about. She would utter words like 'herpes', 'gonorrhoea' and 'unwanted pregnancies', and the local Assembly would nearly fall off their collective chairs. She asked the elected leaders to consider a needle exchange because, yes, the island did have a drug problem. She would talk of the depression and anger and community angst which had gone unrecognised and untreated since 1856.

Buoyed by her success with condoms at the shopping mall, Adrienne Coles was now pushing for condoms at the airport. She approached the Assembly, which told her, 'Well yes, but only on the way out.'

After I paid my thirty-dollar departure tax I ran into the finance minister, Graeme Donaldson. He'd managed to avoid every follow-up interview I tried to arrange. He glanced past me and said, 'You're leaving? Make sure you write nice things.'

At customs an overzealous officer handled my PC with about as much care as he'd handle a coconut. It was then swabbed for bomb residue as part of the island's new anti-terrorism focus.

By the time I entered the small departure hall Bob Peters was already in position, his passport and boarding pass standing at attention in his breast shirt pocket. He looked happy to be going home and was reading a potboiler, a crime novel called *Blood on the Wire*.

I said, 'You actually read that stuff?'

He gave me one of his wry detective smiles and said, 'It's all they had in the newsagency. I don't mind it so much . . .' He paused mid sentence as he's prone to do, and then said, 'It eases my mind.'

I sat down in the chair opposite and closed my eyes.

EPILOGUE

Six weeks after the inquest into Janelle Patton's murder ended, another killing took place on Norfolk. Minutes before midday on Monday 19 July 2004, 25-year-old Leith Buffett walked into the old military barracks at Kingston. Slung over his shoulder, police allege, was a Lee Enfield .303 calibre rifle. In Leith's sights lay his father, Toon Buffett, the Norfolk Minister for Land and Environment.

Leith walked to a nearby building and opened the door. At that very moment Sergeant Brendan Lindsay was on the phone to Toon, not to warn him of his son's approach, but to ask if he knew where his son was because there was some concern over his state of health. In that moment, Toon Buffett knew the answer. According to Sergeant Lindsay's statment, he overheard Toon say in an upbeat voice, 'Hey! Hello lad,' before hanging up the phone. Police allege Leith Buffett shot his father point blank in the head. A single bullet entered above the right ear, leaving a wound 12 mm in diameter. Ivens 'Toon' Buffett died instantly at his desk. No one heard the shot.

According to police evidence, Leith Buffett then went home and had the following conversation with his mother: Shelley asked her son, 'Where have you been?'

'It doesn't matter now Mum,' he told her, 'you don't have to worry.'

'What do you mean I don't have to worry? What don't I have to worry about?'

'Well I have disposed of the evil prophet.'

'Who is the evil prophet?'

'Dad.'

'Leith, are you telling me you shot your father?'

'Yes.'

Shelley Buffett then fled the house and waved down police on Headstone Road, who cordoned off the property. In December 2004 Leith Buffett was committed to stand trial for his father's murder. A hearing before the Mental Health Tribunal found him fit to plead. He is expected to plead not guilty on grounds of mental illness. His trial is scheduled for July 2005. Buffett's lawyer is John Brown, a minister in the Norfolk Island government and one of Toon's former colleagues.

Toon Buffett was no prophet, although many regarded him as the next Chief Minister. He was a pragmatic politician and the only member of the Asembly to tell me the island's 'tax honeymoon' was over. He said what everyone knew, that the tax system wasn't equitable or tenable, but it wouldn't change until the community agreed to make a greater contribution. The key to shaking off Canberra was for the island to prove itself; otherwise, he said, it would never stop meddling. 'Antagonising Canberra is pointless,' I remember him saying on the veranda of the Golf Club after a heavy night's drinking. This was the only time I saw him drink a soft drink. In 2004 Toon was debating getting out of politics and was openly saying he would not stand for re-election. He told me he was tired of dealing with the same old issues. One evening in the Leagues Club I watched Mike King give him a tongue lashing for not wanting to stay in office. When Toon challenged him about his own time in government, Mike yelled, 'They voted me out mate, they got rid of me, but I stuck with it until the end.' It's then I realised just how all-consuming and claustrophobically intimate living on Norfolk must be for those born into its land and culture. I knew some looked fondly at the prospect of being laid to rest in their plot by the golf course and the ocean, for there at last lay peace from the tension of island life.

In his final months, Toon Buffett was looking more and more like his ancestral mutineers, his moustache flared into a beard, a rugged sea-going growth which made him appear old, haggard and fierce in a salty, swashbuckling way. He was one of the few elected politicians who popped his head into the Patton coronial inquest and now he is dead too.

For the second time in two years, Norfolk Island had a murder on its hands. Except this time it wasn't an outsider, it was one of the brethren, allegedly killed by a family member. It was a double tragedy. It left a wife without a husband and a mother without a son. It was a sorry business and it pained the community because it was a death of everything it holds close to its collective heart.

In the wake of Toon's death the local Assembly tackled a problem Bob Peters had notified it of two years earlier—that Norfolk had no jurisdiction to transport prisoners on remand to the mainland. Bob Peters gave the Assembly a copy of the relevant ACT legislation but nothing came of it until it was faced with the dilemma of moving Leith Buffett out of the Norfolk Island lock-up where he had been for seven weeks after being charged with the murder of his father.

Leith Buffett had to literally sit on his hands until the Assembly amended its Crime Act. In the end NSW agreed to change its Act as well and Buffett was transferred to the prison hospital at Sydney's Silverwater Jail.

———

As the island awaits the trial of Leith Buffett, it also watches closely the movements of Bob Peters. In December 2004 the investigation of Janelle Patton's murder took a new turn when the detective placed an ad in the *Norfolk Islander*. It asked the community to help find a white 1984 Honda sedan. The police were interested in this car because it had been driven by a new lead. The car was out of registration and hadn't been driven for several years but old cars on Norfolk never die, they just rust on people's properties. The Honda sedan was located, abandoned in someone's backyard. Police seized it, searched it and towed it back to the copshop. Meanwhile another car was found—this time a white Hyundai hatchback. Bob Peters could have seized control of the rental car but he knew nothing would be left once the forensic team finished combing it for clues so he paid $900 for it; he says it's the only exhibit he's ever purchased.

In early 2005, Bob Peters was back on the island, this time with a three-person forensic team, as well as his two colleagues Tony Edmondson and Mark Elvin. By now Dem Tull was flowing thick and fast about who these cars once belonged to and what forensic clues they may yield, if any. Could police link either vehicle with Janelle, her body or any other exhibit?

The walls and floor of the police garage were lined with black plastic to protect the integrity of the evidence and in stifling, suffocating conditions of heat and humidity, the forensics team systematically dismantled the two vehicles, swabbing, tape-lifting and analysing their way from bonnet to boot. When the work was finished more than several hundred exhibits were bagged and labelled and shipped to the lab in Canberra.

While the cars were being dismantled, Bob Peters was also searching a property several kilometres from where Janelle once lived—a flat at the end of a small cul-de-sac known as Little Cutters Corn. It had never been searched before and in 2002 was next door to a house under construction (a building that Stevie Cochrane worked on as a carpenter).

Locals watched these developments with great interest because they suggested a new direction in the investigation. Neither the compounded cars nor the property are linked to the sixteen Persons of Interest. The focus of Bob Peters' investigation had now shifted from those named to another individual he will not name.

What is known is the investigation is now concentrating on a New Zealand national, a 28-year-old former-TEP who lived on Norfolk Island for two years and left six weeks after Janelle's murder. This man was not named or mentioned during the coronial inquest. It's unclear if this man knew Janelle Patton but it appears the two did not socialise. There is no obvious motive.

The island community is relieved the police focus has switched from *them* to *someone else*, especially as this latest person is an outsider. Bob Peters will not say if the sixteen Persons of Interest are now of no interest at all, or if his latest lead will produce a suspect. The Patton family waits patiently for a resolution and as the months drift into years they worry that it will never arrive. Justice is a slow ship and a trial and conviction is a long journey from a charge sheet and arrest. The family prays justice won't pass them, or Janelle, by.

———

In the October 2004 elections, Geoff Gardner was easily re-elected as Chief Minister but Ric Robinson's old mix of firebrand nationalism failed to entice Islanders. He won 4.9 per cent of the vote and came fourth-last.

The new Assembly immediately earned praise and damnation by not passing traffic laws that threatened to make the wearing of seatbelts mandatory. The government decided to give drivers the choice and make seatbelts optional.

After forty years running the *Norfolk Islander* Tom Lloyd and his wife Tim printed the headline, 'The Time Has Come' and announced in February 2005 they had sold the paper to two staff members, thus ensuring the publication stayed in house and on-island.

Meanwhile, the federal government in Canberra is yet to respond to the damning parliamentary report into the island—which leaves Norfolk doing what it likes best, taking care of its own business in its own way. It leaves the island's reformists exasperated and everyone else relieved that Norfolk will see another day just like the last.

ACKNOWLEDGEMENTS

To Kirsten Garrett who first sent me to Norfolk Island and Richard Walsh and Helen Thomas who persuaded me to return for the book. To the team at Allen & Unwin: Sue Hines, Clare Emery and copy-editor Jo Jarrah.

To Carol, Ron and Mark Patton for their all their help and assistance. To Bob Peters who always did his best to field my inquiries, answer my questions and smile at my dilemmas.

To all on Norfolk who were prepared to break ranks and talk, however little. Special thanks goes to Mike King who never shied away from helping me out and laughing about life on the rock.

For their hospitality thanks to Laurie 'Bucket' Quintal, Steve Borg, Adrian and Lynn Cook, Robyn Murdoch and Jap Menghetti. Thanks to Graham 'Struts' Struthers, Shane, Fiona, Adrienne and all the helpful staff at the Court Registry. To the many I spoke with who didn't want to be named or quoted—I appreciate your trust.

Finally, thanks to my close friends and colleagues who encouraged me to keep writing and stop complaining. Especially Joan, David and James. To my sister Rebecca for reading early chapters, to my parents for their endless support and to Tara, who kept me on course and ensured I had some fun on the way—I couldn't sail without you.